THE REAL AMBASSADORS

THE REAL AMBASSADORS

*Dave and Iola Brubeck and Louis Armstrong
Challenge Segregation*

Keith Hatschek

Foreword by Yolande Bavan

University Press of Mississippi / Jackson

The University Press of Mississippi is the scholarly publishing agency of the Mississippi Institutions of Higher Learning: Alcorn State University, Delta State University, Jackson State University, Mississippi State University, Mississippi University for Women, Mississippi Valley State University, University of Mississippi, and University of Southern Mississippi.

www.upress.state.ms.us

The University Press of Mississippi is a member of the Association of University Presses.

First printing 2022
∞

Library of Congress Control Number: 2021049367

Hardback ISBN 978-1-4968-3777-6
Trade paperback ISBN 978-1-4968-3784-4
Epub single ISBN 978-1-4968-3778-3
Epub institutional ISBN 978-1-4968-3779-0
PDF single ISBN 978-1-4968-3780-6
PDF institutional ISBN 978-1-4968-3781-3

British Library Cataloging-in-Publication Data available

Prejudice is indescribable. To me it is the reason we could lose the world. I have been through Asia and India and the Middle East and we have to realize how many brown-skinned people there are in this world. Prejudice here or in South Africa is setting up our world for one terrible letdown.

—DAVE BRUBECK IN RALPH J. GLEASON, "YOU CAN'T PLAY HERE,"

SAN FRANCISCO CHRONICLE, SEPTEMBER 21, 1958

CONTENTS

FOREWORD

Serendipity. It entered my life when, at the age of sixteen, I left my home in Sri Lanka and traveled by myself to Melbourne, Australia. When I look back, I realize how apt the word is. "Serendib" was the name given to Sri Lanka, formerly Ceylon, by Arab travelers in the 1600s when they survived a major storm and landed on the island. The name means "fortuitous happening."

In Australia, I met the great Dixieland jazz musician Graeme Bell, who became my manager. It was the beginning of my singing career. At a party given for Louis Armstrong's band performing in Melbourne, Graeme introduced me briefly to Mr. Armstrong. I was wearing my long hair in plaits. At age twenty-six when I attended a rehearsal for the premiere of *The Real Ambassadors*—to be performed at Monterey Jazz Festival, September 1962—Louis turned to his wife and said, "Mama, I know that girl." He remembered my plaits. Serendipity?

But the greatest serendipity of all was how I came to be a part of Lambert, Hendricks & Bavan.

Living in London during the late fifties and early sixties, I befriended several jazz musicians who would invite me to ride along in the coaches they took to their performances. I had the good fortune to meet Dave Brubeck on one of these rides. He asked me to meet him at his hotel, as he had some music he wanted me to look at. "Can you sight-read this?" he asked, pointing at the top stave. Being quite young, I was not immobilized by fears or ego: I had faith in Divine source. I sang. "What is this music for?" I asked. "A jazz opera called *The Real Ambassadors*," he answered. "The part I had you sight-read is written for Annie Ross." I was not very familiar with Lambert, Hendricks & Ross. I continued working as an actress.

My close friends Don and Sandra Luck hosted great parties and invited touring musicians. At one such party, I was helping empty ashtrays while a Dizzy Gillespie album was playing. Without thinking, I sang the final note, and a voice next to me asked, "Did you just hit that high note? Are you a singer?" I answered, "No, I am an actress." The person asking me was Dave

Lambert, whom I did not know. That was April 1962. Two weeks after the Basie Band, Jon, and Dave—minus Annie—returned to New York, I received a phone call from Jon Hendricks, whom I also did not know. He invited me to New York to sing with them. I giggled and said I could not because I was not a singer and not capable of singing their style of music and certainly could not hit high notes. His call came on May 1st. He said they had arranged a plane ticket, visa, and working permit at the US Embassy, and they wanted me there on May 3rd. I declined, saying I could not come until May 5th. Four months later, I was performing in the premiere of *The Real Ambassadors* at the Monterey Jazz Festival. Serendipity? Jazz shone a beacon of magical light on my life.

I remained in the US and was surprised and dismayed that jazz—America's music— and its creators were treated like second-class citizens. Racism baring its fangs. Of course, racism is not only in the United States; when, at sixteen, I prepared to go to Australia, I had to prove I had 60 percent white blood before I could go, according to Australia's immigration law. Luckily my mom took me to the Dutch Burgher Club, where the records showed I had the desired amount. The fangs are global.

I am honoured to write this foreword. Keith has done extensive research, and his words show such love, patience, and dedication. In this book, he shares the truth and joy of *The Real Ambassadors*, created by Iola, Dave, and Louis, with whom I was blessed to share the stage.

Fifty years later, I was part of *The Real Ambassadors* concert at Lincoln Center, celebrating Dave Brubeck.

Serendipity.

YOLANDE BAVAN

PROLOGUE

On the evening of September 23, 1962, as civil rights momentum was escalating to a fervor, a cast of thirteen talented artists came together at the Monterey Jazz Festival to perform *The Real Ambassadors*, a jazz musical challenging racial inequality. The culmination of five years' work, the musical was written by well-known jazz musician Dave Brubeck and his wife, Iola, expressly to feature the most celebrated jazz musician in the world, Louis Armstrong. That night, they performed a slimmed-down one-hour "concert version" of what was envisioned as a three-act Broadway show, and their hope was that this premiere would help make that full production dream a reality. Supporting players included Carmen McRae, the vocal trio Lambert, Hendricks & Bavan, and Armstrong's All-Star band, along with Dave Brubeck, Eugene Wright, and Joe Morello.[1] Iola Brubeck, who wrote the book and cowrote the lyrics for her husband's songs, provided narration from a separate temporary stage to frame the musical numbers and explain the show's themes.

The musical was inspired in part by the US State Department and its cultural ambassadors program, which had been sending American jazz musicians abroad beginning with Dizzy Gillespie's 1956 tour. These jazz ambassadors toured overseas as a form of cultural diplomacy, promoting jazz as a uniquely American art form and touting it as a product of a free society. The Brubecks' *Real Ambassadors* offered a nuanced portrait of these jazz ambassadors, drawing heavily on the experiences the couple had during their own State Department–sponsored global tour in 1958. Selling the notions of freedom and equality abroad was intended to present a contrast to the opposing totalitarian model offered by the Soviet Union. Ironically, however, while America's Black jazz ambassadors were treated as royalty abroad, they still suffered racial prejudice at home on a daily basis.

The Real Ambassadors told the story of this irony, chronicling the hard road traveled by jazz musicians on tour for Uncle Sam in the 1950s. Led by a charismatic trumpeter and vocalist, "Pops," and his love interest, the band's vivacious female singer, "Rhonda," the show's lyrics and dialogue made plain the Brubecks' belief that segregation must be overturned and that artists should take a stand to work toward social justice. *The Real Ambassadors* tackled controversial themes head-on, and some of its concepts could be considered blasphemous at the time—for example, posing the question "Could God be Black?" in the one of the musical's most memorable songs, and dreaming aloud of a time when integrated music groups might be able to perform in Mississippi. Historian Penny Von Eschen argued that bringing the show to the stage at the height of the civil rights movement was not without risk. She stated:

> From our present day perspective, these types of statements defending civil rights and egalitarianism seem relatively mild, but when this was produced, America was at the height of the violent civil rights movement, and the federal government had not yet begun to take a stand to defend civil rights advocacy on a formal level. It was a very bold, controversial act at that moment in time."[2]

In evidence reconstructing the musical's rocky path to the stage, we see that music industry power players such as Columbia Records president Goddard Lieberson warned the Brubecks to avoid such controversy if Dave and Iola wanted to see the musical realized.

In the early 1960s, the battle over civil rights in the United States was front and center on nightly newscasts, and the musical and its message were perfectly attuned to the national debate. At the time, powerful governmental, economic, fraternal, and institutional groups in the US were aligned to prevent the end of racial segregation by working actively to sustain the centuries-old practices of Jim Crow, ingrained practices that restricted the civil and societal rights of Black Americans and relegated them to second-class status. Even though the landmark 1954 decision reached in *Brown v. Board of Education* outlawed school segregation, local leaders scoffed at the law and maintained strict segregation throughout society, most prominently in the South. Powerful leaders such as Dr. Martin Luther King Jr., Medgar Evers, and Dr. Ralph Abernathy, and organizations such as the National Association for the Advancement of Colored People (NAACP), had raised their voices and were taking action to demand an end to segregation. Nonviolent actions including marches, boycotts, sit-ins, and teach-ins led by ministers, students, and activists were reported regularly in the media—especially when such peaceful acts caused violent responses from those strongly opposed to breaking the grip of Jim Crow. The nation was undergoing a crisis of unprecedented scope.

Within twelve months of the show's debut, the tragic evidence of a nation divided would be apparent to the whole world. Only a few days after the show's 1962 premiere, James Meredith enrolled to attend the University of Mississippi, the first African American student to do so. This led to riots that left three persons dead, six policemen shot, and dozens injured on the campus. A few months later, in May 1963, the Southern Christian Leadership Conference rallied students of all ages to march peacefully in protest to downtown Birmingham, Alabama, where the notorious commissioner of public safety, Bull Connor, ordered fire hoses used on the children, knocking many off their feet and shredding their clothes. This inhumanity was documented everywhere, from major networks' nightly newscasts to the front page of the *New York Times*, where on May 4th, an iconic photo spread showed a Black high school student, Walter Gadsden, being attacked by Connor's police dogs. Four months later, on Sunday, September 15, 1963, the murder of four young girls in the 16th Street Baptist Church bombing further stunned the nation. News coverage of the protests dominated every form of media, and every day, Americans were reminded of the sacrifices being made by citizens of color.

Given this context, it is no surprise that *The Real Ambassadors'* road to the stage was neither straightforward nor simple, spanning five years of the lives of Dave and Iola Brubeck, the creators and evangelists who were determined to bring the show to life. As Dave Brubeck's own music career blossomed, he made his position on civil rights a cornerstone of his identity, both as an artist and an American. He was quoted frequently in interviews with a courageous mantra: that society would benefit from becoming color-blind. His ideals had come from observing how his father, Pete Brubeck, managed the large ranch in California's Central Valley where the family lived in the 1930s. His father treated everyone with respect, hiring ranch hands who were white, Mexican, and Native American. The young Brubeck worked summers and after school as a ranch hand, side by side with these men, while attending the local public school in Ione, California, where he had a number of friends who were Native American. The pianist's humanistic values advanced through his subsequent experiences as a young GI leading what was likely the first integrated US Army band, the Wolfpack, during World War II.[3] After the war, Brubeck hired African American bassist Wyatt "Bull" Ruther as a member of the Dave Brubeck Quartet in 1951–52.[4] In 1958, another Black bassist, Eugene Wright, became a mainstay of the quartet. Due to Jim Crow restrictions on integrated bands performing in the South, the Dave Brubeck Quartet had to cancel twenty-two dates of a 1960 Southern college campus tour. Brubeck refused to replace Wright with a white bassist, losing an estimated $40,000 in income. Having witnessed firsthand the sting of discrimination through his many musical friends and colleagues, Brubeck and his wife developed a deep-seated commitment to equal rights for all.

The Brubecks used their wits and resources to enlist the aid of every like-minded show business contact they had in order to make *The Real Ambassadors* a reality. Still, the performance itself was nearly torpedoed in the weeks leading up to the festival by Armstrong's manager, Joe Glaser, a powerful man who saw much to lose and little to gain from such an endeavor. Likewise, Armstrong's own wife, Lucille, feared that tackling difficult new songs might have been beyond her husband's reach at that time, as he had suffered a near-fatal heart attack in 1959 while on the road in Italy and was weakened by forty years of nonstop touring.

The night of the premiere belonged to the cast. At its conclusion one critic noted that "the performers were rewarded with a standing ovation by 5,000 fans. Everyone applauded, some wept."[5] Critics unanimously praised the work as a bold statement supporting equal rights, telling the story of African American musicians with dignity and sensitivity in a way that deserved national attention. With these endorsements ringing in their ears, the Brubecks' five-year effort to bring the full production to Broadway or television felt within reach. But the growing success of the Dave Brubeck Quartet, which came to be the most popular small jazz ensemble in the world, eclipsed *The Real Ambassadors*, until it reemerged in the 1990s as a vital, if overlooked piece of Brubeck's and Armstrong's careers. In the twenty-first century, it has enjoyed three revivals, which have proven that the timeless messages in it still ring true today.

Documenting a largely untold history of Black and white jazz artists teaming up to challenge Jim Crow, with Cold War tensions and the emerging civil rights movement as a backdrop, the tale of *The Real Ambassadors* is a story within a story. Wrapped around the production's fictional plot was a very real account of struggle in the civil rights era, as Louis Armstrong and Dave and Iola Brubeck fought to present a musical designed to foment social change. Understanding its complicated road to the stage against the backdrop of its underlying message can provide insight today, at a time when race relations are once again at the forefront of national discourse. These talented artists demonstrated that challenging racism, xenophobia, gender bias, and other hate-based creeds requires logic, compassion, wit, and above all, dogged persistence—and that the reward may come in unexpected forms and on unexpected timelines. Dave and Iola Brubeck and the cast of *The Real Ambassadors* collectively made a bold social and political statement at a time when many Americans were angry, confused, and in search of answers—lifting their voices to help bring about social change one song at a time. They can be seen as part of a wave of mid-twentieth-century American musicians, filmmakers, and artists who spoke out loudly against discrimination in direct response to their troubled times. This story illustrates the vital role that artists can play as ambassadors of the truth, speaking for equality and justice, both in their own time and through their art, for all times. It demonstrates the importance of keeping our eyes on the prize, even if we may never see that prize fully realized in our own lifetime.

THE REAL AMBASSADORS

CHAPTER 1

MEET THE BRUBECKS

The original idea to create a jazz musical was conceived by Iola Whitlock Brubeck in 1956. She had been married to David Warren Brubeck, her college sweetheart, for fourteen years. His star was rising as one of the most celebrated jazz pianists and small-ensemble leaders of his time, while she simultaneously managed Dave's career and a family of seven in their busy Oakland, California, household.[1] Iola had been involved in theater, drama, and broadcasting through the formative years of high school and college, starting at Shasta High in Redding, California, through her many stage and radio performances at College of the Pacific, in Stockton, California. Her early performance career peaked when, through a radio contest, she won a speaking role in the cast of the nationally syndicated melodrama *Red Ryder*.[2]

Iola continued to develop her artistic voice, studying creative writing at Mills College in Oakland. She published two short stories in *Pacific*, Mills College's literary review. "The Tiger Kite," published in 1947, tells the story of a young Black boy, Mannie, growing up in a predominantly white small town. His grandfather helps him to make a white kite with a fierce tiger's face painted on it, a symbol of the freedom that he and his family long for in the restrictive, segregated society in which they live. Flying the kite with both white and Black children, together they revel in its flight. Mannie feels a strong urge to let the tiger kite go, to be truly free; however, at the urging of his family, he pulls it back to earth. In the process, it catches on a wire and is destroyed. The young boy is angered by the loss and returns home utterly alone, his symbol of freedom destroyed.

Her second short story, "The Miracle and Arva Topper," published the following year, drew on her own experiences growing up in rural California.[3] This story demonstrates her fruitful imagination and vividly descriptive writing style. In it, Arva Topper, a young, visually impaired, awkward third-grade girl, is treated as an outcast by her peers. However, a fellow student who serves as the story's narrator stands up to the bullies. Iola accurately portrays the poverty of the Depression in describing the peculiar gait Arva

Portrait of Iola and Dave
Brubeck, taken in September
1942, their wedding month,
in Stockton, California.
Brubeck Collection, Holt-
Atherton Special Collections,
University of the Pacific
Library, © Dave Brubeck.

had developed as a result of the gunny sacks and newspapers her family used
to keep her feet dry and warm. The Topper family invites the protagonist to
attend a revival prayer meeting, at which little Arva becomes the subject of
the revivalist's healing efforts. Appearing to go into a trance, she throws off
her glasses and swoons into the minister's arms, at which point the narrator
thinks she has died. He is very upset and runs out to cry in the back seat of
the Toppers' old car. When Mr. and Mrs. Topper bring Arva out to the car
later, the narrator is amazed that she is alive and also that she seems stronger.
"I was healed," she says, staring at him with her one good eye.

These portrayals of poverty and isolation, and the sting of being ridiculed
as "the other," mark the beginnings of Iola's explorations into social justice.
The stories were informed by her own observations and experiences growing up in the midst of the Depression. She continued to explore these topics
nearly a decade later in *The Real Ambassadors*.[4]

Iola and Dave had first met in 1940 while students at College of the Pacific
in Stockton. He was three years older, but their paths crossed when he was

selected as accompanist for the school's Friday afternoon live radio broadcast, a variety show that was being produced and directed by Iola. After only a few dates, they realized they were falling in love. Less than a year later, Dave graduated and enlisted in the US Army. He got a three-day pass in September 1941, and the couple eloped to Reno, Nevada. During the early years of their marriage, Dave was assigned to Camp Haan near Riverside, California, and Iola joined him there for a time, interrupting her studies. She got a job working at the local radio station, first writing news and advertising copy and eventually serving as what today would be termed music director, preparing the playlists of songs aired by the disc jockeys. This experience helped to broaden her appreciation and knowledge of the jazz genre.

In 1944, Dave served in the European theater, first as a rifleman in Patton's Third Army and then leading an integrated jazz band dubbed the Wolfpack, entertaining troops throughout France and Germany as Allied troops occupied more German territory throughout 1944 and 1945.[5] Once Dave shipped out, Iola returned to Pacific to complete her studies. Private Brubeck returned home in 1946 and began studies in composition on the GI Bill with Darius Milhaud, the lauded French composer who had taken up residence at Mills College to escape persecution during the German occupation of France in 1940.

The first performance outlet for the experimental compositions Dave and his fellow Milhaud classmates were writing became known as the Dave Brubeck Octet, which included Paul Desmond on saxophone and Cal Tjader on drums.[6] Brubeck first met Desmond in the military, and after the war, he played regularly with Brubeck in his octet. The group's avant-garde sound limited engagements to colleges with strong music programs.[7] Gigs were few and far between for the experimental ensemble, so Brubeck assembled a trio, with Cal Tjader playing drums and vibes and Ron Crotty on bass. The trio played both jazz standards as well as popular dance music that had broader appeal, generating income that helped support Brubeck's growing family. Throughout the late 1940s, as Brubeck tried to get more work with his trio, his path often crossed with that of Desmond, who unfortunately ended up stealing a number of gigs from Brubeck, which did little to strengthen their relationship offstage.[8]

Things were looking glum, as Dave was having to support his family of four on forty-two dollars a week ($450 in 2021 currency), playing long sets five nights a week at a bar in rural California, before he finally got his break. Jazz DJ James L. "Jimmy" Lyons debuted the Dave Brubeck Trio's early recording of "Indiana" on the Coronet label on San Francisco's KNBC radio in 1949.[9] The listener response was strong. Lyons then invited

Brubeck's trio to perform on the air weekly. As a result of this exposure, Brubeck began to land better and better gigs around Northern California.[10] "You need somebody like Jimmy when you're unknown and struggling," Dave Brubeck remembered.[11] Lyons was not only instrumental in helping to launch the career of Dave Brubeck; he also was the first West Coast DJ to spin records by Dizzy Gillespie, Milt Jackson, and Miles Davis.[12] With the help of additional airplay and the backing of Lyons, the trio was soon playing at other better-known San Francisco Bay Area nightspots, first at Oakland's Burma Lounge and eventually moving up to the more prestigious Black Hawk and the Cellar in San Francisco.[13] Unknown to many who only were introduced to Dave Brubeck's music in the mid-1950s when he joined Columbia Records, Brubeck's inventive musical approach was the key to his popularity. Jazz historian Ted Gioia states, "By the start of the 1950s, word had begun to circulate of an exceptional young jazz pianist . . . who was applying contemporary compositional techniques to jazz music."[14] Brubeck was then leading a trio, which, although it was as unconventional as his earlier octet, caught the ear of the general public, as he built his early repertoire using well-known pop tunes, such as "Stardust" and "Indiana." Using devices that would become standard Brubeck approaches over his career, including polytonality, polyrhythms, unexpected key changes, and thunderous block chords that echoed the contemporary classical composers he admired, Brubeck used melodies and chord changes that everyday listeners were familiar with as a jumping-off point. Gioia concludes that this was what made his music sound fresh and exciting. "This strange modern mixture—half Tin Pan Alley and half progressive classical music—would become a Brubeck hallmark."[15]

Lyons's radio show, dubbed *Lyons Busy*, went out via the powerful KNBC clear-channel broadcast and was heard throughout the West. *San Francisco Examiner* music critic Philip Elwood explained the significance of the radio exposure:

> The show generated an astonishingly large Brubeck following not only in California but also in Oregon, Washington, Idaho, Utah and Nevada. These were the young people who bought the first Brubeck 78s; these were the college students who packed auditoriums on his first tours.[16]

In summer 1951, with prospects and cash flow starting to improve, Brubeck decided to let bygones be bygones and invited alto saxophonist Paul Desmond to join his group. Desmond was a highly gifted player who proved to be Brubeck's perfect musical partner, and their improvisations were like intimate conversations that revealed a close relationship both musical and personal.[17] The interplay on their live and studio recordings is a master class in listening and improvisation.[18] The sax player became a fixture in the group and a regular at the Brubecks' home, referred to by the Brubeck children as "Uncle Paul." With Desmond's often understated and refined sound, lyricism, and instantly recognizable tone, the Dave Brubeck Quartet became one of the most notable proponents of what jazz critics dubbed West Coast jazz, to differentiate it from the harder, driving bebop sounds of Charlie Parker and Dizzy Gillespie.

From 1952 to 1964, the Dave Brubeck Quartet regularly appeared at San Francisco's Black Hawk Club.[19] According to Elwood,

> It was the center for modern jazz in the region by 1952, and the Brubeck Quartet, following in the footsteps of the Trio, used it as a home base. There was seldom a month during this period that the Brubeck Quartet didn't put in a few nights at the Blackhawk [sic]—they even did some recordings there.[20]

In her role as de facto manager for the group, in 1953, Iola conceived and executed a letter-writing campaign to colleges up and down the West Coast, offering the quartet's services for a sit-down listening concert. "I went to the Oakland Public Library and, using the various telephone directories there, wrote down the mailing addresses of every college from Seattle to San Francisco and sent them a letter," she recalled.[21] This effort was one of the first in an ongoing series of initiatives and strategies that were to have a dramatic impact on her husband's career. Iola Brubeck displayed sharp business acumen and offered frank assessments of the group's prospects over the length of Dave's career.

Within each letter, Iola included reviews of some of the group's successful college concerts as evidence of its positive reception. She incentivized the concerts by offering student body groups a share of the proceeds. Dave remembered, "Some of the colleges answered back, and this led to our first real tour. We drove up to the University of Washington, University of Idaho, and others."[22] This innovative strategy proved very successful and led to a measured growth in the band's earnings. Jazz critic Doug Ramsey argued that "the Brubecks' pioneering opened the college market as a source of work for jazz artists and helped open society's ears to a wide acceptance of jazz as a mature cultural element."[23] Since the group was expressly creating jazz for listening, rather than dancing, their sound caught on with college crowds, leading to a packed calendar of much better paying concert performances.

Eventually, the college touring was so successful that the quartet's drummer, Joe Dodge, recalled at one point playing sixty one-nighters in a row.[24]

With growing success found on the college circuit, the quartet finally attracted the attention of a major national booking agency, Associated Booking Corporation, headquartered in New York City, which took over bookings in late 1950.[25] In large part, the 1953 release of *Jazz at Oberlin* on the Fantasy label created the national breakthrough for the group, as it appealed to radio programmers, record buyers, and influential jazz critics. Now the Dave Brubeck Quartet could count on three steady income sources: being a successful recording ensemble with resulting royalties, being an established concert draw on college campuses, and continued engagements at a range of well-regarded nightclubs, such as the Black Hawk and the Both/And in San Francisco. The *Jazz at Oberlin* recording had also gained the attention of music industry insiders, leading to the group being signed by producer George Avakian at Columbia Records after he heard them perform in San Francisco.[26] Avakian was one of the most influential music producers of the twentieth century and was widely heralded as the father of the long-playing record, having developed the first jazz LPs while still a student at Yale.[27]

Capitalizing on the success of the Oberlin recording, Columbia rushed out *Jazz Goes to College*, a compilation of additional songs recorded at Oberlin College and the University of Michigan. With the promotional clout of Columbia behind the release, the record quickly sold more than one hundred thousand units, an astounding feat for a jazz album at that time.[28] A November 8, 1954, *Time* magazine cover and accompanying story featuring the quartet widened the group's appeal even further. The story was an immediate dividend of Brubeck's affiliation with Columbia Records. Avakian, who at the time was an A&R (artists and repertoire) executive at the label, recalled, "Debbie Ishlon was the Columbia Records publicist and a damn good one. She liked jazz and went out of her way to publicize Brubeck, Armstrong, Ellington, and Miles, in particular. She did wonders."[29]

By the late 1950s, fueled by the Columbia Records publicity machine and a series of successful releases, the Dave Brubeck Quartet emerged as a standard-bearer of West Coast jazz. It was a sound that offered a more melodic alternative to pure bebop, which some listeners felt had become increasingly complicated and less accessible. While essential to the overall evolution of jazz as an art form, the adventurous bebop played by Dizzy Gillespie, Charlie Parker, and their peers appealed to a smaller segment of the overall listening public. Conversely, West Coast jazz emphasized melody and improvisations that were firmly rooted in song forms that the average audience member could follow.

With Brubeck trading solos on piano with Desmond's instantly recognizable alto saxophone, by 1960 the Dave Brubeck Quartet was considered one of the top jazz groups in the world when measured by record sales, airplay, and popularity polls. The quartet won the *DownBeat* readers' poll five times: in 1959, then in a string of consecutive wins from 1962 to 1965. It was recognized as the top jazz combo in *Billboard*'s 1962 disc jockeys' poll, as well as by that magazine's readers, a larger group made up of music industry insiders, in 1965 and 1966. Demonstrating the staying power of the group, they also topped the *Playboy* readers' poll for twelve consecutive years, from 1957 to 1968.[30] An extensive 1961 profile in the *New Yorker* described the Dave Brubeck Quartet's success this way:

> What no one can dispute, though, is that the Brubeck quartet, which is ten years old, is the world's best paid, most widely travelled, most highly publicized and most popular small group now playing improvised syncopated music. It grosses a couple of hundred thousand dollars a year from its night club dates and concerts. It has made thirty-odd long-playing records whose combined sales are well into seven figures.[31]

Further cementing the group's cultural relevance, the same essay reported that comedian Mort Sahl, one of the first nationally known entertainers to single out the quartet for praise, had a regular line in his act referencing the global fan base Brubeck had developed: "Whenever [secretary of state] John Foster Dulles visits a country, the State Department sends the Brubeck Quartet in a few weeks later to repair the damage." Sahl was referring to Uncle Sam's use of America's jazz ambassadors to help spread American influence and thereby promote the nation's policy interests throughout the Cold War.

Regardless of the commercial and critical acclaim, the nearly nonstop touring by the quartet put a substantial strain on family life, especially as the Brubecks' five children became increasingly involved in extracurricular activities like music and dance lessons. During the times when the quartet was not out on the road, Brubeck would accompany his wife in the car as she chauffeured the children to their lessons. Recalling that time period, he stated that work requiring concentration and quiet could be better taken care of in a parked car than at home, due to the hubbub generated by their children:

> For a while, Iola was driving the children to twenty lessons a week; it was like a taxi service. And if I was around, I'd go along and sit in the car and work. The musical she and I wrote together for Louis

Armstrong, it was about jazz ambassadors . . . was done mostly while
we were waiting for [son] Michael.[32]

Cathy Brubeck Yaghsizian, one of the Brubeck children, shared a similar
recollection. "My mom loved those yellow legal pads, and since it just wasn't
worth driving home [during my lesson], she would sit in the car and do stuff
on those yellow pads each day."[33] Oldest son Darius concurred:

> The yellow pads were indispensable. I have a mental picture of sitting
> in the car, and they had a clipboard that was also a folder that held
> a yellow pad inside. I remember a green folder and a blue one, and I
> don't think that was by chance. It was probably meant to distinguish
> business stuff from lyrics or show stuff."[34]

To help increase family time, Iola would on occasion bring the children
to New York City and set up quarters in a hotel while Dave was on tour, so
that the whole family could spend more time together when school was out
for the summer. These junkets would correspond with the plentiful summer
concert, festival, and club dates on the East Coast for Dave and his group.
During the summer of 1956, a classmate of Iola's from College of the Pacific,
actress Barbara Baxley, joined her to see a number of the leading musicals
then playing on Broadway.[35] Baxley was the godmother of Iola and Dave's
son Chris, who recalled that Brubeck family members would sometime stay
over at Baxley's New York apartment. "She was my mother's closest lifelong
friend," he said.[36] The close friends enjoyed the range of offerings on and off
Broadway, but it was a free jazz concert held one evening in Central Park
featuring vocalist Joe Williams that sparked Iola's imagination. Iola recalled,
"Joe Williams really reached me, emotionally, more than any of the Broadway
shows with the lavish sets and complex story lines that went into a musical."
She thought, why not combine two great American art forms: jazz and the
Broadway musical? She shared the idea with her husband, who loved it, and
the couple immediately set to work conceiving what would become the first
version of *The Real Ambassadors*.[37]

CHAPTER 2

WORDS AND MUSIC

From the musical's genesis in 1956 to its performance at Monterey in 1962, Iola firmly grounded her narrative in the present, carefully combing news stories, editorials, and current events for timely issues that would inform the show's evolving story lines.[1] The earliest extant outline for the musical is a three-page typewritten synopsis from 1957 that provides a broad overview of the characters and narrative structure.[2] The Brubecks felt that the work might not only address social issues but also be a pivot point to widen Dave's milieu beyond leading a jazz quartet, adding Broadway and perhaps even film or television scoring to his resume. To help protect their original ideas they sent themselves a copy of the three-page treatment via registered mail and placed the unopened envelope, which could be used to verify the date of origination, in a safe deposit box at First Western Bank in Oakland. In a cover letter attached to the sealed envelope, a memo signed by Iola Brubeck documents the provenance of the packet, the post office registration number, and the postmark date, October 3, 1957. It ends by stating, "Said letter placed in Safe Deposit Box unopened. Letter contains a musical synopsis of the musical comedy, 'World Take A Holiday'" (emphasis in original). The memo was witnessed and signed by two officers at the bank.[3]

At the center of the musical would be two couples. The first was bandleader and star "Pops" Anderson (also referred to as the "hero" in the final version of the show) and "far-out chick" vocalist Rhonda Brown. Pops's dedicated manager, Saul Hoffman, and Hoffman's wife, Ellie, would be a second couple in the narrative, providing the additional dramatic and musical pairings needed for a full-scale musical stage production.[4] Iola initially set the action in the fictional European country of San Cristobal, which is about to hold elections to select either a communist or democratic ruling government. The show's book and songs were grounded in then-contemporary life and featured Cold War politics, mistaken identity, two parallel love stories, and a strong thread of social commentary that clearly challenged segregation at a time when many artists chose not to speak out in fear of possible damage to their careers.

Iola introduced the main characters by framing their work as jazz ambassadors touring to promote democracy:

> "Pops" and his five-piece band, the Jazz All-stars, embark on a Government-sponsored world jazz tour accompanied by his dedicated manager, Saul Hoffman, and Saul's wife, Ellie, who cannot understand why he is so dedicated; and a "far-out" chick, the band vocalist, Rhonda Brown.
>
> They are received with wild enthusiasm and "Pops" personality and his music leave an indelible impression on the people of every country they visit. Heady with success, "Pops" and Saul decide to pay an unofficial call on the tiny country of San Cristobal while flying on their way back to Paris. Saul has read that the election immediately following the Festival of San Cristobal is predicted a victory for the Communists because of the spectacular exhibitions that Russia and neighboring Red states have exported to influence the citizens.[5]

This scenario accurately reflected the global Cold War struggle of the US and USSR to curry favor with emerging nations. While the Soviets dispatched the Bolshoi Ballet, the US countered with Dizzy Gillespie and other jazz ambassadors.

Trumpeter Pops and his band, known in the early script as the All-Stars, take San Cristobal by storm and win over the populace, leading the country's king to offer his throne for one day to Pops to help solidify support for democracy. The setting of San Cristobal would eventually be replaced by the newly independent fictional African nation of Talgalla, to better mirror actual world events. In addition to naming the lead character Pops (Armstrong's own nickname), his band's actual name, the All-Stars, is also used in this early synopsis. In doing this, Iola further blurred fact and fiction. This conflation is embedded throughout the musical, so much so that by its finale, the jazz chorus backing Pops calls him "Satchmo" in the lyrics to the song, in spite of the character being named Pops throughout the rest of the show. The magnitude of Armstrong's aura as the world's most beloved jazzman was such that listeners had no problem with such references, even if they broke with standard theatrical practice. Whatever moniker was used to describe Armstrong, the public knew his sound, image, and character well and loved him for his candor, joie de vivre, and artistry.

The musical was originally titled *World Take a Holiday*, but as the show took shape, it was renamed *The Jazz Ambassadors*.[6] Using a number of Dave's existing instrumental compositions, the Brubecks crafted the lyrics for the fifteen songs that would make up the staged version of the musical. In a 1962 interview with Arthur North of the *New York Daily News*, the couple confirmed that they had to work on the show's plot and lyrics whenever Dave was home off the road. This often included the hours the couple spent alone "parked in their car outside the music studio where one or the other of their . . . progeny was taking a lesson."[7] Darius Brubeck shed some light on how the couple worked together on developing the lyrics for the musical:

> What I recall is that Dave would create a lyric which would be rubbish. It wasn't even an attempt to be something usable. But he was really very expert at scansion, a technical term for [identifying] where the stresses, the long notes and short notes would be. He could do that faster than Iola because she wouldn't want to write rubbish. She would think about what the lyric meant, but he would write anything, and it would be a perfect fit for the music. And if she couldn't come up with something that fit the music perfectly, then the music would have to be adjusted.
>
> I recall one example, and it's not as bad as many of the ones he came up with, in the bridge of the song about the real ambassadors. The final lyric is, "We're the real ambassadors, though we may appear as bores." That came from, "I'm the real ambassador, but I can't get past the door." That is how they worked on everything. Dave always presented something in writing with words. It wouldn't be dictation; it would be, "The message is this." Then she set to work to polish the prose or lyric.[8]

In advance of the show's 1962 premiere, Iola hit upon the idea of using a narrator to substitute for the dialogue and onstage action that she and Dave had envisioned in the full-blown musical theater version of the work. Thus, the extant version of the musical was referred to by the Brubecks as the "concert version." In this version, Iola used the narrator's voice to establish Pops's origins and impact, which closely paralleled Armstrong's own rise to fame:

> **Narrator**: Our story concerns a jazz musician not unlike other musicians you may have known. The personal history of our hero reads like the story of jazz—up from the shore of Lake Pontchartrain to Chicago and beyond—from New York to San Francisco, London to Tokyo, and points in between. The music which poured from his horn became his identity—his passport to the world—the key to locked doors. Through his horn he had spoken to millions of

the world's people. Through it he had opened doors to presidents and kings. He had lifted up his horn, as our hero would say, and just played to folks on an even soul-to-soul basis. He had no political message, no slogan, no plan to sell or save the world. Yet, he and other traveling musicians like him had inadvertently served a national purpose, which officials recognized and eventually sanctioned with a program called cultural exchange.[9]

Immediately after this introductory dialogue, the song "Cultural Exchange" recounted the stunning victory scored in 1956 by Dizzy Gillespie and his big band when they calmed rioting students in Greece by making an appearance on behalf of the US State Department. The students had taken up rocks and were stoning the offices of the United States Information Service in response to American support for the country's current right-wing dictator. When Gillespie arrived in Athens later that same day, he recalled that the group played for

> . . . a seething audience of Anti-American students. . . . They loved us so much that when we finished playing they tossed their jackets in the air and carried me on their shoulders through the streets of the city.[10]

The headline in the local newspaper the next day ran, "Students Drop Rocks and Roll for Dizzy."[11] Iola used these news reports to inspire the song "Cultural Exchange." In it, she introduced the idea of the agency jazz ambassadors now wielded:

> From reports on Dizzy Gillespie
> It was clear to the local press
> He quelled the riots in far off Greece
> Restored the place to comparative peace.
> That's what we call cultural exchange! [Repeat four times]
> When Diz blew, the riots were routed
> People danced and they cheered and shouted
> The headlines bannered the hour as his
> They dropped their stones and they rocked with Diz.
> That's what we call cultural exchange! [Repeat four times][12]

Gillespie was known to hire the best musicians for his orchestra, regardless of race. His 1956 orchestra that played Athens was integrated, a point the bandleader used to reinforce the notion that segregation was absurd. When he toured on behalf of the State Department with this group, he would point to the band just before the next number and instruct the audience, "Watch them work together." The implication was that people of different colors could blend harmoniously to create the band's signature sound. Upon hearing Dizzy's concise comment on American race relations, one observer in Zagreb reportedly remarked, "One concrete example is worth a million words."[13] The Brubecks recognized the power that jazz ambassadors wielded and used their agency as the primary engine to drive the plot of *The Real Ambassadors*.

Another song, titled "Remember Who You Are," was written as a parody on the briefing that had been given to the Brubecks and their entourage by delegates of the State Department before leaving the US on their 1958 jazz ambassador tour. The lyrics are sung by a diplomatic representative giving the musicians their last-minute instruction and emphasizing both the importance of good behavior and the need to avoid discussion of any controversial issues. They clearly acknowledge the elevated role that jazz had achieved in America's cultural arsenal.

> Remember who you are and what you represent.
> Always be a credit, to your government.
> No matter what you say or what you do,
> The eyes of the world are watching you.
> Remember who you are and what you represent (represent, represent, represent).
> Remember who you are and what you represent,
> Never face a problem, always circumvent.
> Stay away from issues. Be discreet.
> When controversy enters, you retreat.
> Remember who you are and what you represent (represent, represent, represent).
> Remember who you are and what you represent.
> Jelly Roll and Basie helped us to invent
> A weapon that no other nation has,
> Especially the Russians can't claim jazz.
> Remember who you are and what you represent (represent, represent, represent).[14]

However, prior to "Remember Who You Are," the Brubecks decided to introduce the inherent tension that resulted from Uncle Sam relying primarily on African American jazz musicians as cultural ambassadors during times of intense cultural struggle at home.[15] This section of spoken and partly sung script clued in the audience to the ironies that would be unfolding in *The Real Ambassadors*:

> **Narrator**: And there were other serious questions on our hero's mind. Like . . .
> **Voice I**: Look here, what we need is a goodwill tour of Mississippi!
> **Voice II**: Forget Moscow, when do we play New Orleans!
> **Narrator**: Despite such impertinences, our musician was persuaded that an official tour was not only an obligation but an honor. When the band gathered at the New York International Airport the morning of their departure, members of the President's Committee of the People-to-People program for Cultural Exchange appeared to give the musicians a last-minute "briefing."

[Set rhythm with brushes on drums]

> **Voice II**: Passports
> **Voice III**: Shots
> **Voice I**: Identification
> **Voice II**: Visas
> **Voice III**: Pamphlets
> **Voice I**: Verification
> **Together**: When you travel in a far-off land / Remember you're more than just a band.
> You represent the U.S.A. / So watch what you think and do and say.[16]

Although the narrator had claimed that the character of Pops "had no political message, no slogan, no plan to sell or save the world," the lyrics and narration that would make up the show clearly present the character of Pops as both an agent of change and as a spokesman for African American equality. The script's reference to Mississippi, New Orleans, and Moscow shone a light on the absurdity of sending jazz ambassadors around the globe, and even to the Soviet Union, when mixed-race groups like the Dave Brubeck Quartet and Louis Armstrong and His All-Stars were not allowed to play throughout the American South. In these ways, Dave and Iola Brubeck joined a cadre of artists who took a clear stance against segregation and its underlying fear and hatred throughout the turbulent 1950s and '60s.

The Real Ambassadors introduced the notion of artists becoming cultural diplomats able to bring about change, if only for a short time, in a far-off country. The first two verses of the song "The Real Ambassador" were to be performed by actors portraying US Talgallan ambassadors in their tuxedos and top hats. The Brubecks were lampooning the attitudes expressed when they were briefed prior to their own State Department tour. After explaining their charge, these stuffy diplomats still had to acknowledge the unplanned victory Pops has scored with the people and leaders of an emerging nation that promoted democracy ahead of the socialist agenda:

> **Ambassadors**: Who's the real Ambassador?
>   It is evident we represent American society,
>   Noted for its etiquette, manners, and sobriety,
>   We have followed protocol with absolute propriety,
>   We're Yankees to the core.
>   We're the real Ambassadors.
>   Though we may appear as bores.
>   We are diplomats in our proper hats,
>   Our attire becomes habitual, along with all the ritual.
>   The diplomatic corps,
>   Has been analyzed and criticized by N.B.C. and C.B.S.
>   Senators and Congressmen are so concerned, they can't recess,
>   State Department stands in awe, your coup d'état has met success,
>   And caused this great uproar.
>   Who's the real Ambassador, yeah, the real Ambassador?

As the song continues, Pops takes over center stage and gives a much more nuanced reading of the realpolitik situation that the jazz ambassadors often found themselves in during the Cold War era. Pops's lines in "The Real Ambassador" reveal a manifesto that elegantly lays out the complexities surrounding the US jazz ambassador cultural exchange program. Addressing both US ambassadors to Talgalla, who were surprised by the jazz ambassador's tumultuous reception and the fact that the local populace mistakenly identified him as the diplomat sent from Washington, DC, Pops lays out his views:

> I'm the real Ambassador!
> It is evident I wasn't sent by government to take your place.
> All I do is play the blues and meet the people face to face.
> I'll explain and make it plain I represent the human race,
> And don't pretend no more.
> Who's the real Ambassador?
> Certain facts we can't ignore.

In my humble way, I'm the U.S.A.
Though I represent the government, the government,
Don't represent some policies I'm for.
Oh, we've learned to be concerned about the Constitutionality.
In our nation, segregation isn't a legality.
Soon our only differences will be in personality.
That's what I stand for.[17]

The Brubecks took a stand to say that segregation, which had been banned in American schools by *Brown v. Board of Education* in 1954, must be rooted out so that in time peoples' only differences would be personality. The clever statement "Though I represent the government, the government don't represent some policies I'm for" allowed Pops to distance himself from the day-to-day practices of Jim Crow laws that kept African Americans back and instead use his own agency to support equal rights for all. In just a few lines, the irony is made plain.

Insight into the creative processes that Dave and Iola Brubeck used in creating the lyrics for the musical, and this song in particular, may be gained by reading over a lyric sheet for the song that was originally typewritten but then crossed out and revised in the unmistakable hand of both Iola and Dave Brubeck. At the top of the page is an annotation, "For Louie," in Dave's scrawl. The lyric to be sung by Pops starts by acknowledging the actual State Department envoys, but knocks their comparative stuffiness to his jazz-infused hipness. The earlier draft concludes the passage by citing integration as a reality, and his own recognition of each person's unique personality, ending by asserting that it is these values which make him a more authentic ambassador:

He's the real ambassador, (and a bore)
Why I can't get pass [*sic*] the door,
I am déclassé, in the U.S.A.
Though I represent the government
The government don't represent
The things that I stand for.

We have learned to be concerned about the Constitutionality,
Integration in our nation is now a legality
He who tries to recognize the human personality
And what it stands for.

I'm the real ambassador
Yeah, the real ambassador.[18]

On the same sheet, Iola's handwritten revision changes the last two lines to a question for the audience—"Who's the real ambassador?"—rather than the declaration in the earlier draft above. Now Pops would ask the Talgallans to choose, "Who's the real ambassador?" skillfully putting the question about political versus artistic agency to both the citizens of Talgalla and, in turn, the audience present at the show's performance.

Alongside its political messages, the musical included a second story line: love. The love interest in the musical would primarily play out through the interactions of Pops and the band's new girl singer, Rhonda. Initially, when Rhonda joins the band just prior to the State Department–sponsored tour, she's characterized as a free spirit, enjoying life as a single female jazz singer working with an established all-male band. She's experienced in life and love, and likes to be the center of attention. An early version of "Holiday," an ensemble number designed to be performed early in the first act that didn't make it into the final version of *The Real Ambassadors*, allows Rhonda to tell her new bandmates and the audience what's important to her:

> Every day's a holiday,
> They're all the same to me,
> Cause life's too short to sing the blues,
> In a minor key.
> I prefer up tempo,
> Swingin' all the way.
> When the ball is never over,
> The blues refuse to stay.
> Let's have that worldwide party,
> Give life a great big cheer.
> Don't mean to be a smarty,
> Just want to spread joys,
> Meet me some new boys,
> Miss Rhonda Brown is here![19]

Rhonda starts out as a party girl; however, as she gets to know the members of the band, and especially Pops, her perspectives begin to change and she longs for a stable relationship. In her notes to future producers found in the published preface to the score, Iola wrote of Rhonda's character, stating:

Their tour progresses smoothly, except for the inevitable trouble that comes with a new and designing female traveling with a group of men. Everybody vies for the Girl's attentions; except the man she wants most—our Hero. She [later] sings to him a revealing ballad in the form of a confession, "My One Bad Habit is Falling in Love." Obviously overstating her ethical qualities, she reveals to our hero that the shopworn chanteuse still possesses the soul of the angel she'd like to be.[20]

Dave and Iola credited Ella Fitzgerald as a cowriter on "My One Bad Habit Is Falling in Love," as one night after they had both performed at a jazz festival in Atlantic City, Dave was having a late dinner with Ella, who was clearly feeling down. When he asked what the matter was, she told him, "You know, Dave, my one bad habit is falling in love." He shared that line with Iola, and the song title was born.[21]

"My One Bad Habit" starts out with Rhonda's tongue firmly planted in her cheek, as she winks at the audience before singing directly to the object of her desire, Pops. As the song evolves, she reveals that the carefree life has taken its toll and she's ready to settle down, if our hero is willing:

> I neither smoke, nor drink, nor swear.
> My habits are sublime.
> And at the risk of seeming square,
> Resist temptation all the time.
> One weakness I possess,
> In all meekness I confess,
> My one bad habit is falling in love,
> And falling right out again.
> My resolution: forget the past,
> Don't fall too fast,
> And make it last.
> The dreams that mattered,
> Have all been shattered.
> They're long since scattered—gone!
> My grand illusion,
> Was all delusion.
> My revolution is on.
> To break that habit of falling in love,
> With someone who doesn't care.
> I'm out to conquer.
> So love, beware!

No more despair
In this love affair.
It's now or never,
My last endeavor
To love forever more.
So please treat me gently.
For evidently,
Your bad habit,
Like my bad habit,
Is falling in love.
Just one little shove
And I'll start falling again
Yeah!
I'll start falling again
Oops!
Let's start falling again.

Pops responds with a contemplative ballad, "Summer Song." Rather than directly answering Rhonda's implied invitation, the song uses simile to paint a vivid picture, comparing love to fond memories of Pops's youth:

Love to me is like a summer day,
Silent, cause there's just too much to say.
Still and warm and peaceful!
Even clouds that may drift by,
Can't disturb our summer sky.
I'll take summer,
That's my time of year.
Winter shadows,
Seem to disappear.
Gayest, warmest season!
That's the reason I can say,
That I love a summer day.
I hear laughter from the swimmin' hole,
Kids out fishin' with a willow pole,
Boats come driftin' round the bend,
Why must summer ever end?
Love to me is like a summer day.
If it ends, the memories will stay,
Still and warm and peaceful.

Now the days are getting long,
I can sing my summer song.[22]

By the end of the number, Pops and Rhonda are staring into each other's eyes, and romance has begun. Before the next song begins, the narrator simply tells the audience that "Pops and his singer have come to an understanding." Their relationship is tested later in the show via a solo number, "In the Lurch," in which Rhonda explains that she's tired of waiting for Pops to more publicly return her affection, and, as a result, she is thinking about moving on. Pops has been distracted by the celebrity he has become in Talgalla after being elected "King for a Day," and has overlooked Rhonda's recurring romantic signals. However, he comes to realize late in the show that he really does care for her. The Brubecks then provide the couple with a duet in which Pops has to fight to get Rhonda to stay: "One Moment Worth Years." Whether intentional or not, this part of the plot development neatly paralleled Armstrong's own early failed marriages before he settled down for the rest of his life with his fourth wife, Lucille. "Since Love Had Its Way" brings the romantic couple all the way back together just before the finale, as Pops declares, "That ol' marriage vow now seems worthwhile."

As the musical evolved, the barrier between facts and fiction continued to dissolve, as one of the key songs was eventually titled "Blow Satchmo," a nod to Armstrong's most common public nickname. Pops plans to start a world peace movement during his one day of holding office in Talgalla. He invites world leaders to abandon their statecraft and instead attend a jam session to distract their attention from hair-trigger Cold War politics and its omnipresent threat of nuclear annihilation. Even in the early 1957 synopsis, some of the most important musical numbers that would appear in *The Real Ambassadors* are referenced, including "They Say I Look Like God," "Remember Who You Are," "He's the Real Ambassador," and "World [Take a] Holiday." Iola initially titled the tune portraying Dizzy Gillespie's triumph in Athens "Dizzy Ditty," clearly showing the song's inspiration. After the soundtrack album was recorded, its title was changed to "Cultural Exchange."

The couple not only hoped to address cultural exchange and segregation through the ambitious project; they also wanted to highlight the ever-present fears of nuclear war. An early version of the song "World Take a Holiday" made this explicit:

The world should take a holiday,
Free itself from fear.
A holiday from atom bombs,

And all the threats we hear.
In this age of missiles,
No one's out of range.
We had best bombard each other,
With cultural exchange.[23]

From the first time Dave and Iola put pencil to paper, the goal of the musical was clear: through music, address the major societal concerns of the day and offer it as a tonic to bring healing in troubled times.

The last scripted text read by the show's narrator frames the overarching messages of dignity and acceptance for all mankind.[24] This passage further refuted segregation and discrimination of any type as inhumane practices. Just as the Talgallan people had voted to embrace a democratic government, the dream of an America where racial equality meant true freedom should be championed.

> Narrator: In a remote spot in Africa, a flickering dream of human dignity had been kept alive. No one had yet succeeded in wresting from the citizens of Talgalla the remnant of democracy . . . the freedom to run through the streets shouting their simple, if untenable, dreams.
>
> Each year their ritualistic drama was enacted with fervor and hope that somehow, someday it could be translated into action. With the arrival of the trumpet-playing, swinging Ambassador from the United States, the people of Talgalla felt that day was about to dawn. Talgalla would become a monument to freedom . . .
>
> On the morning of July 10, 1961, a small child, clad in white, with a garland of flowers upon her shoulders, placed a crown upon our hero. The real ambassador was the symbol of the universal dream.

These final words of the narrator bring full circle the concept that art and artists could unlock the potential within mankind to a better life, one where people would no longer be judged by the color of their skin. The Talgallan practice of crowning a popular leader for a single day provided the ideal construct to place Pops in a role where he might change society. If Talgalla could crown a Black man as its leader for a day, why couldn't America accord some level of dignity to its African Americans? The musical's function was to rally the nation to put an end to segregation, the universal dream that the show's cast all sought to realize. However, the path to bringing it to the stage in the fall of 1962 would prove to be fraught with a series of significant obstacles.

CHAPTER 3

BECOMING JAZZ AMBASSADORS

In 1955, in a page-one story, Felix Belair, foreign correspondent for the *New York Times*, had proclaimed jazz as America's greatest "secret weapon" in the Cold War, and Louis Armstrong its most potent agent in the struggle to assert US cultural supremacy over the Soviet Union.[1] Soon after, Dizzy Gillespie became the first official Uncle Sam–sponsored envoy with his twenty-two-piece big band's 1956 world tour. This officially inaugurated the US-sponsored jazz ambassador program, which would run for the next twenty-two years. Benny Goodman followed in 1957. That April, as the Brubecks were working on the initial treatment for their jazz musical, negotiations were underway between Brubeck's representative at Associated Booking Corporation and the American National Theater and Academy (ANTA)[2] to send Brubeck abroad on a State Department tour.[3]

By the end of 1957, it was clear that the State Department tour would take place directly on the heels of a series of commercial dates across Western Europe arranged by Brubeck's European agent, Harold Davison, who worked collaboratively with Associated Booking. Davison was one of the most influential agents in England, having been instrumental in negotiating the means to allow US performers to tour England by setting up reciprocal touring agreements for UK artists to perform in America. Prior to his efforts, American performers were banned from performing in the UK in an effort to preserve jobs for English performers. Davison's client roster ranged across the entire spectrum of UK performers, from rock to jazz. It was Davison who used his international connections to help first bring the Rolling Stones to America, but he also assisted American jazz performers with bookings in Europe and Great Britain. Davison struck up an immediate friendship with Dave and Iola Brubeck, which would play a key role in the *Real Ambassadors* saga.

Brubeck recognized the opportunity that such a tour would provide, not only to bring his music to a much wider global audience but to also learn more himself about people, cultures, and music that would broaden his own artistic palette. Although the State Department was against the idea, Brubeck insisted that his wife and two oldest children, Darius (age eleven) and Michael (age nine), accompany him on the tour.

The tour officially began with a series of US performances, in part to help break in new bassist Eugene Wright, who had joined the quartet at the last minute. Wright was a seasoned performer who fit in quickly with the rest of the group. He had been performing for twenty-five years, having led his own group, the Dukes of Swing, during World War II, then going on to tour with some of the most noted musicians of the postwar era, including Count Basie, Gene Ammons, Arnett Cobb, Buddy DeFranco, Red Norvo, and Cal Tjader.[4] Wright had stepped in to take the place of Norman Bates, who was unwilling to leave home for three months of performing internationally. The overseas portion of the tour was broken into two segments. As mentioned, the former part was strictly commercial, with no association with the State Department, while the latter would be in service of US cultural diplomacy.

After the group's last concert in Copenhagen, the commercial leg of the their overseas tour was completed. The second and lengthier portion of the tour, sponsored by the US State Department, began as the Brubecks' entourage left Denmark, heading to a Cold War hotspot, West Berlin. From there, the jazz ambassadors went to work for Uncle Sam, crisscrossing Asia and Europe from March 5 to May 10, 1958. They performed forty-six concerts and attended many after-hours jam sessions, visited music schools, gave interviews to the press, attended receptions and social events, and visited foreign family residences—all of which contributed rich material to Iola's continued work on the musical.[5]

Throughout 1957, while preparations were taking shape for the upcoming global tour, the Brubecks shared ideas for their musical with two powerful and well-regarded producers, Paul Gregory and George Avakian. Avakian signed Brubeck to Columbia Records in the mid-1950s, and he remained a close confidante of Dave and Iola throughout their careers.[6] Avakian also had a close relationship with Louis Armstrong, as he had conceived and produced a string of Satchmo's most commercially successful albums in the mid-1950s on Columbia.

Paul Gregory's rise to prominence as a producer on Broadway reads like a Horatio Alger novel. He was one of five children in an Iowa family. As a teen, his mother sent him to England to live with an aunt and uncle after his father ran off with his mother's money. Soon Gregory was enjoying the finest schooling and being exposed to a full range of arts and culture, which would serve him well in his future career as a producer and director. He developed a solid work ethic and eventually returned to the US, finished high school, then headed west to make his fortune in Hollywood. He got his start in the late 1930s, working at a soda fountain in a Hollywood Boulevard drugstore, where he met a number of artists for whom he soon booked performances, using money he had saved up from his job to promote the concerts. His early shows were successful, and soon MCA's powerful head, Lew Wasserman, learned of the budding impresario and offered him a job as an agent in the firm's New York office. Although Gregory was handling personal appearances for some of the leading artists of the day, such as Horace Heidt and Carmen Cavallaro, he didn't enjoy the work.[7]

One night in 1950, over dinner at a diner he saw British actor Charles Laughton reading from the Bible on the *Ed Sullivan Show* and was riveted by his dramatic reading of the book of Daniel. He immediately made his way from the diner to the studio and waited outside the exit. Ambushing the actor as he left the theater, he brashly talked his way into joining Laughton and his companion for the evening. Gregory eventually persuaded Laughton to sign with him for stage performances across the US. His instincts for what would be popular in the theater proved to be excellent, as the young agent secured more than $200,000 in bookings for Laughton's dramatic readings.[8] Spurred by this success, Gregory left MCA, as at this time the agency only represented musical talent.

Gregory built Laughton's profile to successively greater roles, first on television and then on Broadway. Gregory's 1953 Broadway production of Stephen Vincent Benét's epic poem *John Brown's Body*, starring Laughton, Judith Anderson, and Tyrone Power, drew rave reviews and was a box office hit. Gregory followed that up by producing *The Caine Mutiny Court-Martial*, based on the Pulitzer prize–winning novel, directed by Laughton and starring Lloyd Nolan and Henry Fonda. It too was a commercial and critical success, running for 415 shows.

It was clear that Paul Gregory had the connections and experience to help the Brubecks realize their vision for their musical.[9] While no correspondence survives between him and the Brubecks, Iola Brubeck joined her husband in Los Angeles to preview the show for Gregory in the fall of 1957. She recalled:

> The meeting was arranged by Joe Glaser. I had the feeling that Gregory was not really interested but listened out of politeness. Dave played the tunes and I read the lyrics and dialog for the first act. We had been told that we had one hour, so we quit at the end of the first act and just described the second act. I do recall his asking if Louis Armstrong would really be available.[10]

An experienced producer such as Gregory understood that Armstrong's commitment would be a linchpin in generating enough interest to finance such a production. Dave noted in follow-up correspondence that Gregory advised the Brubecks to rethink and simplify the staging and production in order to gain support for the show. In a December 13, 1957, letter to George Avakian that accompanied the story outline, song list, and first act of the book for *World Take a Holiday*, the Brubecks shared a detailed reflection on the preview of the show they gave Paul Gregory. Gregory, who was known for a minimalist approach to his productions, had suggested they "use a bare stage (Gregory approach) that would greatly reduce the cost . . . as well as keeping a simple, direct and fluid approach more in keeping with jazz."[11] The Brubecks told Avakian that Gregory liked the music and concept and had asked them to not show it to any other producer until he returned from an overseas trip, where he was making a new film.

Having successfully attracted the attention of a very successful Broadway producer, Dave and Iola now felt confident that their continued efforts to engage an established producer might be fruitful. The letter accompanying the December 13, 1957, package sent to Avakian at Columbia Records' New York City offices bubbles with excitement at the prospects the couple saw developing. That enthusiasm was the result of a prior phone conversation (referenced in the letter) between Avakian and Dave Brubeck about the musical and how to best move ahead to make its production a reality. The correspondence discussed which songs would be in the show and described their relationship to a recently completed session recorded in Chicago by Avakian's assistant, Cal Lampley. The Brubecks also expressed concern that the record-buying public might resist purchasing the show's soundtrack, since it looked as if most of the songs would be updated versions (adding vocals) of songs previously released by Brubeck. A note at the bottom of this letter, handwritten in Brubeck's distinctive scrawl, instructs Avakian: "Call me if you get any ideas immediately."

While the Brubecks' enthusiasm was certainly engaging, Avakian, like Gregory, was concerned with the complex structure that the couple was integrating into the musical. For instance, in a story outline prepared by Iola, act 1, scene 3 features six individual dance numbers strung together to represent the traveling jazz ambassadors' stays in England, France, Spain, Russia, Japan, and India. A chorus is called for, along with the musical's principal actors and extra musicians. When interviewed in 2010, George Avakian reflected on this letter and recalled that at the time he also felt the production might be too complex, stating, "Simplification was one theme of any discussion with Dave and Iola. I was concerned about the many changes of settings [in the show] and what that would cost. Since the project was not something universal like rape, lust, or vengeance, it had to be budgeted carefully."[12] As the years went by, other producers who met and discussed the show with Brubeck would continue to raise similar concerns about the large cast and complicated staging the couple imagined for the show.

Still, realizing a Broadway production remained a high priority for Dave Brubeck. Writing to his brother Howard, who served tirelessly as his orchestrator, on the eve of the quartet's departure for their 1958 three-month world tour, Dave said, "the orchestrations for the Broadway show . . . will have to wait until I return."[13] Dave understood they would have to temporarily put a halt to the planning process while he was on tour. As they prepared for their pending 1958 departure for Europe and points beyond, however, Dave and Iola brought along the music for a number of the songs to continue refining the lyrics and structure. Meanwhile, actual events were about to unfold that further informed the path the couple would take in detailing the jazz ambassadors' peculiar role as cultural diplomats.

While the Brubecks continued to polish their socially conscious musical, behind-the-scenes concerns about the State Department using integrated groups as jazz ambassadors surfaced, as evidenced by its own back-channel cables addressing the matter. Musicologist Stephen Crist points out that secretary of state John Foster Dulles had previously exchanged a series of telegrams with the US delegations in Poland, Czechoslovakia, and Romania touting Brubeck's quartet, which then still included bassist Norman Bates, as "all-white," implying that such a group was preferable to a mixed-race ensemble in fulfilling the propaganda needs of the State Department. A response from the mission in Prague to Washington confirmed such concerns, as it stated: "For U.S. purposes [a] white jazz group [is] preferable, as this sidesteps regime propaganda linking jazz to oppression [of] Negroes in America."[14] There was no reason to add fuel to the Soviets' effective counterpropaganda messages.

By 1957, bassist Norman Bates had been with the quartet for two years, but his refusal to go on the trip evidently caught the State Department off guard, as the tour's advance photos of the quartet (distributed by the State Department) still featured Bates, representing the quartet as all white. By the time the State Department realized that the quartet would be mixed race, it was too late to cancel the tour. Such a cancellation would have also played directly into Soviet propaganda, which trumpeted the double standards in the US with regard to segregation.

Serving as jazz ambassadors meant that the musicians were charged by the State Department to engage in daily "people-to-people" dialogues as a way to provide foreign nationals with a more complete and sympathetic understanding of life in America.[15] While on the tour, Brubeck and his fellow musicians became de facto spokespersons, as they were repeatedly asked about the state of race relations in the US, in part because of international news coverage of the steady stream of bus and restaurant boycotts and marches in protest of racial discrimination across the US, and the frequent violent responses that resulted. This coverage raised valid questions worldwide about the quality of life in America, especially for people of color.

Savvy propagandists working on behalf of the USSR constantly amplified reports of racial strife in America, broadcasting it across every continent, to help weaken the American messages of what democracy stood for. Unfortunately, such Soviet counterpropaganda messages were very effective, as they were grounded solidly in fact. As an example of how segregation affected jazz performances, the night before the quartet's departure for Europe, their concert at East Carolina College in Greenville, North Carolina, was delayed long past the billed start time while the mixed-race band waited just offstage for the college president to get approval from the governor before allowing them to perform.[16]

In the late 1950s, the world's eyes were focused on America's race-relations struggles, and this was driven home to the entire Brubeck entourage repeatedly throughout the State Department–sponsored portion of the tour. Their first day behind the Iron Curtain, Dave was interviewed on Polish radio. The initial question asked him to comment on the race problems in America.[17] The official concert program printed by the Polish government for Brubeck's two-week, thirteen-concert tour of the country cited him as a product of white privilege, having had access to the best schools. The program then compared Brubeck's talent to that of saxophonist Charlie Parker, who was forced to rely on his native talent, implying that due to his race, Parker was denied the same educational opportunities as Brubeck. Since the program was created and printed by the Polish government and their arts ministry, it provided a convenient platform to once again poke a finger in the eye of Uncle Sam.[18]

Later, while the quartet was in India, a young man approached African American bassist Eugene Wright and asked him how he could support his government as a jazz ambassador while discrimination was prevalent in America. Wright, who had studied the countries the quartet was touring, turned the question around and asked the Indian man "what business he had asking me about that, when his own country had a much longer history of discrimination" (referring to India's centuries-old caste system). Wright said the man then simply walked away.[19] Iola and the two oldest Brubeck sons joined the group as they toured Europe, Poland, and Turkey, providing a shared cultural exchange experience that the Brubecks would mine as they continued to revise and adapt the show in the coming years. Spending four months touring the world and meeting and discussing music with musicians and the legions of jazz devotees encountered in so many different cultures had a profound impact on Dave Brubeck.

Brubeck believed in America and the ability of a democracy to address segregation. One of the ways he attempted to answer challenges about US race problems was by drawing a comparison that positioned his quartet as a microcosm of society. He argued that the "freedom" he and his fellow musicians enjoyed onstage within the quartet to improvise, listen, and respond to one another equally represented an aspirational model of the same individual rights a good society should afford its people. He didn't gloss over the ugly realities of Jim Crow segregation, but he did offer hope that the situation could and would improve. Summing up the social and political critiques the jazz ambassadors faced, Iola recalled:

> We ran into enough criticism when we were overseas, people asking us "What about your racial problems [at home]," and so we felt this [musical] was a way to bring the two ideas [cultural exchange and race relations] together.[20]

The 1958 tour experience inspired Iola Brubeck to adapt her original ideas on cultural exchange and how the subject would be handled in *The Real Ambassadors*. The Brubecks clearly understood that although the State Department's intent for the jazz ambassador tours was to demonstrate the value of American culture as a product of a free and integrated society, the reality was markedly different, in large part because the quartet was now a mixed-race group. The conversations and debates that resulted on the tours between the musicians and foreign citizens seldom followed the prescribed State Department dictums to avoid any mention of controversy at home. This was especially true for African American jazz ambassadors like Duke Ellington, Dizzy Gillespie, and Louis Armstrong, who faced daily discrimination at home yet were asked to set aside any personal reservations about representing Uncle Sam abroad as jazz ambassadors. It was this dichotomy, made evident over the three-month State Department tour, that inspired Iola to make sure the show would clearly demonstrate the absurdity of discrimination.

Iola and her two oldest sons returned home to California in early April after the group concluded their tour of Turkey. Music writers for the *San Francisco Chronicle* and *Oakland Tribune* briefly mentioned this return from the first part of the State Department tour. In a more extensive interview with *DownBeat* magazine, Iola later explained how important jazz music was to the people she met while touring Poland for two weeks as part of the People-to-People tour:

> The Poles consider jazz an art; it means the free expression of the individual to them. . . . They take jazz more seriously than we do . . . the fact that they continue to play it, even when it was forbidden, shows how much it means to them. It is a symbol of protest to the Poles. They are starved for books, records and U.S. jazz magazines, they pass jazz magazines around until they are in shreds.[21]

This article led to an outpouring of Bay Area readers donating used LPs, sheet music, and jazz magazines to be collected by Iola and sent, via US consular dispatch, to the US cultural attaché in Warsaw to distribute to Polish jazz fans.[22] Dubbed by Poles the "Jazz-Lift," the materials were viewed as manna from heaven upon their distribution to the Polish jazz clubs. Citing the emotional connection that the Polish jazz fans and local musicians made with the Brubeck entourage, jazz critic Ralph J. Gleason reported:

> When the Brubecks left March 20 after their [final] concert in Poznan, the station platform was crowded with persons offering them flowers and small gifts. The jazz buffs who had followed the group for two weeks were crying. "And," said Mrs. Brubeck, "so were we. It was quite an experience."[23]

Iola had been changed by her time on the road with the jazz ambassadors and was even more determined to incorporate some of what she had learned about jazz, its passionate global audience, and the sometimes messy realities of cultural exchange into the show. She made note of the fierce love of jazz she witnessed in different countries, as well as its connection to the notions of individual freedom that nearly all the audience members talked about with her. Dave and Iola clearly recognized the inherent contradiction represented by enlisting Black jazz artists to be goodwill cultural ambassadors for the

US at the same time that the US civil rights struggle dominated the national conversation at home and abroad. This central tenet of *The Real Ambassadors* had been brought into sharp focus numerous times during the tour, as both members of the foreign press and fans persistently asked the musicians about the long-standing struggle for equality in America.[24]

After his family's departure from Turkey, Brubeck and the group embarked on the most physically demanding portion of the tour, going on to India, Ceylon, East and West Pakistan, Iraq, Afghanistan, and Iran. The artists were exhausted by the time they flew back to the US in early May. However, within days of Dave Brubeck's return from the lengthy overseas tour, he and Iola once again turned their attention to the musical. In a May 27, 1958, letter to his music publisher, Ernie Farmer of Shawnee Press, Brubeck asked him to "withdraw any of my material from the commercial-vocal market, such as 'Summer Song,' which you are trying to push for me."[25] The Brubecks had decided to embargo their own vocal pieces so they would be fresh for the audience they hoped to reach with the musical.

After the quartet's return, the tour garnered even more press attention. Among the various news reports of the tour, the most prominent was a Brubeck-penned op-ed that was published June 15, 1958, in the *New York Times Magazine*. Titled "The Beat Heard 'Round the World," this high-profile essay firmly established Brubeck as a proponent of using cultural diplomacy as an effective Cold War stratagem. The lengthy piece, cowritten by Dave and Iola Brubeck with an assist from Gilbert Millstein at the *Times*, captured the excitement and overwhelmingly positive response that the quartet had received, especially in nations where US diplomats perceived the greatest opportunity to win over the people to a positive viewpoint of American culture and values.[26]

A close reading of this op-ed, in light of the themes presented in the 1957 drafts of *The Real Ambassadors*, shows a clear sense of purpose and alignment between the musical and the essay. The vocabulary, tone, and tenets laid out also show that the piece was a collaborative effort by Dave and Iola. In it, they argue that "jazz is welcomed . . . throughout the world as the most authentic example of American culture," and that postwar America "assumes the most moral role of all internationally." Like Dizzy Gillespie, they assert that the "sight and sound of a mixed [race] band improvising" with beauty and precision shows that, in their idealized worldview, racial categorization should be meaningless. The Brubecks argue:

> Jazz is color blind. When a German or a Pole or an Iraqi or an Indian
> sees American white men and colored in perfect creative accord, when

he finds out that they travel together, eat together, live together and think pretty much alike, socially and musically, a lot of the bad taste of Little Rock is apt to be washed from his mouth.[27]

Their direct reference to the highly publicized troubles in Little Rock, Arkansas, refers to the still-festering wounds the nation had experienced less than a year before due to the refusal of Arkansas authorities to allow Black children to attend school, in spite of the landmark 1954 Supreme Court case, *Brown v. Board of Education*. That decision mandated that all US public schools must be integrated to provide equal opportunity to students of all races. Echoing the role that the musical's lead character Pops would play in the show's narrative, the Brubecks cite Armstrong (whom by now they strongly conflated in their minds with the show's Pops character) throughout the essay, as America's most potent cultural ambassador. In language strikingly similar to what she would repeat three years later in a radio interview just before recording *The Real Ambassadors'* soundtrack, and subsequently in the album's liner notes, Iola lauded Armstrong as the "uneducated Negro who, through his genius, has overcome all possible obstacles and who is loved universally. Love walks in, all right, when Louis plays."[28] The Brubecks were well aware of Armstrong's triumphant tours of Europe and Africa and of the heroic status he had achieved in most of the world as the best-loved jazz performer of all time. This irony would provide the perfect setup for their socially conscious musical.

Another anecdote recounted in the *Times* op-ed informed another plot direction of the show. At the final concert during their two-week residency in communist-controlled Poland, the quartet premiered a new piece titled "Dziekuje," Polish for "thank you," as a way of showing the profound appreciation the pianist and his fellow musicians felt for the outpouring of hospitality, fellowship, and musical exchange that had been afforded to them. He wrote a solo piano introduction to the piece that is an homage to Frédéric Chopin, one of Poland's greatest musicians. At the conclusion of the piece, the crowd showed their appreciation with a long round of applause. As the group left the stage, Brubeck recalled, "A Polish government worker said to me backstage, 'Why don't the artists rule the world?' There were tears in his eyes and he almost made me weep."[29] The idea later emerged in the show in the memorable number, "King for a Day," when bandleader and hero Pops becomes the ruler of Talgalla for a day. The Brubecks embraced jazz conventions even further and suggested that if world leaders could only get off the dais at the United Nations and get to know one another personally through a musical connection, the prospects of world peace might also be one step closer. In the same song, the Brubecks claimed that instead of formal summit meetings, which seemed to rarely result in lasting changes, world leaders might instead participate in a Satchmo-led basement jam session as a more effective means of building trust and actually defusing Cold War political tensions.

The platform afforded by the lengthy *Times* op-ed piece highlights the clarity and purpose the couple had in their minds and hearts as they prepared to devote their energy and time to realizing the musical. Reviewing the surviving correspondence, it is clear that Iola and Dave believed they had selected the strongest possible leading man for the musical to help them persuade audiences that segregation was ultimately absurd and must be overturned. Their essay was a public call to action, and they embraced the opportunity afforded to them by the quartet's recent successes as a platform for cultural transformation.

With the tour experiences fresh in their minds, and the validation of jazz as a potent cultural and geopolitical tool, Iola and Dave continued to fine-tune the book and lyrics. Over the ensuing four years, from late 1958 through the show's premiere in fall 1962, they would produce what became the final version of *The Real Ambassadors*. Still, dreaming about its hoped-for path to Broadway wouldn't make it a reality. They had to think practically: the Brubecks needed a legitimate producer.

CHAPTER 4

FINDING A PRODUCER

By May 1958 at the end of the State Department tour, the Brubecks knew that to get on Broadway, they must convince a successful impresario that the musical and its message were bankable. Thus, they widened the circle of music and entertainment industry executives to whom they pitched their ideas to include Broadway producers Joshua Logan, Leland Hayward, Marshall Jamison, and Jerome Robbins. They undertook their campaign with zeal, as they next consulted with the president of Columbia Records, Goddard Lieberson.

On June 9, 1958, less than a month after Brubeck's homecoming, Lieberson arrived at the Brubecks' Oakland residence to discuss their plans for the show.[1] Lieberson had been head of Columbia for two years. He was himself a trained musician and composer, and had firsthand knowledge of the risks and rewards of investing in Broadway shows. In 1956, it was Lieberson who had convinced his boss, CBS chief William Paley, to invest $400,000 of the firm's money into a new Broadway show titled *My Fair Lady*, giving Columbia a reported 40 percent interest in the hit show ($4 million in 2021 currency). The resulting original cast recording soared to number one on the *Billboard* popular music charts, a position it held for fifteen weeks, and then continued to reside on the bestseller charts for an unprecedented 480 weeks—slightly more than eight years.[2] Dave and Iola Brubeck were well justified in looking to their own record label as a prospective backer for the musical. Although Lieberson was unwilling to lobby for Columbia to back the show's production on Broadway, he offered to introduce the Brubecks to a potential producer. He even suggested lyric changes to the song "My One Bad Habit."

Iola Brubeck recalled that Lieberson cautioned them that

> sometimes what is popular and acceptable in concert is not the same as onstage In other words, he was warning us that even though we had Louis Armstrong [in mind as the lead], that didn't necessarily mean that we had a viable vehicle for Broadway.[3]

Soon after the meeting, Lieberson offered an introduction to an even more prominent Broadway figure, producer Joshua Logan, for whom Dave would preview the show in November 1958.[4] Logan's credits included Broadway smash hits such as *Annie Get Your Gun, Mister Roberts, South Pacific, Fanny, Wish You Were Here*, and the Pulitzer Prize–winning *South Pacific* with Rodgers and Hammerstein.[5] Logan, like Paul Gregory, was reportedly enthusiastic about the show and asked Brubeck to return in a month's time to go over it in detail. Although no record of that second meeting exists, during the first meeting, Logan must have made clear to Dave that securing a firm commitment to have Louis Armstrong appear in the lead role would be necessary in order for any serious producer to consider backing the show, because not long after that meeting, the Brubecks began a lengthy correspondence with Joe Glaser, who not only headed up Brubeck's booking agency but also served as Armstrong's personal manager. An extensive series of letters cowritten by Dave and Iola between 1958 and 1960 asked for Glaser's support in their efforts to secure Armstrong in the musical's lead role.

As a result of the continuing dialogue with Broadway producers, including Gregory and Logan, by November 1958 the issues of the show's substantial production cost and access to the musical's lead, Louis Armstrong, had become crucial barriers to its possible realization. Dave and Iola Brubeck listened carefully to each comment and suggestion they received and continually adapted their vision as they persisted in seeking a backer. In a detailed two-page letter to Joe Glaser on November 28, 1958, Dave explained to Armstrong's manager and agent how he and Iola had reworked the show based on Gregory's suggestions, with an eye toward a more streamlined staging.[6] He told Glaser, "The rewritten version will be far less expensive to produce." He summarized the meeting with Joshua Logan one week earlier, previewing the show from the piano in Logan's Manhattan apartment while Logan's wife went in and out of the room. "He was most enthusiastic about the music, and in a month or so I am going to go over the entire show with him," he wrote. Dave then tackled the crux of the problem in the next paragraph, writing that although both Gregory and Logan were "excited about the possibility of Louis Armstrong appearing in a Broadway show," he understood well the economics of constant touring. He suggested that an extended residency for Armstrong might result in diminished revenue for all parties, since Satchmo could "earn far more on a concert tour than a musical can pay."

Ever the creative problem-solvers, the Brubecks then proposed a truly novel solution. They suggested that Armstrong and Brubeck might concurrently pool their resources to purchase or rent a nightclub in Manhattan during the show's run to offset the loss in income from the higher nightly earnings Satchmo would earn on the road. The proposal suggested that Brubeck would do an early set before the curtain and Armstrong would perform an after-show set. Dave proposed, "With me performing the early part of the evening at the club and Louis coming in for one set after the show, [it] would probably make the week's combined gross equal to what Louis normally gets [on the road]."

This innovative solution had a solid precedent in Armstrong's own history. In 1929, while appearing in a review called *Hot Feet* at famous Harlem nightspot, Connie's Inn, Armstrong would leave the club and head down to the theater district to do his showstopping rendition of Fats Waller's "Ain't Misbehavin'" as part of the successful *Connie's Hot Chocolates* review, which played 219 shows at the Hudson Theatre on Broadway. Armstrong would play in the orchestra pit each night, perform his featured number from the pit, and immediately after the show, rush back uptown to Harlem to play the final set of the evening. Some evenings he even played another after-hours show at the Lafayette Theatre just a block away from Connie's Inn.[7] The Brubecks' notion that nightclub performances by Dave's band, as well as a late performance by Armstrong, could be sandwiched around a Broadway staging of the show was based in Armstrong's own history. By keeping Satchmo in New York City if the musical was successful, he would be home each night to enjoy his wife Lucille's famous red beans and rice, Brubeck argued. He concluded this letter with a direct ask: "Can [I] secure Louis Armstrong for a Broadway production?"[8] When queried about this letter and its outside-the-box proposal to jointly own a club in a 2009 interview with the author, Iola commented that, though she did not recall writing it, "it doesn't surprise me, though. We knew we had to secure Louis if we wanted the show to be produced." With their minds made up that Armstrong was the only choice to play the complex role of Pops, the couple redoubled their efforts to earn manager Joe Glaser's approval for Satchmo's involvement.

Meanwhile, as the afterglow of the successful 1958 world tour faded, the need to keep food on the table and his band fully employed meant that Brubeck was back out on the road within a few weeks of the group's return from Asia. As had been the case just before their departure with the snafu in Greenville, North Carolina, the quartet continued to run into situations that forced them to cancel engagements, both at home and overseas. On September 21, 1958, Ralph Gleason reported that Brubeck's group had to turn down a $17,000 booking for a week of concerts in South Africa. Once the offer had been made to Brubeck's agent, a message came through to Brubeck explaining the conditions that would be required to book the dates:

As regards one of your group being a Negro, it is absolutely impossible for him to come to South Africa. Not only is there an ordinance
prohibiting the appearance on the stage of a mixed [race] group, but
also he would not be allowed in the country and therefore, the tour
would need to be made without him.[9]

The South African performances were to be a key element in another globe-
trotting journey for the quartet, who planned to play first in Spain and Italy,
then cross the equator to South Africa, before heading east to dates in Ceylon, Australia, New Zealand, and finally, Hong Kong. While disappointed
to have to cancel the ambitious plans without the South African bookings,
Brubeck simply stated, "We called it off." The next year, the *New York Post*
reported that a March 4, 1959, concert scheduled for the University of Georgia was canceled when the school learned that bassist Eugene Wright was an
African American.[10] Ironically, the call canceling the University of Georgia
engagement was made to Brubeck during his weeklong residency at Harlem's
famed Apollo Theater, where his mixed-race group was regularly welcomed.
Brubeck offered up a more succinct indictment of the harm being caused to
America and its reputation overseas to the editors of *Jet* magazine:

Race prejudice is going to make this country lose the world if it is not
changed in a hurry. It's losing us Europe, the Middle East, Asia, South
Africa—what else is there. When I write a Broadway show or play, it
[will] be on the racial problem . . . blatant hypocrisy is what is holding
our country back.[11]

Developing *The Real Ambassadors* offered a very real pressure-relief valve
for Brubeck's frustration with the lack of what he viewed as meaningful
progress in the daily lives of American Blacks. Adding even more fuel to the
Brubecks' desire to challenge segregation through the musical, in 1960, the
Dave Brubeck Quartet was forced to cancel twenty-two of twenty-five college
concerts in the South due to Jim Crow restrictions on mixed-race ensembles
performing at state-supported institutions. The net loss to the group was
$40,000.[12] Brubeck's integrated quartet had also received numerous threats
of violence during Southern tours in an attempt to intimidate the group
into canceling performances, Iola Brubeck remembered, "but nothing came
of them." At one point, the concerns were such that the FBI sent an agent
to provide additional security at a concert in the Deep South, according
to Eugene Wright. He recalled, "We learned there would be extra security

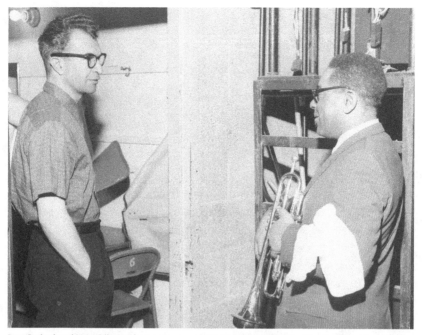

Dave Brubeck and Dizzy Gillespie sharing a moment backstage at Harlem's famed Apollo Theater. Brubeck's group performed regularly at the venue. Brubeck Collection, Holt-Atherton Special Collections, University of the Pacific Library, © Dave Brubeck.

because of some threats at one particular concert. I remember a man coming up to me backstage and introducing himself, saying, 'Mr. Wright, I'm with the FBI and will be here in case of any problems.'"[13] Such bias was not limited to the American South. Iola noted that shortly after the family had first moved to Weston, Connecticut, in 1960:

> Eugene [Wright] had come to the house to rehearse and may have stayed the night. It's hard to believe . . . I don't know the provocation, but I did receive one of those nasty name-calling phone calls. Incredible."[14]

Leading an integrated group meant that unsavory manifestations of the fear and hatred of segregationists were nearly always in the Brubecks' purview. The musical offered a chance to present their view of a potentially better world where music, and jazz in particular, might help counter decades of systemic racial bias.

But to make it work the way they envisioned, they needed Louis Armstrong, and Louis had a very powerful gatekeeper: Joe Glaser.

CHAPTER 5

JOE GLASER

Joe Glaser plays a pivotal yet complicated role in the behind-the-scenes efforts to bring *The Real Ambassadors* to life. As Armstrong's manager, booking agent, financial steward, protector, and sometime enforcer, he presents an enigmatic character who was wholly offstage; however, without Glaser's actions, Armstrong would have never become what amounted to a global superstar in an era before that term was even coined. There is currently no biography of Joe Glaser, but Armstrong biographer Ricky Riccardi provides the most detailed account to date of Glaser's life in his 2020 Armstrong biography, *Heart Full of Rhythm: The Big Band Years of Louis Armstrong*, looking closely at Glaser and Armstrong's early years together.[1] Another Armstrong historian, Michael Cogswell, asserts that the reason there is no biography of Glaser is the manager's almost obsessive focus on maintaining a shroud of total secrecy about his business dealings. He was intensely private about his affairs and shunned interviews for most of his life, deriving power from his intentionally low profile. Glaser would aggressively defend Armstrong or any of his other artists, but he could also be shockingly patronizing, taking the artists for granted and often referring to them as if they worked for him—rather than the other way around. As anecdotes reveal, Glaser was a street-savvy brawler, fiercely loyal, and a masterful negotiator, not unlike Elvis Presley's infamous manager, Colonel Tom Parker. He could also hold a grudge and mete out punishment for any who crossed him. John Levy, who worked for Glaser on occasion as a tour manager, remembered Glaser's over-the-top manner during one of Levy's regular visits to Associated Booking's office:

> As soon as I hit the front door of [Glaser's] office suite in the Squibb Building at 745 Fifth Avenue, I could hear him cussing as usual, in his loud, shrill voice. As I walked down the long hallway toward his office, I passed all the agents working for him. Everyone was on the phone making deals, and most had their free hand over their ear to block out the sound of Joe's voice.[2]

Joe Glaser, who managed the career of Louis Armstrong from 1935 to 1969, on the phone at the New York City offices of Associated Booking Corporation. Courtesy of Louis Armstrong House Museum.

Armstrong's and Glaser's professional lives and finances were inextricably bound together for more than thirty-five years. Viewed by the ethical standards expected of an artist manager today, Glaser would be seen as taking grossly unfair advantage of Armstrong. However, one cannot apply today's conventions and business practices to the music industry of the mid-twentieth century. Glaser also provided much more than just a booking agency, as will be discussed shortly. If one looks strictly at Satchmo's apparent income and celebrity, Glaser's efforts led to impressive results, as Armstrong was consistently one of the highest-paid African American entertainers of the day. To better understand Glaser's ways of conducting business and their effect throughout *The Real Ambassadors* narrative, it's essential to go back to his beginnings in Chicago.

Glaser was born into a prominent Chicago family ca. 1897.[3] After failing as a medical student and a car salesman, he found his calling in the sports and entertainment businesses. In the early 1920s, Glaser managed a few prizefighters in Chicago and became known for tipping reporters on which fights were fixed, going so far as to sometimes predict in which round the fight would end, according to Laurence Bergreen's biography of Al Capone.[4] The mob was mixed up in the boxing business, so Glaser was most likely surrounded by gangsters with a stake in the fight world.

By the mid-1920s, Glaser had graduated to a much more lucrative position, managing the Sunset Cafe nightclub and its upstairs bordello, two of Al Capone's most profitable properties at the time.[5] For musicians during Prohibition, club engagements such as those provided by the Sunset offered a modest, steady paycheck, while the club owners made enormous profits from selling illegal alcohol. There was a distinct power imbalance between the talent and management. "That was one of the reasons why Joe's contracts were very lopsided with artists," stated George Avakian. "They were an outgrowth of his training as Capone's South Side 'Director of Entertainment' in the twenties."[6] Rollicking music was an essential part of the speakeasy experience, but musicians would be paid just enough to keep them alive. In the same letter, Avakian further demonstrated Glaser's lack of refinement, as he recalled the first time the manager introduced his wife to the Columbia record executive. "He described her as the [former] madam in charge of the South Side brothels, and . . . the best wife [his] money could buy." From the recollections of those artists who worked with him, as well as his history running speakeasies and bordellos during Prohibition, Glaser had earned a reputation as an influential and often intimidating power broker. His consistent need to "win" any business negotiation and nonstop in-your-face attitude were further artifacts of his coming of age under the tutelage of the Capone Mob in Chicago. It was there that Glaser first worked with Louis Armstrong in 1926 and recognized the immense talent that the young musician possessed, billing him as "the world's greatest cornetist" on the signs outside the club.[7]

The lawless era of Prohibition brought criminal enterprise and violence to the entertainment industry on an unprecedented scale. Here's an example of what musicians sometimes faced in the crossfire that could erupt between volatile bootleggers. An original member of Armstrong's All-Star band, Barney Bigard occupied the clarinet chair for longer than any other musician. Like Satchmo, Bigard was a New Orleans native who had followed King Oliver to Chicago.[8] Bigard remembered:

> Sometime toward the end of 1926 things around Chicago were getting really bad with gangsters and so on. I remember one night at the Plantation. You see, Joe Glaser, he had the Sunset right across the street from us, and he was somehow tied in with the gangsters. We were taking all the business from him, so one day these gangsters were up on the roof of the Plantation. They were planting bombs all over the roof, and of course people saw them up there in the broad daylight but just figured they were up there to fix a hole . . . [later] the first set started

and we were playing "Animal Crackers" when VROOM! Debris started falling everywhere. I was stunned, I didn't know what was going on. Then another shot, VROOM! Right over the bandstand. A guy came running up to the bandstand yelling, "Play, play!" It seemed like my horn was playing itself. The whole place was in a turmoil . . . people were running to the vestibule to get outside when another one hit the front of the place. I took off like a bat out of hell and went home. Those were rough days.[9]

Glaser's amorality, assuming he was at least partially responsible for the above crime, wasn't limited to bombings with innocent patrons and musicians in the line of fire. Armstrong biographers cite Glaser's frequent run-ins with law enforcement early in his career, including two charges brought for having sexual relationships with underage girls in Chicago in 1928.[10] Evidently, he avoided a ten-year prison term in the first case, which involved a 14-year-old girl, by marrying her. Not long after, a second girl brought charges against Glaser, and although he was acquitted with the help of Capone's fixers, he was evidently told to return to managing boxers, as public awareness of his predilection for teenage girls posed a liability, even for the Mob.[11]

Glaser became Armstrong's personal manager in 1935, when Satchmo was out of money and in poor health.[12] He promptly rescued Armstrong from a ruinous relationship with manager Johnny Collins. It was Collins who had convinced Armstrong to run away to Europe in 1932 to escape competing organized crime syndicates that each believed they controlled his contract with Collins. Prior to the trumpeter's European exile, one of Dutch Schultz's gang members had forced him to return to New York from Chicago at gunpoint to fulfill a prior commitment to perform at Connie's Inn. Using his connections with the underworld, Glaser was able to promptly resolve the gang dispute over Satchmo's contract, earning the trumpeter's lifelong loyalty in return. Longtime Armstrong collaborator and confidante George Avakian explained the details of how Glaser rescued Satchmo from the dangerous dilemma he was facing, revealing that it was in fact the weary trumpet player who sought out Glaser's protection:

When Armstrong returned to the U.S. after fleeing for nearly two years to Europe to escape the tug of war to take over his career between the remnants of the Chicago mob and gangster Arthur Fleigelheimer (aka Dutch Schultz) in New York, Pops went to Joe and proposed a deal which lasted until his death in 1971. That Joe protect and manage him, pay for Louis's expenses, taxes, etc., whatever they may be, and never mind the rest—Joe could keep everything else. As Pops himself told me, he and Lucille also got a good living allowance, a new Lincoln, and new mink coat for Lucille every two years . . . "What else do [we] need?" he said. Sheltered by Joe from the law, Pops also had his lifetime quota of marijuana every day without interference from the fuzz.[13]

Glaser may have literally saved Armstrong's life, which explains how he and his successors remained Armstrong's managers until Louis's 1971 death, operating with nothing more than a handshake agreement. Cogswell summarizes the resultant change in Armstrong's quality of life post-1935, after Glaser took control of his career:

> With a simple handshake, Glaser became Armstrong's manager. The handshake contract lasted for the rest of their lives. Glaser took care of everything—marketing, bookings, itineraries, payroll, taxes, royalties, residuals, hiring (and sometimes firing) Louis's backup musicians— all Louis had to do was walk out on stage and play. Under Glaser's management, Louis was transformed from star to household name.[14]

Cogswell argues that, due to his absolute control of the most bankable name in popular music, Glaser "became one of the most powerful figures in the booking of black entertainment." In 1940, Glaser and Armstrong relocated to New York City and established Associated Booking Corporation to handle Satchmo's career, in the process attracting other top musical talent to sign up with the fledgling agency. Over the years, Glaser still represented a few boxers.

In addition to filling Armstrong's professional needs, Glaser also worked closely with Brubeck, booking the Dave Brubeck Quartet for two decades— commencing in 1950 and continuing up until Glaser's death in 1969—roughly spanning the period when the group was at its peak in popularity.[15] The Brubecks' oldest son, Darius, has enjoyed a long career as an international jazz artist, bandleader, and educator, including the years he toured with his father as part of Two Generations of Brubeck and the New Brubeck Quartet, an all-Brubeck ensemble. With his perspective as a veteran performer, he looked back on the relationship his father had with Glaser, noting that as a teen he had met the powerful manager a number of times.

> [My father] admired his power, but was careful not to become a close friend. It was known that Glaser had Mob connections, but I don't think his clients were intimidated by this. It was rather an advantage,

because they were protected from club owners who didn't pay, they were protected, to some extent, from racial discrimination, especially if you were a Louis Armstrong or perhaps less famous Black client. They were treated differently than artists who didn't have a Joe Glaser. . . . There was a tacit understanding [by artists] that a Joe Glaser was a necessity in that world, as there are things you don't want to know and you never know.[16]

One of Brubeck's other sons, composer, trombonist, and bassist Chris, also recalled that his father "perceived Joe Glaser as a 'tough guy,' someone Dave wanted to be on his side. He told me stories where Joe went to the mat to protect an artist."[17]

Glaser routinely used his image as a Mob-connected power broker to advantage as a subtle form of intimidation in his daily business. Avakian shared what he ironically described as "his fondest memory" of Glaser:

> As I was leaving his office one day, someone else was going in to see him. Joe put his arm around my shoulder affectionately and he introduced me to the new arrival. "This is the only man," he said, "whoever hung up on the phone with me." Then he smiled and added, "And lived."[18]

Nonetheless, Glaser made a profound impact on jazz artists, who often struggled to get paid and support themselves, especially in the era of Jim Crow. He used every ounce of his influence, both within and outside of the bounds of the law, to advance his own interests and those of his clients—so long as the two were in alignment. Glaser would often leverage his exclusive control over Armstrong's availability as a performer to increase the frequency and fees paid to his other performers. He would negotiate by offering, "You can have Louis in your club that week if you have Charlie Shavers in your club the following week."[19]

Drawing on written accounts and recollections of those that knew the man, the portrait that emerges is of a larger-than-life character who would have been at home in one of Damon Runyon's tales of New York life, such as *Guys and Dolls*. A few examples substantiate this claim.[20]

John Levy, a bass player and music manager cited earlier, shared one such story. In 1948, Levy was invited to play in the backing ensemble for Billie Holiday's March 27 comeback concert at Carnegie Hall. Although Joe Glaser had represented Holiday for some time, her contract had expired while she had been in jail on drug charges. Glaser was fighting through a contentious divorce with his wife Lily, and to get back at him, she had convinced a disgruntled former agent from ABC, Ed Fishman, to make the arrangements for Holiday's concert and its promotion to further upset her soon-to-be ex-husband. Levy was hired to back up Holiday and reported that Glaser was trying to hide his financial assets from court purview leading up to any divorce settlement with his wife. Speaking to Levy, Oscar Cohen, who in 1948 was an assistant at the agency, recalled,

> Joe took $700,000 in cash out of the bank before she could get to it. He came back to the office late one afternoon, just before I was to go home. He handed me a paper bag and told me not to look inside it. He said I should take the bag home with me and bring it back in the morning. I lived with my mother up in the Bronx, and I took this bag with me on the subway. Next morning, my mother wanted to know what was in it, so we looked. In those days, $700,000 might have been $700 million.[21]

Duke Ellington, another one of Glaser's internationally famous Black clients, also ran afoul of Glaser's strong-arm tactics. In the late 1950s, George Avakian had conceived an idea for an artistic collaboration between Armstrong and Duke Ellington. Avakian remembered that he discussed the idea separately with both men, and that they both enthusiastically endorsed moving ahead. Avakian mapped out specific repertoire for Duke and his Orchestra that would feature Armstrong, including a new composition to be titled "Portrait of Louis Armstrong," written by Ellington to pay Armstrong his due as one of the greatest jazzmen of all time. Unfortunately, Armstrong's contract with Columbia was set to expire before any recordings could be booked. Then, Glaser told Avakian that Armstrong would no longer be signing any standard recording contracts requiring multiple albums. Instead, he would consider so-called one-off deals, and Avakian was free to propose whatever he had in mind for Glaser's consideration. This was in spite of the fact that in the mid-1950s Avakian had resurrected Armstrong's recording career with a string of hit records such as *Satch Plays Fats*, *Ambassador Satch*, *Armstrong Plays Handy*, and the million-selling single "Mack the Knife." Glaser planned to collect any offers from Columbia and other record labels, then use them as leverage to increase his take on any future project by offering Armstrong's services on a comparable project to the highest bidder. This money-first approach torpedoed Avakian's Armstrong-Ellington collaboration, which both artists had hoped to realize. Although such high-profile collaborations were rarely easy to pull off, it's clear that money, not artistry, was the driving force in whatever music Glaser would allow Armstrong to record, resulting in a loss of what might have been a crowning musical achievement for Ellington and Armstrong. In the aftermath, it was Ellington who provided the sad epitaph to the failed project. Avakian recalled:

> Joe could stall his answer until he had shopped my idea with other companies, and then name any figure he chose as the amount I would have to pay to top another bidder. The terms [he offered Columbia] were suicidally unacceptable. I rejected them, and Louis was crushed, but explained that he was deeply beholden to Glaser. He was in tears but assured me that it would never affect our personal relationship. Duke was totally cool about it. He saw how shaken I was, but simply said, "George, I'm surprised at you. I've dealt with gangsters all my life, but your idea of a gangster is Edward G. Robinson or Humphrey Bogart."[22]

Avakian's assessment of Glaser's strategy was spot-on. When Columbia refused the outrageous costs proposed by Glaser for Armstrong's participation in the Ellington project, Glaser then took the project to Roulette Records. The resulting album, titled *The Great Summit*, stood Avakian's original idea on its head and featured Duke sitting in with Armstrong's band. The set list was made up entirely of Ellington standards played by the All-Stars and sung by Armstrong.[23] Lyrics were added to the Ellington standard "C Jam Blues," which was now titled "Duke's Place." The recording did not include the proposed new Ellington composition, "Portrait of Louis Armstrong."[24] Avakian commented, "It was a simplified reversal of my idea—Duke performed with Armstrong's band. A nice album, but a far cry from what I had in mind . . . and the label [Roulette] was owned by a mobster."[25] Morris Levy, Roulette's director, had known ties to the Genovese crime family.

Continuing Glaser's run of profiteering, Sidney Frey, founder of independent label Audio Fidelity, paid the then-astronomical sum of $40,000 ($376,000 in 2021 currency) to secure Armstrong to record an album of the King Oliver repertoire he had played during his meteoric rise in the 1920s. This amount was far beyond what artists such as Miles Davis and Dave Brubeck were receiving as royalty advances from Columbia, proving Avakian's claim that at this point in his career, Armstrong could name his price and would be available only to the highest bidder. The album was recorded in August 1959, featuring Satchmo with the Dukes of Dixieland; however, neither Glaser nor Frey cleared the repertoire with Decca, who blocked its release due to contract rerecording restrictions that remained in effect even after Armstrong had left Decca. Those tracks were not released until 1970.[26] Stymied for the moment, Frey called in Armstrong's regular band, the All-Stars, to record Audio Fidelity's *Satchmo Plays King Oliver*, which was released immediately, providing some return on Frey's substantial investment in working with Glaser and Armstrong. The twelve tracks were recorded at Los Angeles's venerable Radio Recorders in late September 1959, and released soon after.[27]

During the postwar years, Glaser built his organization into one of the most powerful and successful talent agencies of the mid-twentieth century, with offices in New York, Hollywood, Chicago, and Miami.[28] He hired musicians who were tired of the road and trained them to be effective bookers. As evidence shows, without Glaser's approval, Louis Armstrong would be unavailable to any promoter, record label, or Broadway producer throughout the remainder of his career. Over the years, in addition to Armstrong, ABC's roster boasted a who's who of jazz stars, including Duke Ellington, Dave Brubeck, Lionel Hampton, Benny Goodman, Billie Holiday, Woody Herman, Ella Fitzgerald, Cab Calloway, Sammy Kaye, Les Brown, Pearl Bailey, Stan Kenton, and Dinah Washington, as well as pop artists including Peggy Lee, the Kingston Trio, Barbra Streisand, the Rascals, and Bob Marley. During the latter part of the 1960s and '70s, chart-topping rock acts including the Allman Brothers, Alice Cooper, Rod Stewart, and Creedence Clearwater Revival also relied on ABC to handle their live bookings.

Glaser's handling of Armstrong's career centered on two things: maximizing Armstrong's earning opportunities and ensuring that his marquee talent could focus solely on music and never have to worry about money again. Judged strictly on those criteria, Glaser performed exceptionally well on Armstrong's behalf. After solving Satchmo's Mob-related dilemma at the start of their artist-manager relationship, Glaser skillfully navigated the changing tides of the music industry, the end of the big band era, finessing Hollywood and radio contracts, and every other moneymaking aspect of Satchmo's career to mutually benefit both parties. Armstrong biographer Ricky Riccardi offered that "Glaser provided Armstrong with great freedom and peace of mind over the last 35 years of his career. Maybe not always artistic freedom, but that was the least of it."[29] Armstrong repeated hundreds of times throughout his career that Joe Glaser was his "best friend" and had earned his complete trust to manage his finances, taxes, business ventures, and catalog of song compositions. While the two men may not have socialized together, the evidence found in voluminous correspondence—among the hundreds of hours of candid audio recordings of Armstrong's musings found in his library of home tapes—and the bequests left to Louis and Lucille Armstrong at the time of Joe Glaser's death all point to the fact that the tough-talking Glaser continued to look out for Armstrong, even after his death on June 6, 1969.

That's why the jazz community was surprised when, in 2003, Newport Jazz Festival founder and jazz impresario George Wein published an account of a 1970 meeting with Armstrong, attended by Wein, his wife, and a third party, during which Armstrong reportedly lambasted Glaser as having ripped him off for his entire career. Wein had come of age as both a performer and jazz promoter in the post–World War II jazz age, opening his first club, Storyville, in Boston in 1950, and going on to found the Newport Jazz Festival in 1954 and its folk festival counterpart in 1959. He also created various Newport-branded jazz tour packages that kept artists working and visiting countries around the world.[30] According to Wein's account, Armstrong was shocked to find out that Glaser had left his partner in profits no shares in Associated Booking. Wein wrote that Satchmo angrily declared:

> When we started [in Chicago] we both had nothing. We were friends— we hung out together, ate together, went to restaurants together. But the minute we started making money, Joe Glaser was no longer my friend. In all those years, he never once invited me to his house. I was just a passport for him . . . I built Associated Booking, there wouldn't have been any agency if it wasn't for me. And he didn't leave me a percentage of it.[31]

Wein's report left many who knew both men perplexed. While Glaser and Armstrong did butt heads on occasion, the long history of financial successes they had enjoyed, and Glaser's tenacious protection of Armstrong's right to live his life exactly as he wanted, including keeping Satchmo supplied throughout his life with his daily supply of marijuana, was diametrically opposed to such a diatribe. Armstrong biographer Ricky Riccardi questioned the veracity of this account, if not the motivation for Wein including such an attack in his own autobiography. Evidently, there was a long and bitter history with frequent battles between Glaser and Wein, who were at odds for most of their relationship as agent and promoter. Riccardi did significant research in Armstrong's voluminous written, audio, and video archives to determine if there was a basis for the claim Wein had made in his book.[32] Drawing on dozens of sources, including rare backstage homemade tapes of Armstrong discussing his relationship with Glaser with other artists, correspondence with many business associates and researchers, and Armstrong's own extensive writings, no hard evidence supports Wein's narrative of an embittered artist accusing his manager of thirty-five years of fleecing him.

Furthermore, Glaser's will left substantial assets to Louis and Lucille Armstrong, which further rebuts Wein's assertions. The will left complete control
of ABC's music publishing arm, International Music, Inc., in the hands of
the Armstrongs. Not only were all of Louis's song copyrights held here, those
of other ABC artists were as well, along with the important song catalog
of Lil Hardin Armstrong from Louis's Hot Five and Hot Seven days. Additionally, James Lincoln Collier, another Armstrong biographer, interviewed
Lucille in 1970, and she confirmed that shortly after Glaser's death, substantial
funds held in trust for the Armstrongs were turned over to them, and ABC
arranged for a new, independent financial manager to take over the multiple
savings accounts, annuities, and trust funds that Glaser had set up to benefit
his longest-tenured client. With regard to the inference that, without shares
in ABC, Armstrong may have been broke, an IRS audit completed in 1976
reset the value of the 1971 Armstrong estate at the time of Satchmo's death
as $1.11 million dollars ($7.36 million in 2021), nearly double what had been
reported on tax documents filed in 1971. This was due to the failure to report
$560,000 ($3.75 million in 2021) in music publishing royalties for that year
alone, which were now going directly to the Armstrongs. With such a pre-
ponderance of evidence, it appears as though Wein may have embellished
Armstrong's statements to serve his own purpose of calling out Glaser as a
controlling and racially insensitive person. Positioning the beloved Satchmo
as a victim of Glaser's purported unethical behavior may have suited Wein's
purpose of fostering the idea of a feud between the two men, even after Glaser's death. Wein's report of Satchmo's alleged postmortem attack on Glaser
became one of the inspirations for Terry Teachout's popular play *Satchmo
Plays the Waldorf*, which, according to the play's introduction, "is a work of
fiction, based freely on fact."[33]

One last point about the ownership of ABC came to light in the wake of
Glaser's death. At that time, it was discovered that a majority of ABC's shares
had been transferred to Sidney Korshak, an infamous gangland lawyer and
fixer. Court documents from 1962 recorded the stock transfer from Glaser
to Korshak, which included Glaser's voting rights. So, in fact, at the time
of his passing, Glaser did not actually own ABC any longer. He worked as
an employee at the pleasure of the stockholders, likely with the controlling
interest held by the Mob, and would have been in no position to provide any
type of ownership interest to Armstrong, adding further credence to Riccardi's thesis that Wein's account of the angry Armstrong was most likely an
invention. While no definitive evidence has surfaced yet as to what leverage
Korshak wielded to get Glaser to give up control of his agency, in *Satchmo at
the Waldorf*, Teachout implies that it was most likely some form of blackmail

that Glaser feared even more than losing control of the agency he spent the latter part of life diligently building into an industry powerhouse. The power dynamic between Armstrong and Glaser is one of the most fascinating in the history of the often colorful music business, but it is safe to conclude that both men had a deeply symbiotic relationship and relied on each other's strengths over more than three decades to keep the gears oiled and the money coming in to both of their benefit.

A careful analysis of the surviving correspondence between the Brubecks and Glaser shows that the manager respected Brubeck's commercial appeal. The fact that Columbia's widespread promotion had brought the Dave Brubeck Quartet's music into middle-class American households, as well as a growing list of college campuses, afforded Associated Booking's agents the opportunity to keep the group constantly working. Glaser and his staff also worked diligently to ensure that the quartet was compensated fairly. Initially, when Dave laid out the concept for the jazz musical to Joe Glaser during a 1958 meeting at his New York office, Glaser seemed encouraging and offered to introduce the Brubecks to a few veteran Broadway producers in his circle. True to his word, Glaser and his staff did provide introductions to Paul Gregory, Joshua Logan, and Leland Hayward, who each play a role in this story. Still, at that first meeting with Glaser, Brubeck recalled that he "foresaw problems tying up Louis for a long Broadway run, when he could make much more money from individual concert fees."[34] With Joe Glaser holding the purse strings, in time this economic reality would become the nexus of the Brubecks' ongoing struggles to bring *The Real Ambassadors* to life.

CHAPTER 6

STANDING UP TO SEGREGATION

Although Glaser and ABC did provide access to Broadway producers and even helped to publicize the nascent project in the press, the Brubecks never gained Glaser's unqualified support. Glaser's vacillation caused an undercurrent of ongoing tension throughout the couple's five-year campaign to bring the show to the stage, as any commitment from Louis Armstrong required Joe Glaser's full cooperation. As a result, the show enjoyed only two performances with Armstrong in the lead role: the 1962 soundtrack album (recorded the year before) and the subsequent concert performance at Monterey. Despite the Brubecks' best efforts to bring the show to the stage, Armstrong and Glaser's tangled business and personal relationship kept their focus primarily on maintaining the most rigorous touring and performance schedule possible for the legendary jazzman. In so doing, Glaser maximized his take of Armstrong's earnings, and Armstrong continued to enjoy the life of a traveling musician feted around the world as America's truest musical ambassador, with all his expenses more than covered. Glaser made sure that Armstrong, his wife Lucille and some of his confidantes and select paramours, were financially comfortable.

To accomplish this, Glaser kept Armstrong in front of the largest and most lucrative mainstream audience possible. The progressive views put forth in *The Real Ambassadors* likely concerned the veteran manager, as they clearly associated Armstrong with a politically charged pro-integration message that could alienate some of his fans. However, the show's message did align with Armstrong's own position on segregation.

The insults Satchmo faced for leading an integrated band continued, and occasionally the hostility became violent. A February 20, 1957, *New York Times* story titled "Satchmo and Trumpet Dull Knoxville Blast" reported, "A dynamite blast reverberated tonight through a municipal building where Louis (Satchmo) Armstrong was playing a concert to a segregated, white and Negro audience of 3,000." The stick of dynamite thrown at the auditorium by a passing car left a four-foot crater near the concert hall. The veteran showman took the intimidation tactic in stride as he quipped to the audience, "That's all right, folks—it's just the phone."[1] Armstrong glossed over this aggression, but like many other attacks, it must have left a scar on his heart, knowing the deep hatred some aimed his way.

In September of the same year, Armstrong publicly raised his voice in anger and condemned American president Dwight Eisenhower and other politicians for not enforcing *Brown v. Board of Education* in the Central High School school desegregation battle in Little Rock, Arkansas. "It's getting almost so bad that a colored man hasn't got any country," Satchmo railed at cub reporter Larry Lubenow in Grand Forks, North Dakota. He accused Eisenhower of being "two-faced" and having "no guts" to solve the problem. He said that there had been discussions about a state-sponsored goodwill tour for him to perform in the Soviet Union, but that "the way they are treating my people in the South, the government can go to hell."[2]

The trouble in Little Rock made front-page news, and eventually the president ordered armed soldiers of the 101st Airborne Division to escort the school's Black students (the so-called Little Rock Nine) as they entered and left the building each day in order to fulfill the Supreme Court's mandate to integrate public schools. This incident further concentrated the world's attention on America's race problems. Immediately after Armstrong's comments were picked up by wire services and broadcast on the evening network news, Glaser's handpicked road manager for the All-Stars, Pierre "Frenchy" Tallerie, called the media to soften Armstrong's statements.[3] He explained that Armstrong "was very sorry he spouted off." When Satchmo heard what Tallerie had told the media, he immediately placed a call to the *Pittsburgh Courier*, the nation's leading Black daily newspaper, to refute Tallerie's rebuttal. Satchmo's resentment is articulated with the force of a man who has endured silently for too long:

> As much as I'm trying to do for my people, this road man, Tallerie, whom I've respected for 20 years, although I've suspected him of being prejudiced, has worked with Negro musicians and made his money off them, has proved that he hates Negroes the first time he opened his mouth. I don't see why Mr. Glaser doesn't remove him from the band . . . I wouldn't take back a thing I said. I've had a beautiful life over 40 years in music but I feel the downtrodden situation the same as any other Negro. My parents and family suffered through all that Old South and things are new now, and [no] Tallerie and no prejudiced newspaper can make me change it. What I've said is me. I feel that . . . My people—the Negroes—are not looking for anything—we just want

a square shake. But when I see on television and read about a crowd
in Arkansas spitting on a little colored girl—I think I have a right to
get sore . . . Do you dig me when I still say I have a right to blow my
top over injustice?[4]

Satchmo's off-the-record thoughts on his Little Rock–influenced tirade and
Glaser's measured response further show that there is no simple reading of
the Armstrong-Glaser relationship. The two powerful men shared a complex
and fully symbiotic connection. Based on Armstrong's rebuttal of Tallerie's
false denials, there could be no doubt about his stance on the civil rights
struggles. Change had to occur, and the jazzman added his powerful voice
to the call for reformation.

Since Armstrong was Glaser's biggest earner, Satchmo's politically charged
comments would be cause for concern. Glaser relied on Armstrong's broad
appeal—a nonpolitical stage act and amiable onstage persona—to keep
him constantly booked in front of largely white, middle-class audiences
around the world. However, after over twenty years of partnership, Glaser
had become a savvy enough manager not to buck Armstrong on his very
militant stance regarding Little Rock and his scathing indictment of President Eisenhower. Both men could be stubborn, but once Armstrong had
made a public statement of this magnitude, Glaser knew he would never take
back his remarks. The manager fully backed his star and even handled the
virulent hate mail that flowed into the ABC offices in the following weeks.

Armstrong appreciated that Glaser stood behind his remarks, especially
when many other Black artists and leaders took the opportunity to criticize
him for speaking out so vociferously—most notably Sammy Davis Jr., who
claimed Armstrong had no authority to speak about integration when he
regularly performed before segregated audiences. Politician Adam Clayton
Powell claimed, "Louis Armstrong isn't up on current events." Armstrong
proved that he did monitor current events closely, however; when Eisenhower ordered federal troops to enforce the order to integrate the Little Rock
high school, Armstrong famously sent the president a telegram in which he
said he would join Eisenhower if he personally escorted the Black students
into the school. He also told the president that he believed the nation's leader
"had a good heart."[5] Ever the pragmatist, Glaser's stance may also have been
the most expedient strategy for letting the considerable storm blow over.

With such strong convictions, Louis Armstrong was the ideal person to
play the lead role in *The Real Ambassadors*. Brubeck recalled that when the
news of Armstrong's broadside against Eisenhower broke, "I sent Louis a
telegram congratulating him for his stand, and for making such a bold and

courageous statement to President Eisenhower."[6] Iola Brubeck kept careful notes of Armstrong's profile in the media, especially when the topic was civil rights. Her handwritten notes accompany a draft for the lyrics to the song "The Real Ambassador" and list the following: "1) Louis' mixed band cannot play in N.O. [New Orleans] and 2) Louis' comment to Eisenhower during Little Rock."[7] The couple would skillfully weave these events into the musical as it continued to evolve.

Returning to the letter of November 20, 1958, in which the Brubecks floated the idea of sharing ownership in a Manhattan nightspot with Armstrong, Joe Glaser wrote a reply letter dated November 28, 1958, confirming that he did take the bold proposal from the Brubecks seriously. A close reading of his reply raised warning flags about the manager's willingness to support the Brubecks' ambitious plans, however. Glaser opens with "Received your letter of November 20 . . . and I have read it very very [sic] carefully." He then comments, "Of course, I appreciate the way you go into detail to explain your feelings as to how I feel about Louis and I am sure you are familiar with our situation." The "situation" Glaser is referring to is that fact that Armstrong had a steady overhead—including his salaried band, his immediate family, and his mistresses—that required him to keep performing. Hence, any change in the regular schedule of lucrative one-nighters would interrupt Armstrong and Glaser's essential income stream. Still, the manager did acknowledge that, in the wake of Armstrong's June 22, 1959, heart attack in Italy, it was clear that Satchmo's schedule was a key factor contributing to his health problems.[8] Glaser continues, "You are definitely and positively right when you make mention of the fact that Louis could well afford to sit down and take things easier much more than in the past."

Glaser than flexes his muscles in the most telling point of the letter: "It is a pleasure to advise you in this letter that you can tell Paul Gregory and Josh Logan or anyone you want that should you write something that meets with my approval, I would be willing and ready to sit down with you and them and discuss the matter in detail."[9] He was telling the Brubecks in the most direct way possible that the road to securing Armstrong ran across Joe Glaser's desk. It would not only require direct negotiation between him and any interested Broadway producer: the content of the show would also have to meet his approval before he would open up a channel of communication with any possible partners.

The content of this crucial letter, while relatively brief, proved to be a bellwether for the succeeding four years of struggles that Dave and Iola Brubeck endured in their efforts to bring *The Real Ambassadors* to the stage with Louis Armstrong in the lead role. Over these years, on the surface, Glaser would encourage the Brubecks with words and slaps on the back, but in reality, at each important crossroads along their journey, Glaser would delay, question, defer judgment, or outright refuse to cooperate with the couple as they sought to enlist partners to bring the show to life.

Dave and Iola replied to Glaser on December 3, 1958. In their letter, they acknowledge Glaser's reference to their request to get a firm commitment for Louis's role in the musical, but since Glaser proposed a two-step process to even determine whether Armstrong's involvement might be possible, the Brubecks must have understood how little they had to offer any producer in the way of star power. It is unfortunate that Glaser appears to have dismissed the Brubeck-Armstrong nightclub idea, since Armstrong record producer George Avakian, when shown a copy of the letter outlining the plan decades later, commented that, based on his familiarity with both musicians, "Louis would have welcomed the idea and had no qualms about repeating his days of doubling between *Hot Chocolates* on Broadway and Connie's Inn after the curtain came down! It is a great idea and Pops would have pulled it off in spades."[10]

One factor that doubtless caused Glaser concern is that to realize a Broadway show would necessarily have involved additional financiers. As a result, Armstrong's decades-old verbal agreement with Glaser, which reportedly gave Glaser half of his earnings, might have been compared to other performers' much lower rates of commission for their managers.[11] Armstrong biographer Terry Teachout wrote that Armstrong's wife, "Lucille, was certain that Glaser was robbing her husband under the cover of their fifty-fifty-deal and tried to persuade him to switch to a percentage agreement."[12] Historian and former Armstrong archivist Michael Cogswell wrote, "There exist few primary sources to document the decades-long financial relationship between Glaser and Louis . . . an accurate accounting of the [sic] how the money flowed may never be discovered."[13]

The bottom line is that Armstrong never wanted for money. Late in Armstrong's career, Glaser gave some sense of how much Armstrong was earning at the time when he was riding the wave of success from the hit record *Hello, Dolly!* In an interview with *Ebony* magazine in November 1964, Glaser crowed:

> Hell, Pops hasn't made less than a half-million bucks in any given year during the past 20 years. . . . It's between us and Uncle Sam how much he actually takes in, but I can tell you this, for tax reasons we won't let it go over a million a year.[14]

Producer George Avakian said Glaser was "holding Armstrong in a steel-vise grip, in which money came first by a wide margin."[15] The prospect of giving up the near-constant touring income for the uncertainty of a musical—particularly one that would provide Satchmo a soapbox to argue for what some might see as a divisive political and social stance—would certainly have worried the astute businessman.

It can also be argued that *The Real Ambassadors'* message was antithetical to Glaser's approach to maximizing income while minimizing risk. Aligning his top star with racial politics could only harm Armstrong's bankability with his largely establishment white audiences. While no direct statements exist documenting Glaser's stance on the civil rights struggle, an anecdote related by jazz journalist Nat Hentoff offers the jazz critic's interpretation of Glaser's mindset. In his May 28, 1992, article in the *Village Voice*, titled "Louis Armstrong and Reconstruction," Hentoff recounts a visit to Glaser's office:

> I do remember the one time I was given an audience with Glaser, who booked a lot of other artists, many of them black—I kept looking at a decoration on his wall. It was made out of black velvet on which was superimposed a scene of antebellum plantation life. The darkies were grinning, some were strumming banjos, and massah was basking in their sweet sounds of gratitude, which clearly, he richly deserved. One explanation for that scene of darkies celebrating their place on Glaser's wall might have been that he had a sardonic streak. But Joe Glaser's dogs had a much more developed sense of humor than he did. And he wouldn't know sardonic from existential.[16]

By placing this image directly behind his desk, where any Black entertainer meeting with him would be faced with that image of America's troubled past, Glaser was making a direct connection to slavery. One might infer that Glaser saw himself as the equivalent of the plantation owner and that the musicians working for him were under contract first and foremost to serve his economic needs.

Glaser felt he knew what was best for Armstrong and with rare exception strictly limited the artist's own business interactions. Glaser or one of his staff hired and fired members of the All-Stars when necessary, after consulting with the bandleader. Armstrong's knowledge of his business dealings was limited to what and where the next string of gigs would be. He could count on Glaser's office to take care of his many financial obligations. Glaser saw that Armstrong's wife Lucille wanted for nothing and ensured that Satchmo always had a bankroll to take care of friends and day-to-day expenses. The system worked for both men, each of whom reliably fulfilled his respective role.

The Brubecks were not deterred by Glaser just yet. A subsequent letter asked him to ensure that the Dave Brubeck Quartet would be working every available night on a January–February 1959 East Coast tour, because it was Brubeck's intention to "spend the rest of the year 1959 here in California, working on the show between West Coast engagements so that the February tour would be as lucrative as possible for both of us, as it is liable to be the only one for the year."[17] Unlike Glaser, Brubeck was willing to take a substantial reduction in his earnings by limiting his performances to the West Coast for the period of March–December 1959, so that he could put the great majority of his efforts into the jazz musical.

CHAPTER 7

SECURING SATCHMO

What of Armstrong's interest in *The Real Ambassadors*?

Armstrong's introduction to *The Real Ambassadors* happened at the end of 1958, due ironically to a meeting suggested by none other than Joe Glaser. With Brubeck's star rising, Glaser was savvy enough to encourage the pianist to explore a possible collaboration with Armstrong. The surviving written records from 1958 to 1960 show Glaser supporting the concept, but keeping any firm commitments for Satchmo's involvement under his exclusive control. Brubeck and Armstrong would both be in Chicago the week of December 27, 1958.[1] On Glaser's recommendation, Brubeck had gone to the Palmer House Hotel, where Armstrong was performing that night at the Empire Room, to speak with him about the show and the Brubecks' plan for Armstrong to play the lead role. In typical fashion, to block any access to Satchmo, Armstrong's road manager, Frenchy Tallerie, left word at the hotel desk that no one was to have access to Armstrong and had all phone calls to Armstrong's room routed to himself. Repeatedly, Dave called, and each time Frenchy turned down his request for an audience with Louis.

Dave finally gave up but found a friendly bellman who knew Armstrong's room number. He proceeded to wait outside the room for the door to open. Eventually, room service showed up with Louis's dinner, at which point Armstrong looked out and saw Dave sitting on the floor across from his room.

The two were not strangers, and had developed a friendly mutual respect, as their paths had crossed on many occasions. Both artists were managed by Associated Booking Corporation, so it was not unusual that they sometimes found themselves performing at the same venues. Both had appeared on the *Timex All-Star Jazz* television broadcast in 1957, and one year earlier they had both been featured at a summer concert by the Lewisohn Stadium Symphony Orchestra.[2]

Surprised and delighted to see an old friend outside his hotel room that evening, Louis invited Dave in and asked the waiter to bring up a second steak dinner just like his own. Over dinner, Dave explained the musical and its underlying themes, and Louis enthusiastically followed along as he learned he would be the lead character, appropriately dubbed "Pops."[3] Brubeck recalled, "To my surprise, he seemed interested and told me that Joe Glaser had already spoken to him about it."[4]

Brubeck showed Armstrong the lyrics of one of the show's songs, "Lonesome," which Armstrong then read aloud. His reading had such an emotional impact on Brubeck that he later transformed the song, which had been intended to be sung in normal vocal style, to a recitative (spoken-word) format for its eventual 1961 recording, with Armstrong reciting the melancholy lyrics and overdubbing his trumpet onto Brubeck's understated piano.[5] Brubeck was encouraged by the warm reception he got that night from Armstrong. Little did he know, however, that one more experience awaited him that would help make this one of the most memorable nights of his life. After they finished dinner, Louis invited Dave down to the Empire Room as his guest and invited him to sit in with the All-Stars. Brubeck recalled the moment he took the stage to perform with Armstrong for the first time:

> Louis announced to the audience that I was there and invited me to come up on stage to play with him and the band . . . he called two tunes from the band's repertoire, and fortunately I knew them both. This may have been Louis' sly way of determining if he could work with me. After all, most people considered our jazz styles poles apart.[6]

A bond was forged that night in Chicago. Before *The Real Ambassadors*, Armstrong had never had the opportunity to play a role that fit his personal convictions about segregation. Instead, he had accepted numerous film roles in which he mostly played a lighthearted version of his showman character. "Pops" was a part the veteran entertainer would relish playing. Louis asked Dave if he could send him practice tapes made on reel-to-reel so that he could listen to them using his traveling audio system in hotel rooms. Brubeck agreed to do so. As the project gained momentum, Brubeck recalled that "Louis started telling friends that we had written him an opera. Iola and I had no idea of this being called an opera, but that didn't stop Louis, nor us." With his personal commitment to participate now apparent to the Brubecks, they redoubled their efforts to "give him the vehicle and the opportunity to voice what had been bottled up inside."[7]

The face-to-face meeting between the two jazzmen in Armstrong's hotel room, and Armstrong's response to the invitation, represented a major leap forward in the show's progress. Having Satchmo's enthusiastic support galvanized the Brubecks to ramp up their campaign efforts throughout 1959. Armstrong's natural ebullience, and his clear connection with the message of equality built into the show, left the Brubecks feeling that with Louis on their side, they now had the most important ally of all.

When Dave returned home from seeing Armstrong in Chicago, another event further inspired the Brubecks to push harder to get Armstrong on tape in any sort of demo, performing or even speaking lines from the show. While Satchmo was still in Chicago appearing at the Palmer House, Glaser booked him to make a cameo appearance on the popular ABC television human-interest show *You Asked for It*. As part of a segment on New Orleans and the role of jazz as an internationally renowned American art form, Satchmo would appear near the end of the piece, live from a studio in Chicago. After being introduced by the show's host, Jack Smith, Armstrong provided his own candid take on jazz music's influence on the people he had met touring all around the world.

> **Announcer**: And now we take you from New Orleans to Chicago, to hear from Louis "Satchmo" Armstrong, the King of Jazz.
>
> **Armstrong**: Hi, everybody. Say, Jack. I think you're wrong about me being the ambassador: I think jazz is the ambassador. While I might be the courier, that takes the message over there, but it's jazz that does the talkin'. That's the good thing about our kind of music: it speaks in every language and is understood by everyone that wants to listen.
>
> My horn and me have traveled from Sweden to Spain, and when I played Berlin, a lot of them cats jumped around fences [*sic*] to hear ol' Satchmo. Ha-ha-ha-ha. I was provin' that music is stronger than nations.
>
> I don't know much about politics, but I know these people in foreign countries hear all kinds of things about America—some good, some bad. I'm pretty sure what comes out of this horn makes them feel better about us. One thing sure, they know a trumpet ain't no cannon! Ha-ha-ha-ha. This horn is my real voice; it's my livin' and my life. I've got a lotta high notes in me that haven't been blown yet. Ye-e-e-a-a-h-h-h-h."[8]

Dave and Iola Brubeck happened to be watching the show that night, and Armstrong's soliloquy was further validation to the couple that he was the ideal lead for the show. Later that same night, the Brubecks shared their enthusiasm in an audio letter to Armstrong. On it, after an introduction by

Dave asking Louis to listen to the demo versions of the show's music and if at all possible record a verse from one of the songs, either singing or playing, Iola shared her own enthusiasm for Armstrong's acting abilities:

> Hello Louis, I saw you tonight on that show, *You Asked for It*, and I was very, very impressed with your performance on the show. It thrilled me particularly because I heard you deliver some lines in a way that I knew that it was possible for you to do some of the scenes in the show that I had written for you. Now, I had the feeling all along that you could do them, but I had never heard you do anything like that before, and when I saw you tonight, and saw the sincerity with which you delivered some very deep lines, it impressed me, terrifically.[9]

Armstrong's appearance, and more importantly, his perception that his music was one of the most powerful weapons in the Cold War culture wars, was tailor-made for the messages that the Brubecks wanted the audience to receive from their musical. Armstrong's quip that "music is stronger than nations" neatly encapsulated one of the main themes the Brubecks envisioned for the show: the role of artists in changing the world. Iola and Dave must have been exhilarated to know that Satchmo's views and their own were in perfect harmony.

Just before the Chicago meeting, they had learned that Armstrong would be departing for a four-month European tour on January 14, 1959. In a flurry of activity, the Brubecks recorded a series of audio letters and demos for both Louis Armstrong and the intended female lead, Carmen McRae. McRae was a rising star on the jazz scene. She came of age studying the vocal stylings of Billie Holiday but developed her own unique approach that was also influenced by the emergence of bebop. On the strength of a 1953 release titled *A Foggy Day with Carmen McRae* on the tiny Stardust label, she was selected 1954's Best New Female Singer by *DownBeat*. This led to a contract with Decca Records in 1955. With Decca's distribution and marketing clout, her albums received national attention and were soon acclaimed by critics and listeners. On songs such as 1956's "Yardbird Suite," "Suppertime," and "You Took Advantage of Me," McRae's smoky voice and rhythmic invention established her as one of the preeminent singers of her time.[10] The Brubecks heard McRae's soulful voice and imagined her playing the female lead, Rhonda Brown, in the show. They reached out to McRae, pitched the musical concept to her, and she agreed to participate in the project.

McRae's tapes were sent directly to her, while Armstrong's tapes were sent US Postal special delivery to Joe Glaser's office. Each one included a music-minus-vocal version of the songs so that the two lead characters could add their parts over what the couple had dubbed to the audition tape. Once Armstrong's voice was on it and the tape was in the possession of the Brubecks, they planned to preview the recording for the Broadway producers with whom they had been meeting. They believed that once a producer heard Armstrong's and McRae's inimitable voices portraying the lead characters, the project would take wing, hence their use of the term "audition."

A handwritten draft, in Iola's fluid script, of the letter to manager Joe Glaser that accompanied Armstrong's tape survives. Its eloquence and persuasiveness show how much value the couple placed on securing Armstrong's voice, but it appears that between Brubeck's meeting and the sending of the tapes, there was a phone conversation between Brubeck and Glaser that dimmed their hopes. According to the letter, in a phone conversation between Glaser and Brubeck on January 3, 1959, Glaser said Armstrong was too busy to complete the recording, even though Armstrong had a complete home recording system in his Corona, Queens, home. The letter cites a specific day, January 13, upon which Dave suggested he would be willing to fly to New York City to help Louis make the recording. The letter then goes into great detail about how simple the recording should be for Armstrong, citing the intricacies of what is on each tape and exactly how in one hour Louis and Carmen could complete and record their performance. More than other correspondence, there is an undercurrent of desperation between the lines, as no matter how passionate Armstrong himself was about the musical, the Brubecks now realized that Glaser had the final word. The letter starts out stating, "Dear Joe, I've just talked to you on the phone and I feel somewhat disappointed with the knowledge that Carmen and Louis won't be able to record on the 6th, because as you explained, Louis will be rehearsing all day." It was another example of Glaser feigning support while blocking any tangible involvement by his star performer.

While the Brubecks thought their request to have Armstrong perform just one song to be used for audition purposes seemed entirely reasonable, Glaser astutely realized that if producers such as Paul Gregory or Josh Logan heard the audition tape with Armstrong playing the part of Pops, they would assume that Armstrong was on tap to appear in the show. In fact, the Brubecks stated precisely how and when the audition tape would be used:

> I am at present negotiating with a chorus in L.A. to record the choral numbers for the audition tape which is a tremendous fee. So you can see the audition tape is progressing and will probably be ready to present to prospective backers while Louis is in Europe.

The Brubecks concluded this letter with a fervent plea to Armstrong's manager:

> You must realize how important I think this is to get this done before Louis leaves [for Europe]. I am asking for this favor to be done at the most inconvenient time possible (I know this from my own experience) and I am brave enough to make this request now only because I trust that [it] is of importance to everybody.[11]

Not content to merely ship the letter and audition tape to Armstrong in care of Joe Glaser, the Brubecks also sent a telegram to Glaser's right-hand man, Oscar Cohen. The telegram details that there were sheet music versions of the songs for Louis to accompany the tape, and a second tape for Carmen McRae. It concludes with an appeal to Cohen, imploring that

> Louis should try to record a few things with Carmen for the audition tape on the 13th, the last date they both will be in New York. Joe has told me how difficult this will be, but I can't stress enough how important it is for all of us. Thank you for taking care of this.[12]

The Brubecks knew that this was their best chance to ratchet up the momentum they had started to see with the positive reactions of potential backers such as Gregory and Logan. In a January 5, 1959, letter confirming the receipt of reel-to-reel tapes with the show's songs sent to Armstrong and Carmen McRae care of Joe Glaser's office, Glaser promised Dave and Iola, "I will do everything I personally can do for you and your wife to make the show a success."[13] That statement would ring hollow, however, once again, as the powerful manager did nothing to help facilitate the one-hour January 13 recording.[14] In the entirety of the surviving Brubeck-Glaser correspondence pertaining to the show, Glaser shows a continual pattern of cheerleading the project on paper or in private conversation but, in reality, stopping the Brubecks dead in their tracks each time they fought to get the show in front of a prospective backer, or later on, in front of an audience.

The phone calls and special-delivery letters between Glaser and the Brubecks continued in the ensuing days, and it became clear to Dave and Iola that the audition recording was unlikely to happen. In a letter dated January 8, the Brubecks regrouped and downgraded their request, asking Glaser to simply poll Armstrong on his commitment to the music and message of *The Real Ambassadors*. Certainly, they must have been shaken by Glaser's lack of any action, and their disappointment shows. The couple asked Glaser to simply confirm his own and Louis's willingness to be involved in the show. They wrote:

> Sometimes I think that the years of hard work and personal sacrifice on the part of my wife and myself will all be in vain. But when I realize that you are taking time to personally help us in this big undertaking, I am encouraged and enthused enough to work even harder to meet the deadlines.

This shift in tone in their negotiations with Glaser was strategic, since the direct requests were not achieving what they wanted. The letters indicate that the Brubecks were beginning to recognize that they must involve Glaser in a more central role. They continued:

> The potential backers that must be contacted as soon as possible in order to guarantee a fall production, will be much easier to convince if I have some indication from Louis that he is interested in doing the show. However, I want you to understand that I want Louis to do the show only if he believes in it—its music and its philosophy—and you both are convinced that this show is a proper vehicle for his multiple talents. Please do not consider our friendship a factor in your judgment.[15]

Now, rather than asking a manager to allow his star to sing one song for an audition, the Brubecks had acquiesced to the de facto reality laid out by the manager in his November 28 letter, in which he insisted that he must approve the show's content before any substantive third-party dialogue could even begin about his star's possible involvement. It was a painful lesson.

Trying to salvage any sign that the world-famous trumpeter could be counted on to join the cast, the Brubecks asked Glaser for very little now: "if [Armstrong] sincerely likes the show, maybe he could say so on tape and send it back to me." Alternately, they asked whether Louis might simply read one verse of the lyrics to "Lonesome" that Dave had found so moving that night in his Chicago hotel room. They conclude their letter with a pledge to work "night and day on the show" during Armstrong's four-month tour of Europe, and for the manager to give some clear indication to the couple about whether he would throw his support behind the effort. The final sentence sums up where the tumultuous and emotionally draining period of December 27, 1958–January 8, 1959, had left the couple: "A frank appraisal of what you have heard and seen and some indication of your interest is what I can desire at this time."[16] As things stood, the Brubecks knew that the initial interest they had generated from Broadway impresarios would not result in any meaningful outcome unless Glaser would bless the project and Armstrong's involvement. As a result, they began to consider what other avenues might exist to create enough interest in the project. If the couple could just secure the backing of an established impresario, they hoped that Glaser might change his tune and allow Armstrong to fully commit to the show.

CHAPTER 8

GATHERING MOMENTUM

When the Brubecks' efforts to get Glaser on the bandwagon failed, they began to consider bypassing him to secure the funding and support they needed. An integral member of the Brubecks' team was attorney and confidante James Bancroft. His no-nonsense manner was a much-needed asset to the couple as Dave's career continued its upward trajectory, with album sales, airplay, and performance fees steadily improving throughout the mid-1950s. Bancroft was a trained accountant, tax specialist, and mergers-and-acquisitions man who joined the Brubeck camp on November 30, 1954.

The story of how the two became colleagues illustrates both Dave Brubeck's own temperament and music business naivete, as well as the realities faced by a talented artist self-managing his own business affairs. Just prior to his signing with George Avakian and Columbia Records in 1954, Brubeck had been contacted by a Los Angeles–based company, Milestone Productions, which approached Dave flying a false flag. One night after a performance, a Milestone representative met with Dave and asked him to sign a document to help Milestone incorporate. He said to Dave that the request was simply "doing them a favor." That oral explanation was nothing more than a ruse. The actual contract bore no resemblance to the supposed favor and tied Brubeck up in an exclusive deal for the foreseeable future. Brubeck admitted he had little idea of what was actually in the agreement, which he did in fact sign, trusting that the other party was as honest as he was. Jim Bancroft explained:

> Dave had been assured by Los Angeles promoters that they needed his signature so they could have their corporation, but that it would not involve any liability or obligation for Dave—he was just doing them a favor . . . except for the fact that they owned his soul, Dave was a free man. This led me to refer to the firm as "Millstone" Productions.
>
> And [overturning that contract] took extensive litigation, as their attorney was very able and a very mean and ambitious man, and so my Hollywood friends uncovered an equally competent and equally

persistent lawyer who was his natural enemy. And at Dave's expense and to some extent, at mine, these two fought with each other until they both decided there was no future in it and we made a modest settlement. And since that time, the understanding with Dave has been, if someone presents a deal, Dave is such a good person, he likes to say yes, so go right ahead and say, "Yes, that sounds great to me. The man who handles matters like this for me is Jim Bancroft. Here's his phone number, you call him and tell him I asked you to do it."[1]

In a letter drafted the morning after their first meeting, at which Dave learned just how awful the contract he had entered into with Milestone was, Bancroft advised the jazzman:

> It would be a good idea not to sign any agreements except routine bookings until we have completely evaluated all your commitments. It is especially easy for an artist to find himself over-committed and the victim of lawsuits from all directions.[2]

His advice was taken to heart by the Brubecks, who had learned just how unscrupulous seemingly well-intended people could be, as it took some months to be extricated from the Milestone deal. From the date of the settlement with Milestone until Brubeck's passing in 2012, the Brubeck-Bancroft partnership avoided entanglements of this nature, with the Brubecks concentrating on the creative aspects of their career and Jim Bancroft and his legal associates providing counsel for nearly six decades.[3] Remembering the impact Bancroft had on her husband's career, Iola said that

> Jim was a powerful negotiator and got concessions [for Dave] from Columbia Records that no other person had. He also negotiated with Joe Glaser, a tough agent, and got a very good deal of 12.5% instead of 15 or 20% and no interest in television appearances or recordings.[4]

By 1959, Jim Bancroft and Iola Brubeck had gotten to know each other professionally and personally, and each respected the other's keen mind. So it was on March 8 of that year that Iola typed a lengthy and illuminating confidential progress report to confidante Bancroft, centering almost exclusively on the couple's efforts to advance their musical.

Despite Glaser's brush-offs, the show was attracting the attention of producers. Producer Joshua Logan sent a brief note to the Brubecks confirming his interest. In it, he stated he would continue to listen to the demo recording of songs from the musical that Dave had left with him.[5] Still, by March 1959 the stresses of working to find a backer were taking a toll. Iola's three-page memorandum concisely demonstrates her sharp analytical skills as she recounts and critiques what various advisors had recommended in order to bring the show to fruition. Although buffeted by the tides of varying experts' opinions, the musical's cocreator remained cautiously hopeful that it might someday find its place on the stage.

Iola's memorandum recounts advice from three sources: regular confidante George Avakian, who was then helping to establish the Warner Brothers record company on the West Coast; Columbia Records executive Debbie Ishlon, who reported directly to president Goddard Lieberson; and the Associated Booking Corporation staffers, who offered their own opinions on how to get the musical to the stage.

From the text of the memo, it's clear that Avakian must have been working closely with Warner Brothers' motion picture division on music scores and possible acquisitions. Some discussion must have occurred about the possibility of making *The Real Ambassadors* into a film, but Iola felt that Avakian was not encouraging. Next, she noted that Debbie Ishlon, Lieberson's colleague at Columbia, defended her boss's interest in the musical but was being "realistic" by suggesting the Brubecks must get a theatrical agent in order to have any chance of bringing it to Broadway. Ishlon had offered that Columbia vice president Al Lorber was willing to take an audition recording and the script to Jules Styne, the powerful president of the MCA agency. In addition to MCA, Iola wrote that friends had suggested a theatrical agent at the William Morris Agency, Charles Baker, or someone like him "who is connected with the theater, which can sell the show and its idea, with the imagination to work up enthusiasm in the heart of producers." Those names may have been suggested by Iola's best friend, actress Barbara Baxley, who was plugged in to the Broadway talent system. Ishlon also advised the Brubecks to "forget about Louis Armstrong and concentrate on the show. Stay away from the Negro cast—or at least do not emphasize the color line."

Ishlon's last suggestion went against the very core of why the Brubecks created *The Real Ambassadors*. In her assessment of Ishlon's advice, Iola Brubeck wrote to Bancroft, "Sorry, I cannot agree. I think the show needs Louis—or else to be done over completely. I also don't think that Ishlon gets the point that the show is a mixed cast" [underlining in original].

Finally, in her assessment of how Glaser's office was responding to the various avenues the Brubecks were pursuing to develop the musical, Iola wrote to Bancroft that Ishlon and Lorber at Columbia felt it was essential to determine whether Glaser had the right as Dave Brubeck's agent to represent

the Brubecks on Broadway. She tells Bancroft, "When MCA or William Morris was mentioned, Glaser screamed 'What do you need them for? Just to
slice a percentage off the top? You got me!'" In Glaser's mind, he was the
only agent the Brubecks needed to take *The Real Ambassadors* to Broadway.
George Avakian was not surprised at all when he read Iola's memo in 2010.
He offered, "Though Glaser had absolutely no experience working in the
totally different world of Broadway, his bluster was more 'vintage Glaser.'"[6]

Iola Brubeck explained to Bancroft that Glaser had created yet another
obstacle to the show's progress when he decreed that he would only guarantee Armstrong once "a reliable producer assures Glaser that it is a show
worthy of Louis and one that will help his [Armstrong's] career." It is fair
to assume that they had already done this. The Brubecks had lines out for
possible involvement of much larger talent agencies like William Morris and
MCA, along with positive responses from veteran producers Josh Logan and
Paul Gregory in hand, but Glaser was still demurring. His actions led to a
simple conclusion: the show could only have Armstrong if he, Glaser, estimated that it would be a boost and not a hindrance to the career and wallet
of Armstrong, at that time Glaser's most valuable client by a large margin.

She closes the section on Glaser with what would prove a stark and utterly
realistic appraisal of their absolute dependence on Glaser to advance the
show: "We need his [Glaser's] moral backing—his continued interest—his
Louis—and possibly his money."[7] Perhaps even more so than her husband,
Iola clearly recognized that without the endorsement and support of Joe
Glaser, the couple's dream of shining a bright light on the absurdity of American's racial intolerance might never happen. Still, her last lines echoed a
confidence that both she and her husband felt as they continued to forge
ahead: "There it stands to date. We can still be hopeful. Friends in the theater who have heard and read it say that it is worthy, so I'm feeling more
confident now."[8]

Iola Brubeck's confidence was confirmed the very next morning, March
9, 1959, when nationally syndicated columnist Dorothy Kilgallen announced
to the world, "Brubeck Pens 25 Songs for Musical" in the *New York Journal
American*. Her scoop cited two "prominent New York showmen who've heard
the demonstration records done by Carmen McRae and an obscure male
singer and are so enthusiastic they want to stage the song-and-dancer. Dave
is figuring on a fall 1960 opening."[9] In an effort to light the fires among producers, agent Larry Bennett at Glaser's office tipped Kilgallen to the project
in the hopes that such a prominent mention would stir up more interest. In
a March 17, 1959, letter to the Brubecks, Bennett acknowledges the Kilgallen
plant and says that he was in continuing contact with Josh Logan's office

regarding the next steps in their evaluation of the musical.[10] Mort Lewis, then Brubeck's personal manager, wrote in a March 28, 1959, letter to Australian promoter Art Thurston that "Dave and his wife have written a Broadway show . . . from the looks of things it may be produced sometime soon."[11] Lewis asked that this development be kept confidential until a deal was in place, and further correspondence with various producers demonstrated that interest was indeed continuing to build on the part of top Broadway producers.

Looking over some of the personal letters Iola wrote to one of her closest friends, Mary Jeanne Sauerwein, it's clear that the progress being made in 1959 to find a producer for *The Real Ambassadors* excited Iola greatly. She concluded her Easter card to Mary Jeanne with pride:

> We were in New York for a few days trying to place our show. This summer we will go to New York (all of us) and Dave and I will concentrate on trying to snag a producer to do our "bang up" musical. We are proud of it, if we did write it ourselves.[12]

In a subsequent note to Sauerwein on May 26, 1959, Iola reiterated that the family would soon be decamping to New York City for the summer while Dave performed at Newport and up and down the Eastern Seaboard. Her optimism in placing the show with a veteran producer was high as she confided, "We have to go east this summer to seek our fortune on Broadway."[13]

Such optimism was certainly justified, as soon after, Joshua Logan asked his producing partner Leland Hayward to visit Dave and Iola Brubeck that summer, while they were in residency at the Music Inn in Lenox Music Camp in Massachusetts.[14] Hayward was a successful Hollywood agent and Broadway producer whose credits included the original stage productions of *Mister Roberts* (1948), *South Pacific* (1949), and *Gypsy* (coproduced with David Merrick) and *The Sound of Music* (both in 1959). Simultaneously, a member of Hayward's production team, Marshall Jamison, met with the Brubecks in summer of 1959 to review the project in detail. Jamison was no stranger to production, as he had started out on Broadway as a cast member in the hit show *Mister Roberts* before becoming a successful director. The meeting went well, as evidenced by a mid-August 1959 follow-up letter from Jamison to the Brubecks confirming a commitment on the part of the Hayward organization to helping rewrite and prepare *The Real Ambassadors* for musical theater production.[15] Unfortunately, at the same time, Jamison outlined that with three new Broadway properties in various stages of production for the coming season, the best he could offer was to help the Brubecks identify and hire an experienced writer to rework the show's book. Jamison named experienced writers Ira Wallach, James Baldwin, and William Dufty as possible collaborators and concluded by asking the couple for the green light to explore such a partnership.

Jamison also diplomatically echoed what Paul Gregory had told the Brubecks earlier about their elaborate production vision. Regarding the show's book, Jamison recommended that "it be a deeply fascinating character study of Pops as a human being, with the cultural exchange acting as a back drop on which to play the personal story" [emphasis in original]. Once again, a seasoned producer seemed to suggest that Dave and Iola Brubeck scale back their vision on the show's production. Regardless of that critique, the commitment from the Logan-Hayward camp must have appeared to be just the break that the Brubecks had been working so hard to achieve. However, the frenetic pace of work in the Hayward offices meant that no further action was taken beyond this hopeful letter. Reflecting back on this exchange, Iola Brubeck remembered that "after the initial spurt of interest [from Hayward's team], there was no more follow-up [from them on the rewrite]."[16]

Additionally, a lengthy, detailed letter was sent by the Brubecks to choreographer Jerome Robbins soliciting his involvement, explaining to him the role of the chorus and dancers, citing an "Around the World" ballet sequence with music based on the folk idioms of various countries in Europe, the Middle East, India, and Africa. This letter makes clear that the staging the Brubecks still envisioned would be much more than simply putting a jazz ensemble and a few actors onstage.[17] Robbins politely wrote back deferring any review until he returned the following year from a production in Europe.[18] No matter, the four months that followed Kilgallen's scoop that Dave Brubeck would be bringing a musical to the stage had seen the Brubecks in contact with a diverse set of veteran Broadway producers who all seemed willing to consider some type of collaboration with the couple. The issue was timing, as the Hayward camp would need from one to two years advance notice to begin any substantial planning for a trial run of the show due to their jam-packed schedule, and that time frame would have to follow the necessary and potentially time-consuming rewrite that they felt was absolutely essential. However, a much timelier opportunity soon emerged that led to a real hope that the show might see the stage within the next eighteen months—across the Atlantic in England.

CHAPTER 9

A PROMISING PROPOSAL

The Real Ambassadors in London

London-based agent Harold Davison first became acquainted with Dave Brubeck when he arranged a series of 1958 Western European dates to precede the State Department segment of the world tour. While in London during the Dave Brubeck Quartet's two-week swing through England, the Brubeck family dined with Davison and his wife, and that evening the Brubecks alluded to their efforts on a "secret project" but offered no additional details to Davison. Later, as momentum was building toward a possible production of *The Real Ambassadors*, the Brubecks wrote a letter to Davison on May 27, 1959, revealing the details of the project. In this letter, the Brubecks outlined the musical's narrative and their hopes for casting Armstrong and McRae as the leads, and they inquired about Davison's possible interest in bringing the show to London.

Previous correspondence from the Brubecks to Joe Glaser had made reference to the advice that veteran producers such as Paul Gregory and Marshall Jamison had made—for the couple to greatly simplify the show's intended production aesthetic to focus on the personal story of bandleader Pops. Gregory had even suggested using a bare stage with just the jazz combo for support. While the Brubecks had listened to such advice with their heads, the correspondence with Davison shows that, in their hearts, they still dreamed of a *My Fair Lady*-scaled musical production with chorus, dancers, and costumed actors, in spite of the various show business professionals warning them otherwise.

> It is, in a sense, a jazz musical, because the story involves jazz musicians; but the music itself varies from the almost classical aria, to swinging jazz, to folk music, to spirituals, to ballet. The story is told almost completely by music. It was specifically written for Louis Armstrong

and Carmen McRae although the parts could certainly be played by others. A mixed Negro and white cast is required.[1]

Soon they met in person. Before Brubeck would return to England as part of a George Wein–produced, Newport-branded concert package in mid-September, Davison came to New York City. Iola Brubeck wrote to Davison on July 1, 1959, and suggested that during the agent's visit to New York in the next month, they arrange to meet and preview the show for him. She and the Brubeck children would be in residency at the Music Inn in Lenox, Massachusetts, and able to come down to Manhattan easily. In closing, she noted that "Louis is even more interested in doing the show now so that he can be off the road."[2] Her comments were in response to Armstrong's June 1959 heart attack, suffered in Italy, which made clear that the legendary showman's grueling tour schedule was no longer sustainable. Appearing in a successful Broadway show, the Brubecks hoped, might now appear to be a more viable option for Armstrong and Glaser, to keep him working closer to his home base in New York City.

While Davison was arranging his New York itinerary and Satchmo was recovering from his heart attack, Dave Brubeck continued his campaign to promote the musical at every turn. He shared his enthusiasm for the jazz musical with the press, with the hope that the more media attention the project received, the more likely Iola and he would be to find their sponsor. In an interview given to the *Tulsa Daily World* titled "Sermon in Jazz May Help Man Love His Brother," Brubeck said, perhaps with a wink of optimism, that the couple's newest project was a musical titled *World Take a Holiday*, and he claimed it was set to open on Broadway the following year. The rationale for creating the show was straightforward, as he stated:

> The theme is that he that loveth his God, loveth his brother also, obviously the racial [equality] question," Brubeck argued. "This is the greatest problem and worst danger to the United States—the threat to us is not missiles, not economics, but our attitude toward our fellow man. I want to make it clear that this is not a hate show, but a love show. I feel very deeply on this but I think we can make our point better through singing than preaching.[3]

In the interview, Brubeck related that while appearing in Tulsa with his own quartet as part of a package tour with the Chico Hamilton Quintet, vocalist Chris Connor and her ensemble, the Maynard Ferguson Big Band, and other groups, the troupe had difficulty finding accommodations since some of them were Black. Brubeck complained that the situation had changed little since he was demobilized after the Second World War in 1946, when he witnessed Black veterans from his unit being denied service even though they had won the Purple Heart fighting for their country. Speaking later with filmmaker Ken Burns for his documentary series on the history of jazz, Brubeck remembered:

> When we landed in Texas we all went to the dining room to eat, and they wouldn't serve the Black guys. The guys had to go around and stand at the kitchen door. This one guy, he said he wouldn't eat any of their food and he started to cry. He said, "What I've been through, and the first day I'm back in the United States, I can't even eat with you guys. I wonder why I went through all this."[4]

In the same interview, Brubeck remembered the first Black man he met as a young boy and the lesson about the pain and suffering that racial intolerance could spawn. At the time, Dave was a teen, working as a cowboy all summer long and most days after school on the large ranch his father managed.

> You know, the first Black man I saw, my dad took me to see on the Sacramento River in California. And he said to his friend, "Open your shirt for Dave." There was a brand on his chest [pause]. And my dad said, "These things can't happen." And that's why I fought for what I fought for [during World War II and after].[5]

So while the daily grind of touring to support his family and build his audience was his primary activity, he never forgot the price being paid by those suffering segregation's injustices. Dave and Iola Brubeck were committed to realizing their musical with every fiber of their being, regardless of how long it might take to do so.

After the summer 1959 New York City meeting between the Brubecks and Davison, a stream of detailed correspondence documenting their collaborative efforts to present the show in England continued. Davison enthusiastically embraced the idea of staging the show there, so that when Dave returned to England in September 1959 on the aforementioned Newport-branded concert tour, discussions and meetings resumed between Brubeck and Davison, leading to the firm belief by Brubeck that there would soon be a premiere of *The Real Ambassadors* in London.[6]

Evidently, negotiations had progressed significantly, since by October 22, Brubeck began his letter to Davison with the electrifying statement, "I have spoken with Glaser and he says he has given you the understanding that it would be possible to open the show in London in September 1960 with Louis Armstrong." Glaser's commitment to the London production was not 100 percent, however, as Brubeck noted: "As soon as you can tell me that a working agreement has been made with Glaser and a definite date set, I will curtail my other activities and will start orchestrating the show." So although a tentative date had been set by Glaser and Davison to open the show in London for September 1960, no concrete written agreement was yet in place. Was Glaser merely extending a carrot to Davison with which to gauge his star's worth for a new project, or did the wily manager really see an upside to supporting this latest effort to produce the musical? Evidence proves that the former was Glaser's main motivation.

Glaser's unwillingness to have Armstrong record even a single song from the show on a home audition tape had left a bitter taste in Brubeck's mouth. Glaser wasn't about to provide the couple with audio evidence aligning Armstrong with the show without being much more firmly in control of any such deal. From that point on, the couple proceeded more deliberately in their dealings with Glaser, insisting that a written agreement with Davison should be the primary goal in moving forward. At Brubeck's request, both Glaser and Davison were now providing carbon copies to the couple of all correspondence, so that he and Iola could be kept up to date on the negotiations. The Brubecks had reason to be hopeful, as two seasoned music managers were now working collaboratively to negotiate the details of how the show would be funded and produced. Still, without signatures, no deal would move ahead.

The presentation would be a concert version, without the elaborate costumes, dance numbers, and additional actors originally conceived. This was borne out by a November 5 letter in which Davison explained to the Brubecks that the prospects for a fall 1960 UK presentation of the musical were quite good:

> From our point of view September 1960 would be fine. There has been a tremendous amount of interest with this show and we have had bookers from various organisations on to us about it. I have no doubts that it would be a tremendous success, but the whole thing depends on how much we could get Louis for . . . it would be ideal for the group to be working here during the period you are working with the show, and it would save a lot of problems.[7]

The reference to "bookers from various organisations" can be interpreted as regional British promoters and venues that anticipated strong demand for a touring musical starring Louis Armstrong. The mention of the "group" is a reference to the Dave Brubeck Quartet, which Davison would have booked for a series of concert and club dates to provide the necessary cash flow to support the rehearsals needed to prepare *The Real Ambassadors* for the stage. On paper, it was a winning plan.

However, the cause for delay in finalizing the deal was revealed one week later: Armstrong's fee. Glaser wrote that Davison had stated that he could not guarantee the requested performance fee of $5,000 per week for Armstrong's involvement ($46,680 in 2021 currency). Glaser offered an alternative to the hefty guarantee, asking Davison to inform him "exactly what kind of deal you can work out whereby Louis will be given a minimum guarantee . . . and a percentage of the receipts each and every week."[8] Such deals could carry a significant upside for Armstrong and Glaser if the show was a hit. Glaser took the opportunity seriously and wanted to probe every possible money-making avenue for himself and his star. He also mentioned that Armstrong could make personal appearances, for instance on English television, which would help offset the reduced guarantee for Armstrong and his band when compared to his US performance earnings.

Positioning himself as Armstrong's protector, Glaser added a separate cover letter to Brubeck accompanying the carbon copy of his letter to Davison, in which he justified in some detail the basis for his requested guarantee. Glaser wrote:

> I just want you to know that I am not insisting that he [Davison] pay Louie a minimum guarantee of $5,000 per week although I'm sure you know that after taxes, family responsibilities and paying his staff, he is left with about $2,000 and from the way he and his wife have been living these past 15 years, they need $2,000 per week to live."[9]

Although no known further copies of correspondence between Glaser and Davison exist, by analyzing the Brubeck-Glaser correspondence that followed, it is clear that Glaser and Davison reached an impasse. Glaser wrote directly to Iola Brubeck sixty days later on December 30, 1959, stating,

> I will keep my fingers crossed in the hope that I can eventually work out something . . . to get some of my dear friends to produce Dave's show here in the States, especially since it seems that Harold Davison, in London told Dave he would be in a position to do certain things and he is now not able to do them.[10]

As he would do again and again, Glaser did not come right out and torpedo the proposal; instead he masterfully extended the negotiations to see exactly how he and Armstrong might profit from the opportunity before reaching his final decision. The Brubecks continued to try to build bridges to influential people in the entertainment industry, however.

In June 1960, on the advice of James Bancroft, Brubeck and his family relocated from their native California to Connecticut, mainly to increase the time Dave could spend at home with his growing family. Originally, Dave had become so sick of being on the road away from his family that he discussed with Bancroft the idea of giving up touring and simply playing in the Bay Area. The attorney countered, "Your best years are ahead of you. You should be on the East Coast to take full advantage of the opportunities there."[11] The opportunities he was referring to were connected with New York City, the hub of the jazz scene, home to all the major television networks and record companies, and with a dense population that meant more performance opportunities than in the Western states. The Brubecks got a lead on a rambling farmhouse situated on a large piece of property in Weston, Connecticut, that belonged to Columbia Records producer Irving Townsend. Darius Brubeck recalled that Townsend was his father's primary contact at Columbia, since George Avakian had left the label to help start Warner Brothers Records. Cathy Brubeck Yaghsizian, then seven years old, recalled the move:

> Originally, we were told the move was supposed to be temporary for the summer, but then we stayed on for the school year. We were thrilled to see snow for the first time that winter. There were a lot of great places to sled and it was just beautiful. After the first year there, we kids were told we were going to have a family "sit down" to discuss our future. We were asked if we missed California and [told] that our parents thought about actually staying there. They sincerely wanted input and asked what we thought about possibly staying there permanently. I recall that we kids were all for it.[12]

The historic eighteenth-century farmhouse sat on Newtown Turnpike, roughly a ninety-minute drive from Manhattan, and was situated in an area known as a retreat for busy New York executives. The farm where the family took up residence was part of the land holdings of a wealthy woman, Alice DeLamar, who resided nearby at Stonebrook, a mansion she had built in the 1930s. Dubbed "the richest bachelor girl in America" by the press, she had begun to purchase and renovate properties in the vicinity of Stonebrook to serve as affordable rentals to artists, actors, and musicians.[13] She was a lifelong supporter of the arts, and her tenants were invited to use the large in-ground pool she had built in her own backyard every afternoon between 3:00 and 5:00 p.m. She enjoyed seeing her tenants at play, as Cathy said: "She would sit above the pool on a veranda and be served tea while we all swam in the pool." Cathy recalled that some of their neighbors included the painter Jean Jones Jackson, jazz saxophonist Gerry Mulligan and his partner, actress Sandy Dennis, as well as composer John Cage's former wife, Xenia, an artist herself and the Brubecks' nearest neighbor, whom Cathy recalled "often hosted parties with all kinds of colorful characters showing up next door. Barbara Baxley, who was my mother's best friend and lived in Manhattan, had a getaway on the lane, too."[14]

To this list of who's who in the arts world, Darius Brubeck, then a budding thirteen-year-old trumpeter and pianist, added famed choreographer George Balanchine, founder of New York City Ballet, Fred Hellerman of the iconic American folk group the Weavers, and *Lolita* author Vladimir Nabokov. Darius recalled:

> Just across the street, Columbia producer John Hammond and Benny Goodman had homes, so it seemed as if everybody was there in a world. Leonard Bernstein [who collaborated with Dave and Howard Brubeck to bring Howard's work *Dialogs for Jazz Combo and Orchestra* to the stage] lived fifteen miles away. [Being surrounded by so many artists] was quite transforming."[15]

Townsend's Weston, Connecticut, home proved an ideal place to help the Brubeck children with the transition to a new life in the East. Their new home had a number of outbuildings, including a small barn where the family had a Shetland pony.[16] In addition to the aforementioned swimming pool, which had a tunnel from the dressing room to the pool, the family had access to a lake, so there was more than adequate room for the children to explore.

With the majority of the quartet's most lucrative performing opportunities on the Eastern Seaboard, the move made sense. Proximity to New York City, the hub for the recording industry at that time, would also increase Brubeck's connections to Columbia Records and other business entities, including Joe Glaser. Just before packing up the family for the move, Brubeck wrote to Davison with a hint of resignation, asking that he return the script and tapes for the show. "I think the price that Joe Glaser is asking for Louis would make it impossible to produce the show as it is. Without Louie, of course, it would have to be rewritten completely."[17] He also mentioned for the first

A portrait of the Brubeck family shortly after their move to Wilton, Connecticut, showing the idyllic country home where they lived, rented from Columbia Records executive Irving Townsend. Standing, *rear*, Dave Brubeck; on wall, *left to right*, Darius, Chris, Dan, Michael, Cathy, and Iola Brubeck. Brubeck Collection, Holt-Atherton Special Collections, University of the Pacific Library, © Dave Brubeck.

time Columbia Records' willingness to fund a cast recording for the show at a future date, and that after moving their family, Dave and Iola intended to seek out a seasoned musical comedy playwright to help rewrite the show. Brubeck hoped that the resulting album might interest other producers in his ability to write for the theater. He thanked Davison for his unsuccessful efforts to bring the show to London, saying no one knew what the future might hold for the musical.

Though they had relocated to the East Coast, the Brubecks did continue to mine the wealth of connections they had developed on the West Coast. One such connection was Dick Hyland, an agent at the Hollywood-based Frank Cooper Agency. By August 1960, only a few months after moving to Connecticut, Brubeck was corresponding with Hyland about possible representation for himself and his brother Howard as a composing "team" for film and television. Included in this letter is a reference to a possible complete rewrite of the musical for television production, still starring Armstrong, who, it was learned, would soon be making his historic three-month 1960–61 State Department tour to Africa. Brubeck mentioned that he, too, would be leaving for another State Department tour in March 1961, this time to South

Having grown up on a forty-five-thousand-acre ranch in Ione, California, Dave Brubeck learned firsthand how to ride, rope, and tend to livestock. Here he's demonstrating how to take care of the Brubeck family pony, Playboy. Pictured on the grounds of their Wilton home, *left to right*, are Michael, Dave, and Darius Brubeck. Brubeck Collection, Holt-Atherton Special Collections, University of the Pacific Library, © Dave Brubeck.

America. The letter closes by once again mentioning Glaser's control over any production involving Armstrong's talents: "We would first have to approach Joe Glaser, who is Louis's manager, as well as his agent. Glaser knows about the musical and I think would be very much in favor of a TV show which would show Louis to advantage."[18]

Even though they had been stymied at nearly every turn over the prior three years, Dave and Iola Brubeck retained an innate sense of optimism that somehow they would pull off bringing *The Real Ambassadors* to the stage. While domestic prospects to bring the show to life were ebbing, another foreign connection would soon emerge, providing a new opportunity to stage the musical.

While on a tour to England arranged by Davison in January 1961, on which the quartet was accompanied by the Brubecks' third son, Chris, Brubeck met Bob Roberts, an expatriate American film producer who had left Hollywood after being blacklisted following the House Un-American Activities Committee's McCarthy hearings.[19] Roberts had an office at the Rank Organization, one of England's leading film and television companies. He was planning a film that was a modern update to Shakespeare's *Othello*, using the contemporary jazz scene in London as the tableau, titled *All Night Long*. Starring Richard Attenborough, the film featured music by leading jazz musicians of the day, with the Dave Brubeck Quartet, John Dankworth, and Charles Mingus contributing music for the staged version of the film's nightclub scenes. In Roberts, Dave found a kindred spirit who understood the theme of *The Real Ambassadors*, as it represented a direct parallel to the ostracism Roberts had suffered. They agreed that such injustices should be addressed by artists through any medium available. Brubeck had pitched *The Real Ambassadors* to Roberts and, at the director's request, had forwarded a script and tape to him made with Carmen McRae, backed by Brubeck, previewing some of the music from the show. In a letter to Roberts dated July 14, 1961, Brubeck shared the frustration of the varying responses to the show he and Iola had received since they began previewing it four years earlier, writing:

> So-called geniuses in the field have alternately praised and condemned various sections of the script—each contradictory as to where the praise and where the damnation should be placed. We finally gave up on revisions until the person came along who was 100% sold on the idea and who would know better than we how best to present the idea.[20]

In his letter, Brubeck discounts the earlier-voiced opinions by Columbia's Goddard Lieberson and Debbie Ishlon that race was a concern when casting the mixed-race *Real Ambassadors*, alluding to *A Raisin in the Sun* and *The Blacks*, both of which had successful runs in New York City. Unfortunately, Brubeck was mixing apples and oranges to a certain extent, since those two dramatic plays in fact featured all-Black, nonintegrated casts. And neither was a musical.[21]

Brubeck stated that he and Iola were extremely flexible in adapting their ideas for possible film production, switching gears from their original goal of reaching Broadway:

> Because of all the hassles and risks that occur with a Broadway production—plus the problems of obtaining the right talent at the right time—I think . . . a film version of our musical would be the most ideal for us . . . basically, I am trying to say that we are extremely flexible in our attitude toward the handling of the story, and we are agreeable to almost any changes. All we ask is the right to O.K. the changes. My wife and I are interested in doing the music and lyrics—the choice of writer would be up to you.[22]

Brubeck then mentioned that the following Monday he would be meeting with Joe Glaser to finalize Brubeck's contract renewal at the booking agency. At that time, he would also discuss Armstrong's performance on the forthcoming recording of the soundtrack album for *The Real Ambassadors*, which was to be scheduled for September 1961, assuming the entire cast could be in one place for the requisite amount of time.[23] Roberts enthusiastically responded on July 29, 1961, writing that "the music and the lyrics Mrs. Brubeck wrote are just wonderful!" He added that the book was not ready in its present form for film production, but that he would share the book with a writer on staff at Rank to get his reactions and recommendations.[24] Roberts exuded optimism for the project in the letter's final paragraph:

> As a whole, I feel that the entire project could be very worthwhile, and I hope we can pull it off together. I would really enjoy working with you again. It could be profitable for all of us—but, beyond that, it would be fun to do something good. [emphasis in original][25]

Once again, the message was clear that, in the eyes of the veteran filmmaker, the show would need a major rewrite in order to be considered a possible film property. No further correspondence exists in the Brubeck Collection suggesting that the film possibilities with England's Rank Organization were ever fully explored. So it was that two experienced and interested entertainment industry veterans were unable to help the Brubecks realize their show in the United Kingdom. However, less than eight weeks after Roberts's letter effectively ended the last hope for a UK collaboration, the September 1961 cast recording of the show had been approved. When completed, it would open a new door to realizing the musical that no one, not even the Brubecks, had yet foreseen.

CHAPTER 10

RECORDING THE REAL AMBASSADORS

Although the Brubecks still hoped to stage a musical theater production, their priority in summer 1961 was the pending series of soundtrack recording sessions in September at Columbia's 30th Street Studio. One of a number that the label maintained in and around New York City, the studio was located in a historic church built in 1875 that was renowned for its outstanding acoustics. The building served as a recording studio for the label from 1948 to 1981, and many of Columbia's most successful albums from this period were recorded there.

Glaser had remained steadfast in withholding Armstrong from an offer to produce the show with Harold Davison in London, the most promising offer yet. However, an album recording for Columbia, one of Armstrong's former labels, with members of Armstrong's All-Stars, as well as Brubeck and his rhythm section, was an entirely different matter. Making the record would only require the commitment of a few days for Armstrong, who had resumed a less-demanding touring schedule after recovering from his heart attack. Once the fees had been agreed upon between Glaser and Columbia, the sessions were scheduled.

Preparations for the 1961 recording dates can be traced back to a series of homemade practice tapes recorded by Brubeck and his rhythm section and sent to Armstrong. The first of these tapes, which survive as part of the Brubeck Collection, was made on January 3, 1959. Over the next two and a half years, the Brubecks sent a series of audio letters to Armstrong, keeping him up to date as the show evolved. For each song on the practice tape, Dave would play or sing the melody with accompaniment, then repeat the tune sans vocal for Satchmo's own practice.[1] Armstrong later told Brubeck that he practiced to those recordings frequently while on tour throughout the summer of 1961 in advance of the soundtrack recording, using his portable sound trunk.[2] Armstrong was an avid tape enthusiast and recorded hundreds

Louis Armstrong, ca. 1953, demonstrating his traveling recording trunk, which accompanied him on the road. He used it to listen to and practice music daily, as well as to make hundreds of hours of impromptu recordings of backstage conversations with friends. Courtesy of the Louis Armstrong House Museum.

of hours of his day-to-day life to audio tape—everything from practicing his horn by playing along with operatic arias to uncensored bull sessions that frequently occurred in his dressing room after performances. These tapes, available for study as part of the Louis Armstrong House Archives, form an invaluable record of just what Satchmo thought about practically every aspect of his life and times.[3]

In addition to these practice tapes, Dave recalled that Armstrong "asked us to type out the lyrics in bold print, so that he could Scotch tape them to the mirror and could be looking at them [practicing] while he shaved." Per Satchmo's request, the Brubecks created a customized set of index cards with each song's lyrics, organized by a numbering scheme to help Armstrong keep them in the order of performance; these were mailed to Armstrong. Those cards are extant today in the Jack Bradley Collection and include small handwritten corrections in Iola's hand.[4]

Brubeck had also made considerable efforts to record demo versions of the show's songs that would include chorus. The first planned choral

recording was to be done in Chicago under the direction of Columbia producer Cal Lampley.[5] A second such session would follow in Los Angeles.
Although Brubeck did all the necessary legwork for the choral demo recordings, no funding had been secured, so the idea was shelved.[6] As the clock
wound down on the approaching September 1961 recording dates, Brubeck
decided to replace the chorus with a dynamic vocal trio made up of Dave
Lambert, Jon Hendricks, and Annie Ross. This was a practical and artistic
decision that helped create the onstage ensemble feel that the Brubecks, along
with their album producer, Teo Macero, hoped to capture in the recordings.

Lambert, Hendricks & Ross had been formed in 1957. Prior to the group's
formation, each of the individual members had found different avenues of
musical success. Lambert began singing professionally in the early 1940s with
the Johnny Long Orchestra. Joining Gene Krupa's Orchestra in 1944, he was
part of the vocal quartet known as the G-Noters, and had a hit with "What's
This?," recorded in 1945. Writing about the G-Noters, jazz critic Marc Myers
stated, "Their scatting captured the essence of early bop, thanks to their close
association with Charlie Parker, Dizzy Gillespie and other burgeoning bebop-
pers on New York's 52nd Street." Lambert went on to collaborative work,
singing and providing his signature bop-influenced vocal arrangements for
Charlie Parker, Charlie Barnet, Al Haig, Benny Green, and Kai Winding.[7]

English-born Annie Ross became an actor at the age of seven and wrote
her first song, "Let's Fly," at fourteen; it was recorded by Johnny Mercer and
the Pied Pipers. The vocalist became active in the early 1950s New York jazz
scene, collaborating with Max Roach, Tommy Potter, and George Walling-
ton. She was also experimenting with taking vocal performance in a new
direction, blending bop with vocal versions of jazz solos, similar to Lambert.
What really put Ross on the map was a 1952 meeting with Prestige Records
president Bob Weinstock, who challenged Ross to come up with lyrics to a
well-known jazz instrumental song. The resulting record, "Twisted," based
on tenor saxophonist Wardell Gray's 1949 hit, became an underground sen-
sation and led to Ross being selected for *DownBeat*'s 1952 New Star award.
Starting in 1953, she toured internationally with Lionel Hampton's All-Star
Band, while recording an album of standards in 1956 backed by the Tony
Crombie 4-Tet.[8] While in New York City to perform a series of 1957 nightclub dates, she was invited to assist Dave Lambert in the role of vocal coach
for an ambitious session of Basie tunes arranged for vocal chorus. It was a
fortuitous invitation for all parties.[9]

Jon Hendricks had grown up performing from the age of seven. By the
time he was a teenager, he was singing professionally in Toledo, Ohio, on
the radio and in a nightclub, often accompanied by the legendary pianist

Art Tatum. After service in the Second World War, he attended college, then moved to New York in 1952 to begin the next phase of his singing career. While holding down a day job as a clerk typist, he wrote songs in the evenings and had some success placing them, most notably with Louis Jordan. Hendricks began collaborating with Dave Lambert in 1953, but it took four years for their new approach to jazz singing to catch on. As a songwriter, Hendricks became known for his ability to "put words to improvised solos that captured the musicality of their source material while adding a verbal vitality of their own."[10]

What would become the group's debut album was originally conceived by Lambert as an homage to Count Basie, featuring himself and Hendricks with ten other singers. The studio group would be performing Lambert's arrangements of some of Basie's best-known tunes, such as "One O'Clock Jump," "It's Sand, Man," and "Every Day [I Have the Blues]," with lyrics penned by Hendricks. The original sessions ultimately proved unsuccessful, as the studio singers hired could technically read the music, but couldn't swing the way that was required to capture the essence of the Basie sound. So rather than auditioning more singers to form another chorus, the duo asked Ross to join them to record all the parts themselves, using multitrack overdubbing, which was still relatively new at that time. The group's fresh new sound struck a chord with listeners. Once it was released under the title of *Sing a Song of Basie*, it became a hit, immediately establishing the group as the vanguard of what was soon dubbed "vocalese"—the art of taking a well-known jazz composition and adding lyrics over it, especially the often complex improvised instrumental solos.[11] While their debut album featured a much denser sound with multiple tracks of each singer's voice, due to their outstanding musicianship, Lambert, Hendricks & Ross were able to distill Lambert's arrangements and Hendricks's often witty lyrics into three-part arrangements perfect for the concert stage. Featuring Lambert's bop-influenced arrangements, Hendricks's bluesy insouciance, and Ross's dramatic vocal range, with her high notes emulating Basie's soaring trumpets, the group became world renowned, winning *Melody Maker* magazine's Number One Vocal Group designation for five years in a row (1959–63).[12]

Vocalist Jon Hendricks recalled in a 2009 interview that he first met Brubeck when Lambert, Hendricks & Ross were playing San Francisco. Hendricks had gone to hear Brubeck's quartet after their own show, and at that first meeting, Brubeck mentioned that he didn't have the label support to record a chorus for his musical. Being familiar with the inventiveness of the vocal trio, Brubeck challenged them to take on the role of the chorus for *The Real Ambassadors*. Hendricks said that at first he and his colleagues laughed. "Three people in place of a chorus?" Brubeck answered, "But you're not just *any* three people." Hendricks reflected back on that moment in the Black Hawk nightclub and described Brubeck's confidence in their ability to fulfill the demanding role of a chorus as "beautiful."[13]

At the time of this meeting with Brubeck, the trio and the intended female lead, Carmen McRae, were all signed to Columbia. This was advantageous, as each act was quickly signed and scheduled for the upcoming series of sessions. Iola Brubeck remembered the flood of phone calls to and from the performers, their agents, and producer Macero, checking and double-checking every musician's schedule. The Brubecks were determined to see that each three-hour session would be as productive as possible. The entire soundtrack recording was based first and foremost around Armstrong's availability and the fact that Carmen McRae would also be in town during September. Iola Brubeck recalled, "It was a very intense time. All the performers were booked through Glaser's office so we could make one call to keep up with their [respective] schedules." This allowed the Brubecks to book all of the artists when they would be in or near New York City, and the majority of the recording could be completed in September, assuming the sessions went smoothly.

In preparation, the couple visited Armstrong at his home in Corona, Queens, for a series of afternoon rehearsals to go over the music and reinforce the character of Pops.[14] A young Darius Brubeck attended one of these rehearsals in 1961. He had just started at Wilton High School, and although his principal instrument was piano, he was playing trumpet in the school band.

> Dave was going to a meeting with Louis at his house in Queens and he took me along, with my trumpet. I recall either Dave or Howard had written out some background horn parts for *The Real Ambassadors* to support Louis when he played, countermelodies, to have two voices going. And that to me was such a significant moment—I'm in the room with Louis Armstrong and we're playing trumpet together. Unforgettable.[15]

Plans continued in overdrive for the upcoming recording sessions for the show at Columbia's 30th Street Studio as the Brubecks made more visits to Corona to review Armstrong's songs with him. Just a week before the first session, Iola Brubeck discussed the rehearsals in an interview on WJZZ radio in Bridgeport, Connecticut. She singled out the ballad "Summer Song" as being one of Satchmo's favorites, and said, "When we played through it with him [at his home] the other day, a big smile appeared on his face, and he said 'Lovely.' I think he's going to do great justice to this piece."[16]

According to all accounts, Satchmo embraced both the music and its message. In an exclusive interview he gave jazz critic Leonard Feather a few months after the recordings were completed, he exclaimed, "There was one song that really thrilled me that I did with Lambert, Hendricks, and Ross—'They Say I Look Like God, Could God Be Black? My God!'" In the same conversation, the trumpeter cited the need for US segregation laws to change. "Sad, isn't it?" he said. "I've been all over the world with my band, but we can't play in my hometown . . . someday New Orleans has gotta change."[17]

With Satchmo's support and the rehearsals ramping up, everything appeared to be moving along on a positive note leading up to the recording dates. On September 8, 1961, Iola Brubeck gave a forty-minute live on-air preview of the upcoming recording sessions for the musical with WJZZ. The station was the brainchild of Kenneth Cooper, who bumped into Dave Brubeck at a party in Weston, where the two soon found their shared love of jazz music could be merged into a new all-jazz FM station that Cooper would fund. He hired Dave Brubeck as music director and spokesman when the station went on the air in 1960, and it was one of the first all-jazz stations in the nation, broadcasting twelve hours a day, from 2:00 p.m. to 2:00 a.m.[18] *The Dave Brubeck Show* was a regularly scheduled one-hour show at the station, which was followed immediately by a live weekly remote broadcast from Bridgeport's Hotel Barnum, the home of the Pink Elephant Lounge, which featured local performers.

That first week in September, Dave was unavailable for his weekly radio show since he was recording a second live album at Basin Street East featuring his group and vocalist Carmen McRae. Their first live album, also recorded there, *Tonight Only*, had been a success upon its release in 1960, hence the follow-up album, which was released in 1961 as *Take Five Live*, featuring an entirely Brubeck-composed repertoire. With Dave in Manhattan recording at the popular nightspot, Iola was drafted to appear on the broadcast to talk about the upcoming recording at Columbia studios. The interview reveals her laser-like focus on what was to be the first real manifestation of the musical, and it makes clear Iola's vision for the show, its lead character, and the broader social, political, and cultural context for the work. In an exchange with station manager and host Mike Lawless, Iola explained the reasoning for replacing traditional diplomats with jazz ambassadors, the most prominent of whom was to be played by Louis Armstrong:

Mike Lawless: Alright, let's go on to another tune here. Let's go now to a piano solo album [the 1956 release *Brubeck Plays Brubeck*] that Dave has recorded. And you can explain about it. The [instrumental] bell tune that Dave did?

Iola Brubeck: "Swing Bells" is on the solo piano album, and it was used in the show to really depict bells for me, and in the scene that we'll refer to as the coronation scene. The setting in the show is that Louis and the band are visiting a small kingdom in Africa during a holiday period similar to Mardi Gras or Carnival. And at this time the population of this small kingdom chooses their most popular man of the hour—to be like the King of the Mardi Gras for a day. And because of Louis's band's appearance, the populace is all for him. And much as it happened in real life, Louis is picked up on the shoulders of the people and marched through the streets and is proclaimed King for a Day. And this tune, "Swing Bells," is used to open the coronation scene. The words are simple because [they follow] the tolling of the bells. It just starts off:

> Swing bells, ring bells.
> The great day may now begin.
> Ring out the news.
> The world can laugh again.
> This day we're free.
> We are equal in every way.
> Ring bells, swing bells,
> declare a holiday.

And this is the beginning of the coronation.

ML: There are the words that will be fitted to the music. And here is the music. [Lawless airs instrumental version of "Swing Bells."]

IB: When you play the music, I think the words are so simple. You can see how they will fit exactly with the melody because it is just the sound of bells tolling.

ML: "Swing Bells," an apropos tune here that fits well within the context of the show. Well Oli, I'd like one more lyric, if we might?

IB: Well, maybe we could continue with the coronation scene? Because after the bells are tolling, the crowd of people, the chorus, starts singing, "What are you waitin' for? What are you waitin' for?" And that they want Louis to start playing because they've heard him play the night before. And they look upon him as perhaps a great leader, a bringer of people. And actually the show tries to say that a simple human being such as Louis, who goes about the world, using the gift that God gave him, which is a great musical talent, and really loving humanity—can really do more to bring peace to the world than all of the summits [conferences] that one could possibly bring together. There is one lyric that the crowd sings to him that I think says this:

Can it really be that you can set all people free?
Joshua stood at the wall.
God told him that it would fall.
Blow, Satchmo! Blow, Satchmo! Give that horn your all.
Joshua had just a horn.
Jericho held him in scorn.
Blow, Satchmo! Blow, Satchmo! That's why you were born.
Blow, Satchmo! Walls will tumble down.
Blow, Satchmo! You can wear the crown.
Blow, Satchmo! Take us by the hand.
Lead us to that promised land.

[Pause] And we are all looking for peace, aren't we?

ML: Yes, we are. There you go. Again it fits in with the context. This show is going to be quite a show. Oli, if it is done within the next few weeks, if it is recorded, when could the record-buying audience anticipate in buying it across the counter?

IB: Well, this, of course, will be up to the powers that be at Columbia. But perhaps we could arrange a preview [for listeners].[19]

In this excerpt from the broadcast, Iola makes a number of key points explaining the musical's socially conscious layers, including her decision to set the culminating scenes for the show in Africa, a continent that was then in the midst of throwing off the yoke of colonialism. European nations had kept native Africans completely out of the political process for generations. The lyrics ("This day, we're free. We're equal in every way.") alluded to the fact that in 1960 alone, eighteen African nations gained independent self-rule. This fact contrasted starkly with America's continued denial of rights to people of color.

The couple's view that artistry, honesty, integrity, and love for one's fellow man could be decisive factors in effecting real change was clearly the context for one of the show's most important messages: that artists should and must contribute to the discourse needed to improve society. She also explained how the world depicted in *The Real Ambassadors* was one where artists' voices would be at least the equal of politicians'. That point of view was based in part on the experiences the couple had on the Dave Brubeck Quartet's 1958 State Department–sponsored tour. *The Real Ambassadors* took that experience to the next level, replacing unproductive summit conferences with jazz jams. This was a concept that would appeal enormously to the jazz-loving peoples in the countries Dave and Iola Brubeck had visited on their 1958 tour and that would similarly resonate with many American jazz fans.

In the interview, Iola—addressed using her nickname, "Oli," by interviewer Mike Lawless—ironically refers to Columbia's underwriting of the very substantial costs required to bring together Armstrong's All-Stars, Carmen McRae, Lambert, Hendricks & Ross, Joe Morello, Eugene Wright, and Howard Brubeck as possibly "the most expensive demo ever made." The question of the show's title comes up near the beginning of the interview.

> **ML**: Oli, I wish you would tell people from the start what the title of this project is.
>
> **IB**: Well, that's a good question, too, Mike, because when it is recorded we are not sure of the final name. This project that Mike is referring to started off as a Broadway show, and it was titled *World Take a Holiday*. Then we thought maybe *Blow Satchmo*, because Louis Armstrong was to be the star. I think that is possibly the title of the album, or the opening track on the album is called "Everybody's Comin'." So we have a selection of three that might be the title of the album, and we are fortunate to have the great Louis Armstrong to sing the leading role in an album for a Broadway show that never made Broadway.

The eventual title emerged nearly six months after the recordings were done; Columbia executives felt *The Real Ambassadors* was the most marketable choice for the resultant ensemble-cast soundtrack album.

Iola then explains that their own overseas jazz ambassadors tour had affected the story line:

> **IB**: Now we started, five years ago, just talking about the idea. And we started writing a show based on a jazz band headed by Louis Armstrong on a State Department tour of the world. The writing of the show was stopped in 1958 when Dave actually went on a

State Department tour. We had a little closer view then of what was going on. We threw out what we started and we went on again rewriting the show.

Iola then compared their show to Duke Ellington's short-lived World War II–era musical, *Jump for Joy*, recalling that "the tunes made it, but not the show."[20] Ellington's show ran for 122 performances in summer 1941 in Los Angeles and was praised by critics, but prompted a number of death threats and fights outside the stage door, started by locals who objected to the perceived onstage romance between the show's racially diverse cast. The show featured the light-skinned Dorothy Dandridge and Big Joe Turner, which may have given the Brubecks, who idolized Ellington, some ideas to follow in casting their socially conscious musical nearly two decades later. Lawless and Iola Brubeck also referenced a few other shows that were incorporating jazz music as they aimed for Broadway: Oscar Brown Jr.'s *Worlds of Oscar Brown* and *The Connection*. The latter was a controversial piece at the time, looking at the lives of drug addicts who also played jazz music, thereby making an association between the two practices. The latter show featured the actors playing jazz interludes between scenes.[21]

As the interview proceeds, Iola states that the song "Remember Who You Are" poked fun at the stuffiness of the State Department's pre-tour briefing for the jazz ambassadors that enjoined them to always be on their best behavior when abroad. In the song's lyrics, the Brubecks quoted the State Department briefing they had received before their 1958 tour. In it, they satirized the original message, flipping the script to lionize founding fathers of jazz like Jelly Roll Morton, Count Basie, and Duke Ellington in place of the names the government representatives suggested they share overseas: Washington, Jefferson, and Lincoln.

Later, she speaks of two pieces that she dubs "special material"—"Summer Song" and "Lonesome." By special material, she means that for these songs, the lyrics came first, then the music. For the remainder of the musical, in contrast, Iola explains that she wrote lyrics expressly to fit her husband's existing repertoire.

One of the highlights of this broadcast was Iola's reading the lyrics of both pieces. Her clear, articulate, and artfully inflected voice brings the words to life. She interpolates commentary on Armstrong's reaction to each, including that December 1958 Chicago meeting when Dave explained the concept to him and the couple's wish for Satchmo to star in the musical. She goes on to lay out the inner feelings of the character Pops as revealed through this medley of songs:

IB: I'd like to read you one lyric, which is "Summer Song," which has just before it a pretty lyric called "Lonesome," which Louis sings, which is different from the type of thing he usually does. And it [then] goes [directly] into "Summer Song." Perhaps we could play "Summer Song."

ML: Okay, I'll tell you what. We'll play "Summer Song" first and we'll tag it with the lyric [which is to precede it in the show]. This will be Louis's solo in the song itself. Now is this another case of special material?

IB: No, I think this could stand as a ballad on its own in the show, in which Louis explains to the singer of his band [Rhonda] of his particular feelings for his band as he's growing older.

[*Lawless airs instrumental version of "Summer Song."*]

ML: That's "Summer Song"; that is from *Jazz Impressions of the U.S.A.*[22] "Summer Song" is Louis's solo within the show. And here is the lyric, Oli.

IB: Mike, in this particular lyric, [performed] before the theme of "Summer Song" is sung, there is a sort of choral prelude which will be sung by Lambert, Hendricks & Ross, most probably in which Louis speaks lines that lead into Summer Song.

And if you'd like I can read this lyric because it shows a side of Louis that most people don't know. I will tell you an interesting thing about this; the lyric was written first and then Dave set it for voices. I guess it was about two years ago, he went to see Louis in Chicago and he brought the material to him up in the hotel room. And in Louis's own special voice that no one else has, he read this lyric over and Dave said it was so moving that it brought tears to his eyes right there. And that Louis himself felt it so much he said "Man, that's deep." And he loves the song, "Summer Song," that comes after it.

[*Iola then gives a measured dramatic reading of the words to "Lonesome" over the air.*]

And then it goes into the introduction for "Summer Song" . . .

[*Iola then gives a measured reading of the words to "Summer Song" on the air.*]

ML: Very nice . . . and it sure fits Louis too, doesn't it?

At another point in the interview, when asked by Lawless what tunes she felt were superior, Iola singles out "Summer Song," admitting that "I like the song very much: [its lyrics were] written with Louis in mind, and the [original] melody is lovely. It's close to Louis's personal way of expressing [those emotions]."[23] The Brubecks chose to honor not only Armstrong but also other jazz greats in the soundtrack. The Armstrong-McRae duet "One Moment Worth Years" was based on an earlier tune Dave had written to honor legendary pianist Fats Waller.

> **IB:** Well, that one appeared first as an instrumental on which Dave played, and it was an homage to Fats Waller. Dave wanted something that had a sort of an old-time spirit, liveliness to it. In the show, it's used as a duet with Louis and Carmen, and again from the book, I'll tell you something about the situation.
>
> A man and a woman have had a tiff. The man has been too busy working. In this case, in the show, he has been busy planning what he is going to do to handle the world's situation and not paying much attention to the girl. After having been stood up several times, she feels as if she's just had enough. The verse of the song begins with the girl, which is Carmen, singing, "Must I spend a lifetime just in waiting while others have fun? I'm unequivocally stating that brother, you're done."

"You Swing, Baby," another duet, was prepared for the two lead characters, Pops and Rhonda, using one of Brubeck's best-known instrumental tunes, "The Duke," as its musical base. "The melody depicted Duke Ellington as Dave saw him," Iola offered.

At this point in the interview, Iola speaks at length about how the couple had forged a close and productive creative partnership with vocalist McRae.

> **ML:** Why don't we just talk a minute about Carmen? I know she is one of your favorite singers, and not just because she is doing the show, but you have worked with her. As such, she is in the process [now] of doing an album with your lyrics. I'll let you say it in your own words about her interpretation of your lyrics.
>
> **IB:** I think that Carmen is one of those rare people who has a great musical gift, sings well, and also has a great dramatic gift. When we first talked about writing this show, before we had any specific

people in mind, I said, "You know, of all the girl singers that I knew that were good jazz singers, I thought that Carmen was the one who had a real flair for the stage—for [playing] the dramatic scene." My guess certainly proved right because later . . . when she was traveling in San Francisco, she came over to our house one day. We said, "Carmen, we're writing a show and we would like to see what you think about these songs." She went through them, and immediately seemed to sense what the situation was [for each one]. We didn't even tell her the story line; we were just interested at that moment of her professional opinion of the songs as material for anybody to sing. She obligingly sang over the pieces while Dave played. We became sold on the idea [of her as the female lead], and she has been with us ever since, trying to help us do something with the show, even if she produced it, recorded it, or whatever.

Iola Brubeck and Carmen McRae connected so well that the Brubecks declined requests from other noted vocalists, including Anita O'Day, who asked to record some of the songs that would be included in the show. This period in McRae's career was highlighted by the close musical collaborations that developed with the Brubecks, as Iola mentioned. It concluded with the recording and subsequent Monterey performance of *The Real Ambassadors*.[24] The remainder of the interview ranges into a discussion of songwriting and lyricists, with the host and Iola sharing their favorite lyricists and other related tidbits about music. Iola Brubeck clearly had developed a detailed and nuanced appreciation for what today is referred to as the Great American Songbook, and her work as a lyricist, librettist, and cocreator with Dave Brubeck demonstrates her familiarity with the conventions outlined in this canonic body of repertoire.

At this point in the development of the couple's vision for *The Real Ambassadors*, Armstrong's larger-than-life persona was a key wellspring of inspiration. As for the coronation sequence referenced earlier, Iola had enthused that in their show, "Louis is carried on the shoulders of the populace, which is based on an actual event!"[25] Iola Brubeck had been studying Armstrong's life and work intently, and had woven many of his ideas, actual statements, and experiences into the plot and libretto for *The Real Ambassadors*. This may have been the real genius in the Brubecks' selection of Armstrong as the leading man: by incorporating so much of what made Satchmo the most beloved musician (and American) throughout much of the world, they created a role that only he could play with certitude, and in playing it, Armstrong and Pops would become one and the same to audiences everywhere.[26]

One of the show's most memorable numbers is the duet between Trummy Young and Armstrong, "King for a Day," in which Iola has them bantering during the introduction:

Armstrong: Man, if they'd just let me run things my way / this world would be a swingin' place . . . the first thing I'd do is call a basement session.
Young: Uh-h-h-h, Pops . . . you mean a "summit conference."
Armstrong: Ma-a-a-a-n, I don't mean a UN kind of a session / I mean a *jam* session.

The implications were clear. Music is a universal language that can break down walls, as it has done since the dawn of civilization. The Brubecks had experienced what other jazz artists had discovered: Once they left the confines of America, they had real social, cultural, and political agency. At home, many jazz musicians were diminished; abroad they were respected. Their opinions were invited and reported as front-page news in nearly every country in which they toured. Brubeck, Gillespie, Armstrong, and Goodman were all quoted as saying that during their groups' State Department–sponsored tours, audiences with little or no understanding of the English language nevertheless connected meaningfully with the music and the musicians creating it. Certainly the Brubecks' own 1958 State Department tour, during which they developed lifelong ties to people in a variety of nations, had shown them a clear and compelling case for the effectiveness of jazz diplomacy.[27] Now, using the show as a platform, they hoped that a well-received soundtrack album might move their dream one step closer to reality.

CHAPTER 11

THE MOST EXPENSIVE
DEMO EVER MADE

It seemed as if the Brubecks' luck had changed, as just four days after this illuminating broadcast, on September 12, 1961, the day of the first recording session dawned. At last, they were about to start producing a soundtrack album. Even Joe Glaser, at best a reluctant supporter of the project, wrote to Brubeck recounting his conversation with Louis Armstrong the morning of the recording session. He recounted, "[Louis] gave me to understand he spent several hours with you [at the aforementioned rehearsals at Armstrong's home] and everything is set for the recording date, I am sure it will be a very successful one."[1] One week later he wrote to Iola Brubeck, confirming what she already knew about Armstrong's attitude toward his role in the soundtrack recording, as she had attended all the sessions. Glaser told her, "[Louis] is really and truly very enthused and happy about the recording."[2] Taking a strictly economic point of view, allowing Armstrong to perform at three recording sessions for a substantial advance on the album's royalties did not carry anywhere close to the potential risk that a Broadway run of the musical would represent to either Armstrong's or Glaser's cash flow. Still, the fact that Glaser allowed the recording to occur shows that he understood just how important performing the Brubecks' challenging new material was to Armstrong. The veteran musician was primed to explore new territory with his younger collaborators in the studio, and Glaser supported his star's artistic wishes.

The costs to produce the recordings, compared to those for a typical album release by the Dave Brubeck Quartet, were substantial. According to documents found in the Teo Macero Collection, the expenses incurred in recording the album included the following:

- Session fees totaling $3,476 for the studio musicians (including double union-scale payments for Armstrong's All-Stars)

- Advances against future royalties for the featured guest artists: Louis Armstrong, $5,000; Carmen McRae, $1,500
- Lambert, Hendricks & Ross (collectively): $750[3]

This brought the costs up to $10,726—roughly four times what Columbia normally spent on a top-line new release album for an artist such as Dave Brubeck or Miles Davis at that time.[4] Here was clear evidence that Iola's ironic musing on the WJZZ broadcast about the sky-high cost of the upcoming recording date was fact and not simply hyperbole. *The Real Ambassadors* album cost a great deal more to produce than any prior Brubeck record.

Additionally, due to carrying the greater fees of the many musicians, as well as $7,250 in prepaid royalties to the other featured artists, Columbia proposed that Brubeck would himself become liable for any portion of Armstrong's $5,000 advance that was not earned back through record sales (a process known in the industry as recoupment) twelve months after the album's release.[5] Furthermore, assuming that the typical artist royalty rate on album sales was 5 percent of the suggested retail list price, Brubeck agreed to allocate 3 percent to Armstrong and 2 percent for himself. Subsequently, Columbia Records Talent Budget Request sheets show that both McRae and Lambert, Hendricks & Ross (collectively as a trio) were given 1 percent royalties each on any featured numbers, theoretically leaving the Brubecks to bear all of the expenses for making the album, with less than 1 percent of anticipated royalties coming to them. Brubeck was so determined to record the soundtrack that any caution about his own reduced royalties was initially thrown to the wind. However, once this arrangement became known to Brubeck's attorney, James Bancroft, the Brubeck camp argued to have a one-time exception made, awarding him an additional 1 percent on the album. This would give Brubeck just under 2 percent—pushing the total royalties to 6 percent, as documented in a memo dated May 31, 1962.[6] The star power lined up for the recording was creating a maelstrom of memos shooting back and forth from San Francisco, where Brubeck's attorney worked, and Columbia's New York headquarters.

One other important codicil to the contracts needed to record the album remained to be settled. Under a normal record contract's terms, the monies invested by the record label to record each new album would be recouped from the artist's royalties generated by that particular album. In the case of Dave Brubeck, he was under contract to Columbia for a series of albums over the 1950s and '60s, and if any particular album did not sell well enough to pay back its production costs, the profits from any subsequent albums could be drawn on to pay off Columbia's losses. The process is known as cross-collateralization. The Brubecks realized the likelihood that the soundtrack to *The Real Ambassadors* might not sell at the same level as Dave's other instrumental albums, as they negotiated successfully to have the soundtrack album's production costs and subsequent recoupment set up as a stand-alone deal, with no cross-collateralization to any of Dave's other Columbia releases. Iola Brubeck remembered:

> From the beginning [of discussions with Columbia] Dave had insisted that the album be treated as a separate entity and not be thrown in with all of his other albums, or essentially, he would end up paying for all of it from his royalties. At that same time, Louis Armstrong was not [then] a big seller and it is doubtful that Joe Glaser would have allowed any cross-collateralization either.[7]

There was much discussion around which musicians would play on the three sessions. Brubeck and his rhythm section, consisting of bassist Eugene Wright and drummer Joe Morello, were initially identified as the backing ensemble. Brubeck's saxophonist Paul Desmond, by his own choice, passed on any involvement. As discussions continued prior to the recording dates, the Brubecks decided to also include Armstrong's All-Stars to perform on specific songs, adding both interpretive variety and a level of stylistic authenticity. For a few numbers, a combination of players would be utilized.[8]

On September 11, Brubeck rehearsed Armstrong and his band in the afternoon at the 30th Street Studio, and Lambert, Hendricks & Ross in the evening. The next day, September 12, 1961, recording began. The sessions proved revelatory. Photographs taken by Armstrong's confidante and unofficial photographer, Jack Bradley, as well as Columbia's photographer, Don Hunstein, show the joy and the intensity on the faces of the performers as they worked out nuanced musical points during the recording sessions. While Dave and Louis had an abiding mutual respect, nurtured over the three years they had been collaborating on the show's music, their two bands' members, along with Lambert, Hendricks & Ross and Carmen McRae, came to the project with a focus on making the most of the limited time they had to bring it off. McRae and Armstrong had never met, but they connected immediately over the duets they would interpret together. The detailed correspondence with each performer by the Brubecks, the use of the audio letters with Armstrong, and frequent rehearsals with McRae in California and New York helped ensure that everyone knew their parts. Dave's brother Howard had prepared charts for each musician in advance, so all the pieces were in place to maximize each session's output. Columbia staff engineer Frank Laico

Left to right, Jon Hendricks, Dave Brubeck, and Louis Armstrong going over the music during the recording of the soundtrack for *The Real Ambassadors*, Columbia Records 30th Street Studio, New York City, September 1961. Brubeck Collection, Holt-Atherton Special Collections, University of the Pacific Library, © Dave Brubeck.

Dave Lambert and Iola Brubeck reviewing musical parts during the recording sessions for the show. Brubeck Collection, Holt-Atherton Special Collections, University of the Pacific Library, © Dave Brubeck.

Although they had never met or performed together before, Louis Armstrong and Carmen McRae readily clicked in the two lead roles in the musical. Here, they are seen singing a duet during the recording of the show's soundtrack. Brubeck Collection, Holt-Atherton Special Collections, University of the Pacific Library, © Dave Brubeck.

remembered engineering one of the sessions for *The Real Ambassadors* and stated, "Even for a jaded engineer like myself, it was an exciting session. It was clear that the musicians were very well prepared for the recording."[9]

The Brubecks chose to start the recording sessions by tackling "They Say I Look Like God" right out of the gate. Always one to inject levity into nearly any situation, it came as no surprise that as Armstrong stepped to the microphone, he elicited rollicking laughter from everyone in the control booth as he ad-libbed the song's opening lines. Recalling that moment, Jon Hendricks said:

> Louis sang the first line straight, "They say I look like God," then mugged for the other musicians in his best comedic voice, "But God don't look like *me*!" and everyone collapsed laughing in the studio, it was so funny.[10]

The tension that had been building in the lead-up to the sessions was broken in a moment. Before long, word leaked out to musicians all over the city

Dave Brubeck and Louis Armstrong conferring during a break in the recording of the soundtrack for *The Real Ambassadors*. Brubeck served as both bandleader and cheerleader to the assembled musicians, working to keep morale high throughout the recording sessions that produced the soundtrack album. Photo by Jack Bradley, courtesy of Louis Armstrong House Museum, Jack Bradley Collection.

that something extraordinary was happening at the 30th Street Studio, and soon producer Teo Macero was obliged to close the sessions to all but the performers and technical crew. Brubeck remembered, "All the musicians performing were well respected, and we started getting overcrowded with friends that would have to say hello, and pretty quickly there goes your session." Iola added:

> [Visitors] became a distraction. And I will say that everybody in that recording worked hard and really concentrated, and nobody harder than Louis. He was there early, and he was the last to leave each evening. And he wanted to know what was going to be recorded the next day so he'd be ready.[11]

The majority of the album was completed in a compact seven-day window, with the musicians working two three-hour sessions per day. Considering the complexity of the material, the need to integrate two rhythm sections on some numbers, and the pending departures on tour of McRae and

This close-up shot captures the joy and intensity that Armstrong felt tackling challenging new music written expressly for him. The musical spoke directly to the role jazz musicians could play in changing society, as well as denouncing segregation and its toxic effects. Brubeck Collection, Holt-Atherton Special Collections, University of the Pacific Library, © Dave Brubeck.

Armstrong, the high level of professionalism, preparation, and positivity each musician brought to the project led to the outstanding results.

The initial sessions, held on September 12–13, 1961, also allowed for a heartwarming reunion for Armstrong and vocalist Jon Hendricks after a nearly thirty-year hiatus. Hendricks had grown up performing from a young age in Toledo, Ohio, including recording solo vocal spots with pianist Art Tatum.[12] Hendricks later recalled his earliest years onstage:

> When I was eleven years old, I would perform one song twice each night at the Waiter's and Bellman's Club in Toledo, billed as Little Jonny Hendricks. One night in 1932, Louis Armstrong was playing there and, after hearing me perform with Art Tatum's band, asked me to come down to his dressing room to meet him. The next time I saw him was at the recording session for *The Real Ambassadors*, twenty-nine years later. When I asked him if he remembered the Waiter's and Bellman's Club in Toledo and that I had performed for him, he jumped up and asked,

"That was you!?!" I answered, "Yeah, that was me!" and he grabbed me and pulled me up and we danced around together while he said, "I *know'd* you was gonna be something." And I was just crying, crying real tears when that happened.[13]

This touching reunion further energized the sessions, as the Brubecks recalled that musicians who were not recording became cheerleaders for those that were, helping to inspire one another as the project unfolded.

Dave and Iola realized the Armstrong and McRae duets, as well as those where Armstrong and either Lambert, Hendricks & Ross or Trummy Young, would sing together, needed to be recorded with all involved musicians present.[14] The music was too new and untested to use the overdubbing methods common today, in which one singer records a part and then another artist adds their part to the recording at a separate time or place. Iola Brubeck remembered that Carmen McRae was booked to go out of town on September 14, so McRae's songs were recorded on the second day, including four songs for which she and Armstrong shared vocal duties. All of McRae's songs, with the exception of "Good Reviews," were accompanied by Brubeck's trio. For "Good Reviews," a McRae-Armstrong duet, a mixed ensemble featuring Eugene Wright on bass, Danny Barcelona on drums, Joe Darensbourg on clarinet, Trummy Young on trombone and additional vocal, plus Dave Brubeck's piano, formed the backing track.

Brubeck, working on the arrangements with his brother Howard, employed a dual rhythm section on the songs "Cultural Exchange," "Remember Who You Are," "King for a Day," "Nomad," and "Since Love Had Its Way." To avoid the musicians' musically stepping on each other's toes, the Brubecks would have one bassist play pizzicato and the other use a bow, or one play walking quarter notes while the other played a dotted rhythm, or separate their parts by intervals of thirds or tenths. Likewise, All-Star drummer Danny Barcelona and Joe Morello, drummer in the Brubeck Quartet, would trade back and forth or play complementary rhythm patterns simultaneously to provide a fuller sound.

Another reunion of sorts occurred when Brubeck was able to play with one of his early idols, Armstrong's pianist Billy Kyle, who in the 1930s and '40s had made a few recordings as a leader.[15] Brubeck recalled, "The first jazz recording I ever heard was by the Billy Kyle Trio, and here I was playing with a guy I considered a mentor."[16]

Working six or more hours per day in the studio, Iola Brubeck recalled the intensity of these recording sessions, as in the case of Armstrong and McRae, there was only one shot to get the songs recorded and stay on schedule and

Louis Armstrong	Vocal, trumpet
Danny Barcelona	Drums
Dave Brubeck	Piano
Howard Brubeck	Tubular chimes, arranger
Joe Darensbourg	Clarinet
Jon Hendricks	Vocal
Billy Kyle	Piano
Dave Lambert	Vocal
Irving Manning	Bass
Carmen McRae	Vocal
Joe Morello	Drums
Annie Ross	Vocal
Eugene Wright	Bass
Trummy Young	Vocal, trombone

Table 1. Complete listing for performers featured on the 1961 recording produced by Teo Macero of *The Real Ambassadors* as listed on the 1994 reissue (Columbia/Legacy CK 57663).

budget. The Brubecks secured reel-to-reel dubs of each session, then commuted back to Connecticut to evaluate that day's work.

> Coming back [home] each night after six hours or more in the recording studio, playing what we had, and making decisions. Do we have to do certain things over? Plotting it out very, very carefully. . . . Dave's brother [Howard] was very instrumental in helping us keep on the right track, too. He was our detail man, [keeping track] of *everything* in the score, where he thought there was a miss, where he thought we should go back, and so on.[17]

Howard Brubeck, one of Dave's two older brothers, was a composer, arranger, and music educator who wrote *Pointes on Jazz*, a jazz ballet, and *Dialog for Jazz Combo and Orchestra*, which featured his younger brother's quartet. That piece was premiered and recorded by Leonard Bernstein and the New York Philharmonic. Howard arranged and orchestrated many of Brubeck's works, among them Brubeck's Mass, which was titled *To Hope*, and *The Real Ambassadors*.

As the sessions progressed, fortunately, there was much more to celebrate than to be concerned about, as it seemed that the performers, who normally would not have appeared together onstage or on records, gave their all. Session producer Teo Macero recognized that Armstrong had arrived at a new plateau with his vocal and instrumental prowess on display at the late-night session on September 12. His diligent study of the music and Iola's frequently multisyllabic lyrics had paid off, and his mastery was evident. He also imbued the words with his own inimitable vocal flourishes, for example, pronouncing "personality" as "pouh-son-all-ee-tee" on the tune "The Real Ambassador," resulting in a performance that was pure Satchmo. Armstrong's trumpet playing was also featured on the recordings, and with it, he took on the role of Joshua, adding glissandi up to high F over and over for the show finale, "Blow Satchmo," while incorporating his warm, burnished signature sound to the ballads and mid-tempo numbers such as "Remember Who You Are." With new material, Armstrong's trumpet playing soared, adding a richer and fuller dimension to his part in the recording process.[18]

During the sessions, it became clear that Iola and Dave Brubeck had effectively created an alter ego for Armstrong via the character of Pops, drawing on his varied and often tumultuous life experiences to inform his sometimes-conflicted character's voice. Iola's gift for lyrics is evident in the song "The Real Ambassador," with its compact inner rhyme patterns (evident-government; nation-segregation), while some of the song's other clever lyrics (legality-constitutionality-personality) gave Armstrong all he could handle to enunciate. Drawing on his extensive experience acting in films and onstage, he delivered the line "I represent the government, but the government don't represent the policies I'm for" with "emphatic irony," Dave Brubeck recalled.[19] Armstrong's close friend Jack Bradley, who documented the recording dates on film, kept detailed notes of the sessions' progress and at one point referenced the jam-packed lyrics for some of the songs Satchmo was performing. He recounted his exchanges with Satchmo between takes. Bradley said to Armstrong, "You'll get your tongue worn out with the lyrics," to which Louis replied, "More than that, I'll get my brains wore out."[20] The role of Pops challenged the sixty-year-old jazzman more than any part he had been asked to play in decades.

Since Armstrong had given up being under exclusive contract to any record label after his years with Decca, Macero sent a short note to Glaser dated September 15, 1961, suggesting Louis record another single for Columbia under his direction, "Pennies from Heaven," backed with "Better is Love." He included a lead sheet for the latter tune with the letter to Glaser.[21] This letter provides further evidence that all present recognized how well Satchmo was responding to new material, and Columbia wished to have another Armstrong recording prepared to capitalize on the potential commercial boost the soundtrack release might give to his career.

The following week, they returned to the studio, minus McRae, who had set off on a tour. After rehearsing on September 16, Armstrong's and Brubeck's groups recorded double sessions on September 18, 19, and 20. As they rehearsed the song "King for a Day," Armstrong remarked that the beat was similar to a particular type of dance he had heard growing up. Dave recalled that Louis then proceeded to "demonstrate to me a slow drag dance that involved the lifting of shoulders he had seen in New Orleans dance halls."[22] Armstrong drew on the entirety of his musical experience in interpreting his role for *The Real Ambassadors*, and his enthusiasm is palpable in his dynamic performances. From his introspective readings of "Summer Song" and "Lonesome" to the jive-talking, swinging bandleader Pops, who used then-current hip jazz vernacular to make his points in "King for a Day," Armstrong's versatility was on full display. Jazz critic Dan Morgenstern attended one of the sessions and reported that the ballad "Summer Song" was recorded in only one take, a compelling example of Armstrong's command of the material. Morgenstern recalled that Brubeck and Satchmo ran through the tune once and then made the historic recording. Armstrong's interpretation of the text so perfectly captured Iola's wistful intent that Dave Brubeck was moved to tears. The song afforded Armstrong the perfect vehicle for contemplating the breadth and depth of the character Pops's lifetime of experiences—experiences that, by design, mirrored his own.[23]

Iola Brubeck had specific ideas about how each song would be interpreted after having spent more than four years working and reworking the characters, lyrics, and book. Still, the artists embraced their roles in the musical's tableaux and reinterpreted their lyrics in new ways that impressed the couple. Iola remembered:

> Davey Lambert had rehearsed the vocal trio, so they knew what songs they were going to do. And for "Cultural Exchange" I had sort of a Gilbert & Sullivan approach in mind, and then they performed it [in a completely different way] and it just *hit* me . . . they had transformed it into bebop. I was thrilled with what they had done to it.[24]

Hendricks remembered putting their parts together for *The Real Ambassadors*, stating, "I'd usually sing tenor, Annie did the lead, and Dave [Lambert], the baritone. So we get the three parts . . . and then we're gone." Evidently the trio's technically facile reading of the piece, which includes a verse sung at a breakneck double-time tempo, profoundly impressed Armstrong, who had once derided bebop music as "ju-jitsu music."[25] Upon hearing Lambert, Hendricks & Ross's interpretation of the same song, he exclaimed loudly to the group, "Man, y'all sound like ya gotta mouthful of hot rice!" Jon Hendricks recalled.[26] Based on both Hendricks's as well as the Brubecks' recollections of the sessions, it seems that the artists one-upped themselves with each successive take.

Similarly, Armstrong brought his own inspiration to his reading of "They Say I Look Like God." The hymn-like, blues-based composition was sung somberly by Armstrong, backed by a Gregorian chant–like vocal trio arrangement that featured Annie Ross's pure soprano voice, while Hendricks and Lambert intoned specific excerpts from the book of Genesis in a call-and-response pattern before and after each verse. Underneath it all, sparse playing by Brubeck's trio formed a harmonic base for the performance. Over the four years of efforts to secure support for the show's production, on more than one occasion the couple had heard that at times the lyrics or script veered toward being too much of a lecture. One unnamed producer famously admonished Dave that the public went to see a Broadway-style show to be entertained, to forget their troubles, and not to be preached to. In part, as a response to such criticism, the Brubecks decided to add some intentional irony into Armstrong's opening lines for "They Say I Look Like God" to lighten up the lyrical message of the song, while intending to return to the central theme by the ending. Once again, the spirit of Gilbert and Sullivan provided inspiration for the lines that Iola Brubeck would pen. To that end, after the vocal trio opens with a series of chants, with words from Genesis, "God created man in his image and likeness; In his image and likeness he created them," Pops was to sing:

> They say I look like God.
> Could God be black? My God!
> If all are made in the image of Thee,
> Could Thou perchance a zebra be?
> Can it be? No, not He.

The Brubecks assumed the completely ludicrous reference to a zebra would break the tension and get a big laugh for Louis. It would help to "show the audience how ridiculous [segregation] was," recalled Dave Brubeck.[27] Iola confirmed that the reference to a zebra was simply a "throwaway line, intended to break the tension at the song's beginning" before the shift in tone during its later verses would allow Pops to give voice to the very real pain caused by racial intolerance.[28]

The Brubecks understood that Armstrong was an ardent proponent of racial equality, and they could look back on his iconic and subversive reading of the song "Black and Blue," which he first recorded for Okeh in 1929 and then again for Decca in 1951.[29] This is perhaps one of the greatest examples anywhere of a Black musician reinterpreting a song to create a whole new meaning, one that cried out in anguish about the injustices of racism and segregation, long before the civil rights movement took root in America. Armstrong had a long-documented history of using irony to cleverly make a point, using his guise as a good-natured stereotypical African American performer. One of the most notable of his many performances of this song was in the film *Satchmo the Great*, which documented his successful 1956 tour through African and European nations. It was his first trip to Africa. In a segment filmed in the Gold Coast, Armstrong dedicated the song to Prime Minister Nkrumah, that country's first Black leader, signifying that change was coming to Africa but still had not taken hold in the US.[30] The Brubecks were on solid ground creating the opening lyrics for this song, based on Armstrong's own performance history and his exceptional comic timing and sensibility. After the aforementioned gag that Armstrong pulled to break the ice at the start of recording "They Say I Look Like God," everyone caught their breath and returned to doing a complete take of the song.

Armstrong was accompanied by Brubeck on piano, Morello on drums, and Wright on bass, with Lambert, Hendricks & Ross in the role of the chorus. Having carefully studied the lyrics, he poured the depth of his own sentiments and emotions into the biblically inspired work. Armstrong related deeply, having grown up on the streets of New Orleans, where the price of an African American's life was negligible, as he had recounted in his memoirs. To understand the scars Armstrong bore as he gave his impassioned reading of the song, it bears explaining what type of daily incidents occurred to the great trumpeter as late as the 1960s. More than five decades after Armstrong had emerged as a hustler and musician from "the battlefield," his often-violent neighborhood, photographer Herb Snitzer was assigned to document one of his bus tours in 1960. Snitzer recalled the appalling treatment Armstrong was subjected to at that time simply due to his race:

> We set out on a bright warm Saturday afternoon, headed north with everyone in a good mood. The bus did not have a toilet. Somewhere in Connecticut we stopped in order for Louis to go to the bathroom. I was stunned when the owner of a restaurant, clearly on the basis of race, refused him use of otherwise available facilities. I will never forget the look on Louis's face. Here he was, world-famous, a favorite to millions of people, America's single most identifiable entertainer, and yet, excluded in the most humiliating fashion from a common convenience.[31]

Notably, this instance of discrimination occurred far from Alabama or Mississippi, instead in the heart of the Northeast. Armstrong had endured treatment like this his entire life, and he had certainly developed a thick skin about such indignities. In his personal collection of photographs, Armstrong had saved a candid snapshot from the 1930s when he was barnstorming the US by bus, backed by members of the Luis Russell Orchestra. It shows him with an assortment of band members leaning against the side of the bus on the shoulder of a highway, urinating, since they were not allowed to use public restrooms at gas stations. Armstrong placed a handwritten caption on the photo, titling it "Tire Inspection," using irony to deflect the indignity he and his band faced daily for decades.[32]

Tapping into the wellspring of emotion formed by enduring a lifetime of such deprivations, Armstrong delivered an elegant, understated reading of the lyrics, contrasting effectively with the vocal trio's chant, which quoted Genesis directly, "God created man in his image and likeness," juxtaposing for the audience the commands to love one another, similar to those found in the Bible's John 3:16, with Armstrong's pained expression of the rejection that resulted from centuries of institutionalized American racism. In one of the great but largely unheralded performances of his entire career, Armstrong inexorably builds intensity from the understated delivery of the first verse, then increases his emotions with each successive verse. By the end he reaches an emotional peak, delivering the payoff in the song's fifth and final verse:

> They say I look like God
> Could God be black? My God!
> If all are made in the image of Thee,
> Could Thou perchance a zebra be?
> Can it be? No, not He.
>
> He's watching all the earth,
> He's watched us from our birth,
> And if He cared if you're black or white,
> He'd mixed one color, one just right.
> Black or white. One just right.
>
> Oh Lord, please hear my plea!
> Oh give me eyes to see,
> That our creation was meant to be,
> An act of God to set Man free.
> Set Man free. Set Man free.

You raised us from the dust.
You breathed in life with trust.
And gave to Man the choice to be,
Alone on earth or one with Thee.
One with Thee. One with Thee.

When will that great day come?
When everyone is one?
And there will be no more misery,
When God tells man he's really free.
Really free . . .
Really free . . .
Really free.

With the vocal trio proclaiming "Hallelujah, Hallelujah, Hallelujah" in a hauntingly sung minor chord, Armstrong draws out the word *free* each time, using his characteristic gravelly vibrato to convey an almost ghostly sense of unfulfilled longing and poignancy. The blues-tinged inflections he adds to the words "no more misery" are wrenching. If there was one song that Armstrong could pour his own hopes and dreams into for a world that would someday not be divided by race, it was "They Say I Look Like God," as stirring an indictment of segregation as it was a call to embrace peace and forgiveness as a way forward. By her clever use of contrasting texts within the same song, Iola placed the tenets of Christianity in stark contrast to the worldview prescribed by America's leaders, who upheld Jim Crow rule at the time the musical was created.

As she recalled both Armstrong's performance on the recording and a live performance of it one year later at Monterey, Iola Brubeck reflected on Satchmo's inestimable contributions, for instance his altered reading of the intended throwaway lines in the song's first verse. Instead of taking the Gilbert and Sullivan–inspired route she and Dave had envisioned:

Louis put his own stamp on it. But the intent was the same. So many of the things that we wrote for the show, once they were in the hands of the artists, if they're true artists, they make it their own. And that's exactly what Louis did with everything he was given. It ended up coming out in a seemingly spontaneous performance, like these weren't the words that had been given to him, just handed to him, with instructions to "sing it this way."[33]

"They Say I Look Like God" is Armstrong at his best, artfully interpreting text in a way that illuminated hundreds of years of intolerance and bigotry. His gift for creating distinctive readings of popular songs defined him as one of the most—perhaps the most—original American vocal stylists. His talent has also intrigued scholars and writers, who have written many thoughtful essays on this rich topic.[34]

In the studio, it was as if Armstrong had cast a spell. According to Jon Hendricks, "We were all standing there like we were in church. Carmen, Dave, myself . . . after he finished, we were rapt."[35] Iola Brubeck would describe that moment as one of the "unforgettable memories" of the sessions, along with "the sweet irony of Annie Ross's first 'Hallelujah'" juxtaposed with Armstrong's plea.[36] Dave Brubeck summed up Armstrong's reading as a once-in-a-lifetime moment: "Louis sang with such great emotion that his voice broke a little on the words 'really free' and there were tears in his eyes, and in ours."[37] While there are many highlights throughout the recordings, "They Say I Look Like God" is the emotional apex of the work. It precedes Rhonda and Pops reconciling, which is followed by a transition to the closing scene, in which Pops picks up his trumpet and blows down the walls of intolerance in the show's bravura, show-stopping, six-minute finale, "Blow Satchmo." The lyrics to this last number reinforce that it's going to be up to Pops and other musicians like him to take the initiative to use their talents to "lead us to the Promised Land" [of equality and acceptance]. Fittingly, the Brubecks decided to add a postscript to the album as well as the live setting for the musical, with a sotto voce Armstrong opining:

> Now I leave you / Now I go . . .
> Now you know as much as old . . . Satch . . . mo.

The audience is thus invited to take action. According to the Brubecks, love, not détente, is what was needed to heal the nation and the world. Jack Bradley, Armstrong's close confidante and unofficial photographer, summed up the musical chemistry between Louis and Dave that he witnessed in the studio recording of *The Real Ambassadors*. He said it was really "a love fest between them. Dave would run up and hug and kiss Louis after every take. It was a wonderful session."[38]

The recording was a pivotal moment in the careers of the Brubecks as well as Armstrong. Reflecting back on the recording *The Real Ambassadors*, Iola Brubeck remarked:

The personalized dedication to Iola Brubeck that Armstrong inscribed on his chart for the ballad "Summer Song." It reads: "To Mrs. Brubeck . . . Am very Happy . . . Satchmo . . . Louis Armstrong." The Brubecks had it reproduced and displayed prominently in their Wilton, Connecticut, home throughout their lifetimes. Brubeck Collection, Holt-Atherton Special Collections, University of the Pacific Library, © Dave Brubeck.

> I think one of the important things about *The Real Ambassadors* is that Louis had been in many ways sort of dismissed at this point in his career as an entertainer, not to be taken too seriously. He was [acknowledged] as great when he first began. But there is a very serious and sensitive side to Louis that the rest of the world just didn't see. I think this is why he was attracted to doing the show, because he felt he could make a statement that was important.[39]

Dave Brubeck agreed and added important perspective about why he believed Armstrong so profoundly connected to the musical:

> His appearances were frequently dismissed as "routine." He was often decried as "Uncle Tom" by more militant blacks. And yet, he continued to perform for an adoring public, following the old rules that demanded entertainment as well as music, subtly conquering the world with his trumpet, his songs, and his great humanity. People seemed to forget that he was as subject to the wounds of racial slurs and segregation as any other person of color. One of the happiest moments of his life, when he was crowned King of the Zulus at Mardi Gras [1949] in New Orleans, was marred by the cancellation of his concert in a city

auditorium because he had a white man in his band and integrated groups were against city law.[40]

In fact, in his *Louis Armstrong Encyclopedia*, Michael Meckna reported that as late as 1960, Armstrong ended up canceling a Southern tour with his integrated band due to restrictions on performing in many of the cities that he had been booked to play, just as Brubeck's Southern college tour had been severely curtailed that same year.[41]

After the last remaining pieces were recorded in December 1961 with Carmen McRae, the sequencing of the songs for the album proceeded under the direction of producer Teo Macero. Simultaneously, *New York Times* writer Gilbert Millstein, who had collaborated with the Brubecks on the "Beat Heard Round the World" essay, was hired to assist in drafting the liner notes. In them, Millstein described the genesis for the musical, then Iola added her reflections on the resulting recording, which seemed to exceed both her and her husband's expectations in every way. She also elegantly amplified the thoughts she had first espoused in the WJZZ radio interview more fully, ascribing to Armstrong the role of a magician:

> There was no question in our minds that the central figure of our play *had* to be Louis Armstrong. Louis embodies in magnificent proportions all the elements of jazz we wanted others to understand. His horn is his crown and scepter. The music that pours from it contains magic the musician does not fully comprehend.[42]

Armstrong's enthusiasm clearly matched the Brubecks' own for the rich material they had written for the character of Pops, a role that he fully inhabited throughout this period. At his final session he inscribed Iola's copy of the lead sheet for the wistful ballad "Summer Song" with the simple declaration, "To Mrs. Brubeck, Am very happy. 'Satchmo' Louis Armstrong."[43]

This inscription shows just how much Armstrong, then starting his seventh decade, valued the pieces written specifically by the Brubecks for him. Listening back to that recording of Armstrong performing "Summer Song," in 2014, jazz critic Will Friedwald described it as the most durable number on the album and one that seemed directly biographical.

> Doing some of the most tender singing in his amazing career, the 60-year-old Satchmo comes off like an old warrior at the end of a long campaign, a battered Don Quixote tilting at the windmills of his youth, so long ago, but still vivid in his mind.[44]

Dave Brubeck remembered, "Over the years, whenever or wherever the participants should meet, we recalled that magical time in September 1961 with Louis 'Satchmo' Armstrong."[45] The Brubecks had Satchmo's inscription to Iola framed and displayed prominently throughout their lives in their Wilton, Connecticut, home.

CHAPTER 12

MESSENGERS OF CHANGE

The experience of recording *The Real Ambassadors'* soundtrack transformed Armstrong into an avid cheerleader for the project. Someone in the Armstrong camp spoke with the editors of the Canadian jazz magazine *Coda*, which reported in November 1961:

> Louis and the All Stars . . . recorded tunes from an "opera" penned by Dave Brubeck with lyrics by his wife, Iola. The material was varied from love ballads to spirituals. Everyone seemed very pleased with the outcome, needless to say, Pops was the star throughout.[1]

This appears to be the first reference in the press to *The Real Ambassadors* as a "jazz opera," something Armstrong would repeat in the coming months as interest in the project started to percolate in the jazz community. Iola Brubeck remembered that both Carmen McRae and Armstrong enthusiastically endorsed the idea of taking the musical to the theatrical stage. "Carmen very much hoped to do it on Broadway, as did Louis. He also hoped that it would run in London, too."[2]

It took nearly nine months from the end of the sessions for Columbia Records to release the record, and the soundtrack album went on sale to the public on September 1, 1962. That was just three weeks before the show's premiere at Monterey. In the meantime, the recording did not languish unattended. Producer Teo Macero corresponded regularly with the Brubecks on the sequencing for the album as well as how the artists would be billed and shown on the cover. A January 22, 1962, typewritten memo from the Brubecks laid out their preferred song order for the record, but a sequencing order was placed via an Editing Instruction Sheet on May 14, 1962, that differed quite a bit from the couple's earlier memo. Dave and Iola had planned to retain the original order of songs as they would appear in the musical, while Macero wisely chose to reorder the songs slightly, taking into consideration that the listener would not really know the underlying plot of the work.

Short bits, such as "Blow Satchmo" and "What Are You Waiting For," were edited directly into what was now renamed "Finale." "Lonesome" and "Nomad" were cut from the LP. Some of the bridging dialogue and music, totaling roughly four minutes of material, was never recorded and would only be presented in the concert performance at Monterey. After confirming song orders and timing with the Brubecks, an initial Mastering Instruction Sheet from Teo Macero to Columbia's production facility is dated July 16, 1962, with a corrected version being issued on August 27, 1962. It lists timings, song order, and other pertinent information.[3] A stereo and mono version of the album had to be prepared, which was standard procedure for that era. The gatefold album package included candid photos from the recording sessions, while the back cover was dominated by a photo of Armstrong's triumphant ride in a chair on the shoulders of African tribesmen in the Congo. This photo was similar to the one that had accompanied Millstein's lengthy appreciation of Satchmo's 1960 goodwill tour of Africa, "Africa Harks to Satch's Horn," published by the *New York Times*. The article's subtitle read, "Louis Armstrong and trumpet, speaking a language clearly understood, have done better there recently than a good many statesmen." This was more evidence of steady press recognition that the jazz ambassadors, Armstrong in particular, were winning the propaganda war with the Soviets in nations where the two superpowers were vying for political dominance.[4] The *Times* reported that Armstrong's African reception was so great that Radio Moscow felt compelled to denounce him as a "capitalist distraction."

There can be little doubt that Millstein's 1960 article detailing Armstrong's tour to Africa greatly influenced Iola Brubeck in the constantly evolving musical and the details regarding the character of Pops. The photos of Armstrong being carried into the stadium in Leopoldville, Congo, provided a visual embodiment of the theme represented in the song "King for a Day," in which the character of Pops fantasizes about what a world run on the principles of jazz might be like. Armstrong also is quoted in the *New York Times* essay about his reaction to a well-educated woman's dismissal of his intelligence in comparison to her own valedictory accolades from a famous university. He commented to Millstein, "One of my thoughts would bust her goddam brains from my experience." Within one of the short narrative interludes that tied the concert version of the musical together, Pops interjects a similar sentiment that his character had struggled to keep in check, shouting out, "Lady, if you could read my mind, your head would bust wide open."[5] The Brubecks wanted the world to know that while Armstrong's public knew him best as the consummate showman, beneath that mantle was an intellectual and social critic. Armstrong identified completely with the arguments put

The October 1960 arrival of Louis Armstrong and His All-Stars to perform in Leopoldville, Congo, was celebrated by more than one hundred thousand fans, who attended his concert in the largest soccer stadium in the nation. Here he can be seen being carried triumphantly into the venue on the shoulders of native dancers. Photo courtesy of the Louis Armstrong House Collection.

forth in the show. He detested segregation, Jim Crow laws, and the very real suffering that resulted from them.

Buoyed by the experience of hearing the songs from the musical come to life, in an extensive interview with a local Connecticut newspaper dated May 31, 1962, Brubeck enthusiastically discussed not only the forthcoming album, but why he felt obliged to bring the issues of equality and justice to the public through his music. In many ways, this article demonstrated that his fight for integration represented a clear through line in his own life and career: from his first realization that people of color were systemically abused, when his father showed him evidence of racial violence as a young boy, through his battle to hold together his mixed-race army jazz band when his superior officers wanted to break it up, to the problems that he still faced performing and touring with his world-renowned quartet, Brubeck was sick and tired of racism.

The interview, whimsically titled "He Left the Steers for Stravinsky," alluded to his having grown up on a working forty-thousand-acre cattle ranch. According to an account in the interview, Brubeck originally had hoped to become a veterinarian and started college as a zoology major, then switched to the study of classical music. The interview primarily introduced the album of songs from the unproduced musical and reported that it had taken the couple five years to bring the music to the public. It also claimed that it was undertaken, in part, to get Dave "off the road," an idea that the Brubecks had floated as early as the previously cited 1959 correspondence with Joe Glaser. If the show were produced on or off Broadway, Brubeck could return to the family's Connecticut home each night after the performance. It is also the first public mention of the title that Columbia had finally settled on, as well as the cast. Journalist Alison Murray reported:

> The album will be released as *The Real Ambassadors*, with Louis Armstrong, Carmen McCrea [*sic*], and the Lambert, Hendricks & Ross singing group, as the artists. The Armstrong band and the Brubeck band are both in the album. The music is kept in sequence and a hint of the story remains.[6]

It appears that Brubeck must have previewed some of the music from the sessions to Murray, as she describes the show's lyrics and Armstrong's powerful vocals, commenting on their impact:

> The recurrent theme is "he that loveth God, loveth his brother also." In one section the chorus sings the readings of Genesis almost exactly like Gregorian chant. Louis Armstrong, in counterpoint, gives the Negro reaction to "God tells man he is really free" in his best gravelly blues voice. The effect is dynamic.[7]

Brubeck explained that he had "to face a lot more [segregation] than others" because he had a mixed-race group. Because he insisted on having the same eating and sleeping arrangements for each member of his band, he said that his annual losses in performance fees were close to $60,000 ($540,000 in 2021 currency). He also said that via trial and error, he had learned "which states not to play for equal treatment—and they are not only in the South—but Northern as well."[8] Brubeck cited twenty colleges at which his quartet had broken the so-called color line, meaning they had been the first mixed-race group allowed to perform.

Brubeck then went on to issue a challenge to both the nation's leaders and the public. He went so far as to assign part of the accountability for the lack of progress in changing the status quo to the nation's political and moral leaders. Under the subheading "Combats Segregation," Murray reported:

[Brubeck] feels very strongly about the subject. He states that since Congressmen and religious leaders have failed in complete integration, the only ones who have made it work are baseball players, musicians and artists—and we had better get going if we are going to really accomplish anything.[9]

The "we" Brubeck referred to can be taken as the high-profile sports and entertainment communities, or the broader American public, which matched the couple's goal for who would be influenced by the messages in the show. This article in a tiny local newspaper was dated midway between the last of *The Real Ambassadors* recording sessions in December 1961 and the show's premiere in September 1962. It provides an accurate look at just how crucial speaking out on segregation had become to the Brubecks as they joined the rest of the nation to watch the nightly news and witness the battles being waged for equality by people of color.

Brubeck wasn't the only cast member to discuss staging the show with the press. A few weeks earlier, Louis Armstrong gave an extensive interview to jazz critic Leonard Feather, in which he expressed his delight at being cast as Pops in *The Real Ambassadors*. He said it was his firm hope that the cast would soon be bringing the show to a wider audience than could be reached with an album. In a lengthy interview dated April 28, 1962, for *Melody Maker*, Satchmo explained to Feather that he was ready to break away to some extent from the same repertoire he had been mining for the past three decades. In the article, titled "There's a Lot in Me the Public Hasn't Heard," he said:

> "There's a lot of stuff in me the public ain't never heard yet. Those things I made back in the 1930s, I'm just living off them right now. But there's so many different types of things I can do."
>
> He began to tell me [Feather] in great excitement about an album he had just made for Columbia with Dave Brubeck.
>
> "It was the musical show Dave wrote for me—the one that was supposed to be produced in London a couple of years ago, but the deal never worked out. Maybe, when the record comes out, we can at least do it as a TV show."
>
> "It's all about the world situations and ambassadors of goodwill. I do numbers with Brubeck; with Carmen McRae; and there was one song that really thrilled me that I did with Lambert, Hendricks & Ross." And Louis began to sing, "They say I look like God . . . could God be black? My God!"[10]

Later in the interview, Armstrong went on the offensive with regard to Jim Crow and its hold on the American political and social system. When Feather asked Armstrong about his feelings on prejudice, Satchmo told a story that showed his resolve:

> When I'm hurt, I'll fight back! When I was very young, I said to a boy who was bothering me, "Hit me, 'cause my mother told me to never start a fight." So he started the fight, and my eye was damn near out, but I took care of him.[11]

In this way, Armstrong alludes to the fact that he was committed to fight for civil rights until the day it was won. Throughout the interview, Armstrong's clear grasp of his dual role as both an articulate spokesperson for equal rights and an acclaimed international jazz artist was on display. Addressing the Louisiana laws that for decades had prevented performance with his mixed-race band, he implies that racial discrimination at home was a bigger problem than Cold War struggles with the Soviet Union:

> "I don't ever want to go back there! Not unless they want to take my white bass player, along with all the other cats. I've turned down all kinds of offers." [Feather added,] A Louisiana state law, declared unconstitutional by the U.S. Supreme Court, but still enforced by the Southern racists, forbids the appearance of inter-racial groups.
>
> "Sad, isn't it? I've been all over the world with my band, but we can't play in my hometown. People talk about sending me to Russia. Sure, I'd like to go someday. But this is more important. After all, who knows if Khrushchev's gonna change? But someday New Orleans has gotta change."[12]

Armstrong had always recognized it as his duty and responsibility to speak out, but taking on the role of Pops had galvanized his own desire to speak out more forcefully. With the Brubecks as his partners in this mission and a forthcoming Columbia release of the soundtrack from the musical, the time seemed right to shine a light on the issues at hand.

In addition to his own performance as Pops on record and at Monterey, this lengthy interview with *Melody Maker* demonstrates unequivocally that Armstrong's position on race and his role in *The Real Ambassadors* were in harmony. Without a doubt, he recognized the social importance of the musical and hoped that in addition to the album's pending release, the musical itself would soon be broadcast on television or, better yet, brought to the stage. Even though Joe Glaser had blocked or delayed nearly every opportunity to bring the show to an audience, the veteran trumpeter joined Iola and Dave Brubeck in setting his sights on performing *The Real Ambassadors* for a live crowd. Notably, the Brubecks received a clipping of this interview, and they kept it on file near their other materials pertaining to the musical.

In the late spring of 1962, the high that the musicians had experienced during the recordings clearly had a residual effect. Both Armstrong and Brubeck used the media to showcase their belief in the musical and its message. In the two lengthy interviews cited above, they each spoke out, addressing the role of artists as change agents and the imperative to speak out against segregation.

Still, during the nine months between the completion of the album and its premiere, the Brubecks frequently voiced their disappointment that they had not been able to stage the musical as it had been intended. In that same interview with the *Newington Crier*, the writer's lede had been "The Dave Brubecks' are bringing out the original cast album of a Broadway show that never saw an opening night."[13] Near the beginning of her September 1962 WJZZ interview, Iola declared that she and her husband had so far "failed to bring it to Broadway."[14] Despite the pair's five-year campaign, with Broadway apparently out of reach, they sought a more practical way to bring the musical and its message to the public. Dave had an idea. Writing to Joe Glaser on February 6, 1962, in the aftermath of a phone meeting between Glaser and Brubeck, he suggested a way to sweeten any deal for a possible package tour of the show:

> We are in the fortunate position of having music already rehearsed with my group and Louis'. If they have a bigger budget, they should add Carmen McRae to this package. In other words, the [ABC] office is capable of sending out a really rehearsed show, which we can call THE REAL AMBASSADORS, after the album. . . . To produce all the music in the album at a festival or concert, you would only have to go out of the office to secure the services of Lambert-Hendricks & Ross, and then you would have a product never equaled in the jazz festivals I have played. [capitalization in original][15]

Brubeck concluded his letter by mentioning an upcoming four-day Washington, DC, event, the First International Jazz Festival (May 31–June 3, 1962), and pitching Glaser the idea that it represented a perfect opportunity to present the musical. This festival was being sponsored by the President's Music Committee of the People-to-People program and was envisioned

Dave Brubeck and Paul Desmond onstage at the June 1962 Washington, DC, International Jazz Festival. At one point, the Brubecks had hoped to debut *The Real Ambassadors* for this audience of politicians and well-connected policy makers, but Armstrong was in the midst of an extended tour and unavailable. Brubeck Collection, Holt-Atherton Special Collections, University of the Pacific Library, © Dave Brubeck.

by the State Department as a showcase for the outstanding results that had been achieved in advancing American interests through the efforts of the jazz ambassadors and other cultural exchange initiatives. In a letter inviting Brubeck and his group to perform, festival coordinator Jule Foster explained:

> This Festival was created to provide national recognition of jazz as an American art form and has been planned as a program to benefit the work of the President's Music Committee which, during the past three years, has established and now maintains cultural contacts with 110 countries of the world. . . . Your performance is requested for Saturday morning June 2, 11 A.M., at Constitution Hall, and Sunday afternoon, June 3, 2:30 P.M., at the D.C. Armory.[16]

With the musical's central characters being part of just such an Uncle Sam–sponsored group, the Brubecks saw this as the perfect opportunity to present the show. More importantly, the festival's audience would be a who's who of Washington movers and shakers and influential media. Brubeck was already invited to appear on the bill, but Armstrong was scheduled to be on tour in Europe at the time of the festival. Brubeck argued that Armstrong could benefit from such high-level exposure. Secretary of state Dean Rusk was the chairman of the festival's sponsoring committee; former president Eisenhower was the national chairman for the People-to-People program; and President John F. Kennedy was the honorary chairman for the jazz festival. However, artists were being asked to perform for union scale, plus transportation—many times less than the usual fee that top performers could command.[17] Once again, the potential financial losses of canceling or postponing Armstrong's European tour in favor of making him available to the Brubecks for only a fraction of his normal fees most likely led Glaser to dismiss the opportunity, probably in a phone call to the Brubecks, since no written reply exists. Although the Brubecks never even got to propose the show to the festival's organizers, the Dave Brubeck Quartet did appear at the festival on June 2 and 3, but yet another prime opportunity was lost to showcase the musical and its message in the nation's capital.

The opportunity to bring the musical to a live audience was about to become a reality, however, in large part due to the maverick cofounder of the Monterey Jazz Festival, Jimmy Lyons. Lyons had been a champion of Brubeck and his music since 1949, and Brubeck had leaked some of the tracks from the forthcoming album to Lyons and his Monterey Jazz Festival partner, journalist Ralph J. Gleason. After hearing the tunes and being briefed on the musical's themes, Lyons cooked up an unconventional scheme to sidestep the continual roadblocks that had been constructed by the powerful Glaser. With Lyons's help, the Brubecks would soon bring *The Real Ambassadors* to the stage with their ideal cast—a surprising and triumphant culmination of their five years of determined effort.

CHAPTER 13

THE ROAD TO MONTEREY

Among the numerous regional and national jazz festivals that were evolving in the 1950s and '60s, the Monterey Jazz Festival, which would celebrate
its fifth anniversary in September 1962, had the strongest reputation for
commissioning new music and for bringing original, adventurous programming to its audience.[1] The festival had been cofounded by the influential
San Francisco Chronicle music critic Ralph J. Gleason, whose jazz column
was nationally syndicated in sixty publications. His cofounder was Jimmy
Lyons, the former San Francisco disc jockey who had been instrumental in
launching Dave Brubeck's career. Gleason was a lifelong student, scholar,
and critic of jazz. In 1938, upon his graduation from Columbia University,
he cofounded one of the nation's first jazz magazines, *Jazz Information*. He
contributed to *DownBeat* from 1948 to 1961, and as music critic for the *San
Francisco Chronicle* from 1950 to 1975, he was the first to write about jazz
and popular music with the same attention and depth that classical music
and opera enjoyed. He also cofounded *Rolling Stone* with one of his protégés,
Jann Wenner, in 1967.[2]

The original idea to start the festival was reportedly Gleason's, who wanted
to "take the [jazz] music out of the dark, smoky, smelly nightclubs and into
the fresh air and sunshine," as reported by his successor at the *Chronicle*, Joel
Selvin. The original publicist for the festival, Grover Sales, concurred: "Ralph
was essential to the festival . . . he suggested the whole concept [to Jimmy.]"[3]
Through their combined connections, Lyons and Gleason curated a veritable
who's who of jazz for the debut festival in 1958: Dizzy Gillespie, Billie Holiday,
Dave Brubeck, Sonny Rollins, the Modern Jazz Quartet, and of course, Louis
Armstrong. It might appear as if Gleason's coverage of the performances
at Monterey would be subject to bias, since panning a performance might
impact his own financial interests. But scanning a few of Gleason's reviews
of different 1960s Monterey Jazz Festival performances shows a balanced
voice, praising many performers, but also taking to task those artists whose
performances didn't meet his expectations.

Ralph Gleason was a fiercely independent voice who famously expressed himself with candor throughout his decades of music criticism. In its obituary upon his untimely death at the age of fifty-eight in 1975, the *New York Times* aptly described him as "an acerbic but highly perceptive critic of both jazz and pop music." His maverick nature was encapsulated by one of his own musings:

> "I write about jazz because I want to share my enjoyment with other people," he once said. "And I dig me as a critic, vain and arrogant as that may sound. I don't care if I make it with the musicians. I wouldn't care if Miles [Davis] and I didn't get along—it happens that we do but that could change. The important thing is I stay straight with myself."[4]

He was unconcerned whether an artist bridled under the harsh glare of his criticism. He felt duty bound to provide his insights, often imbued with an edge of irony, to his readers around the world. And when he rated an album or concert as deserving, he would readily lavish praise on the artist's achievements.

Gleason's relationship with the Brubecks had suffered numerous ups and downs. Both were active in the late 1940s San Francisco jazz scene. When Gleason became the first full-time jazz critic for a major US daily newspaper in 1950, Brubeck was paying his dues in the jazz clubs just up the street from the *San Francisco Chronicle*'s offices. Gleason was one of a handful of critics who reported the backlash from some jazz musicians and fans after Brubeck famously appeared on the cover of *Time* magazine in 1954. Many felt an African American jazz artist, such as Ellington or Gillespie, would have been more appropriate. Gleason wrote in *DownBeat* that the massive publicity that resulted from the laudatory feature in *Time* "crystalized the resentment of thousands of jazz musicians and fans." He went on to pan the pianist by stating that he felt Brubeck had made very little contribution [to jazz] for such a well-publicized artist.[5] Eventually, Iola Brubeck defended her husband and wrote a letter to *DownBeat*'s editor decrying Gleason's attacks on her husband, taking the critic to task for attacking the man, rather than criticizing his music.[6] This further incident exacerbated the already frosty relationship between the Brubeck camp and Gleason.

However, by 1959, Gleason's coverage of Brubeck made an abrupt about-face, assuming a new, more laudatory tone, as one of America's most prominent jazz critics began to praise Dave Brubeck, not so much for his music, but for his stance on civil rights, as the Dave Brubeck Quartet lost multiple bookings in the South due to having a Black bass player, Eugene Wright.

The Dave Brubeck Quartet (*left to right*, Brubeck, Paul Desmond, Joe Morello, and Joe Benjamin) poses in 1958 at the Monterey County Fairgrounds, which would be home to the Monterey Jazz Festival beginning with its inception later that year. The close relationship developed over the years between Dave Brubeck and Monterey Jazz Festival cofounder Jimmy Lyons proved especially helpful in gaining the confidence of the town leadership, who were concerned jazz musicians and fans might bring an unsavory element to their sleepy California coastal community. Brubeck and his quartet drove down to Monterey, met the leaders, played for them, and impressed them enough to allow the festival's debut that year. Photo courtesy of the *Monterey Herald* and Monterey Jazz Festival.

Jim Crow's influence at that time limited the option of having mixed-race groups perform at colleges throughout the region. After losing one booking at the University of Georgia in February 1959, later that year, twenty-two of twenty-five concert dates had to be canceled for a scheduled 1960 winter Southern college tour by the quartet. Gleason detailed the sad state of affairs in a January 12, 1960, *San Francisco Chronicle* piece titled "Racial Issue 'Kills' Brubeck Jazz Tour of the South," clearly sympathizing with Brubeck and his band on the injustice such a situation represented. With the same information, Gleason then used his monthly *DownBeat* column to provide Brubeck with a soapbox to rail against racism. Titled "An Appeal from Dave Brubeck," the piece further cemented Brubeck's public image as a musician who would do everything in his power to defeat racism. Brubeck's appeal went to the heart of the matter: "All we want is that the authorities accept us as we are, and allow us—and other integrated jazz groups—to play our music without intimidation or pressure." Gleason followed this up the following month in his regular *DownBeat* column, lauding Brubeck's public stance of "refusing to alter his group to conform to the racial prejudices of the South."[7]

Based on these developments, one can see how the subject matter being addressed in *The Real Ambassadors* would appeal greatly to Gleason's strong support for racial equality, a position he steadfastly advocated throughout his career.[8] The concept of a jazz musical starring Louis Armstrong as a straight-talking bandleader, addressing the ironies of relying on Black artists to promote Uncle Sam's Cold War agenda, neatly aligned with Gleason's own political views. The Brubecks were surprised and pleased to find that Gleason had appointed himself as a champion for the show and the ideas upon which it was built.

During the Monterey Jazz Festival's first five years, Lyons had built a solid working relationship with Monterey's civic leaders, who provided access to the county fairgrounds where the weekend-long event has been held since its inception in 1958.[9] The Monterey business community had enjoyed five years of revenue as thousands of jazz fans annually descended on the small coastal city, which had a population of twenty-two thousand residents.[10] Brubeck had been part of the festival from its inception. In 1957, prior to its inauguration, Lyons invited Brubeck to perform at a meeting of the county commissioners to allay any concerns about the music. Brubeck recalled explaining to the members of his quartet that, even though they weren't being paid to play a few songs to demonstrate the type of music that the festival would present, by doing so, they would be helping to establish a festival that would mean more work for all jazz musicians.[11] Iola Brubeck shared a more detailed recollection of how important that "audition" was for Lyons to gain the trust of the Monterey business leaders. This was in part because the huge crowds that were attending the Newport Jazz Festival had negatively impacted some local residents. Iola said:

> The Quartet did perform for the Monterey officials. I believe it was the town council, at the fairgrounds in one of the Produce Display sheds, to demonstrate to them the type of music that would be performed. It was early in the afternoon. Dave and Paul answered some questions. Dave recalls that it was a friendly atmosphere and that the questions were mostly about the Newport Jazz Festival and how the festival had impacted the town of Newport.[12]

The audition won over the council members, and soon after, the town was in full support of inaugurating an annual jazz festival, as sixty-seven community leaders each invested $100 to create the seed money necessary to host the first Monterey Jazz Festival. Lyons wisely established Brubeck's group as a regular Monterey headliner, an acknowledgment of the group's strong West Coast following.[13] Doing so helped guarantee strong ticket sales for the new venture. The strong bonds between the Brubecks and Jimmy Lyons were about to pay great dividends.

In a letter dated April 11, 1962, from Associated Booking's Oscar Cohen to Iola Brubeck, Cohen refers to a lengthy talk with Carmen McRae, who had spoken with either Jimmy Lyons or Ralph J. Gleason about staging the musical at Monterey. This letter confirms McRae's willingness to participate in a staged performance and is the earliest surviving document to reveal the efforts underway to cast a concert version of the musical at the festival.[14]

Lyons contacted Brubeck to discuss the possibility of premiering the show at Monterey. The pianist recalled:

Jimmy Lyons became aware of the recording of *The Real Ambassadors*. He called me at my home and asked if he could present the premiere at the 1962 Monterey Jazz Festival. I was both excited and fearful of the proposal. I told him that I thought it would be almost impossible to get all the participants to Monterey at the same time, as we were traveling all over the world constantly. Furthermore, it was not something that could be put on stage without some rehearsal. Jimmy's desire to be the first to present it, however, motivated him to call the different agents that represented the various artists. Much to my surprise, he called me a week or so later and informed me that he had hired Carmen McRae, Louis Armstrong and his All-Stars, Lambert, Hendricks, and Bavan (Yolande Bavan had replaced Annie Ross), and the Dave Brubeck Quartet for separate appearances at the Festival. As a finale to the festival, they were engaged for a performance of *The Real Ambassadors* on September 23, almost one year after the dates of the recording session in New York.[15]

Lyons's simple, effective strategy secured each of the musicians featured on the recording as individual performers for that year's festival. Each artist was booked to perform a set of his or her own and then perform in Sunday night's staging of the musical. The artists were secured, according to the dates of the booking contracts held on file at the Monterey Jazz Festival, as follows: Armstrong (May 4), Brubeck (May 7), McRae (May 25), and Lambert, Hendricks & Bavan (August 15).[16]

Ross's contributions to the 1961 soundtrack recording were substantial, from her stratospheric high notes on the "Finale" to her solemn incantation on the sequence of "Alleluias" that ends Armstrong's tour de force, "They Say I Look Like God." Still, if one of the messages of *The Real Ambassadors* was that jazz could create bonds across borders and cultures, bringing disparate peoples together, the addition of Yolande Bavan to the cast at Monterey seems to have been a stroke of perfect casting. She was another jazz ambassador whose path led her more than halfway around the world to a role in the musical.

Born in Colombo, Ceylon (now Sri Lanka), Bavan was first exposed to jazz by her father, who would listen nightly to *Voice of America* jazz broadcasts by Willis Conover. She won a talent contest as a vocalist at the age of fourteen and was soon featured on a regular radio broadcast, *Swing Time*. Her successes led to a move to Australia and further success as the featured singer with pianist and bandleader Graeme Bell. By the time she was eighteen, her musical interests turned to bebop, and she realized she would have to leave for London if she wanted to advance her career.

From 1957 to early 1962, Bavan performed regularly in London and Paris, while also winning more stage and television roles. A full-time acting career was blossoming and had replaced jazz singing, but Bavan still socialized within jazz circles. Brubeck met Bavan on November 18, 1961, at an afterparty of a London show during their November–December European tour. They struck up a conversation about her home country, which Brubeck had toured in 1958.[17] Soon after, Bavan was invited to attend a concert by the Dave Brubeck Quartet as a guest, and the next day, as she was riding in a motor coach with Brubeck to the concert, he pulled out a score he was working on for *The Real Ambassadors*. Bavan remembered that Brubeck said to her, "Come up to my hotel room before we leave for the concert and you can [sight-read] it through." She did, and recalled asking, "What is this?" but he did not reply. "All he asked me to do was sight-read the music, and that was it. No mention of the jazz musical at all." Bavan recalls thinking, "I thought I did really badly."[18]

At an after-party following another concert by the Count Basie Orchestra and Lambert, Hendricks & Ross in London in early 1962, Bavan was helping the hostess serve drinks and clear ashtrays when a song featuring Dizzy Gillespie's soaring trumpet played. Without thinking, she matched Dizzy's high notes. Bavan recalled: "A man whipped around and said, 'Who did that?'

and I answered, 'I did.'" The man was Dave Lambert, and he quizzed the young actress: "Are you a singer?" to which she replied, "No, I'm an actress." He replied, "Can you really hit those high notes?" She said, "Yes." Lambert pressed her, saying, "Are you *sure* you're not a singer?" to which she replied, "I sing a little, but mostly act."[19]

Bavan remembered the exchange but thought little of it at the time. Nonetheless, the impression she made on Dave Lambert was profound, as a few weeks later, he invited her to join the jazz group, and she was notified that airplane tickets and the necessary artist visa were waiting in her name at the US Embassy in London. During the next three years, Lambert, Hendricks & Bavan would perform nonstop, recording three critically acclaimed live albums that still feature some of the finest vocalese jazz singing ever done.[20] Within a few months of her arrival in America, Bavan would be onstage in the cast of *The Real Ambassadors*, going full circle from Brubeck's mysterious sight-reading challenge to premiering the musical at the Monterey Jazz Festival.

As the Brubecks were preparing for the show's debut, Columbia Records set into motion the prerelease activities for the soundtrack album, which would be in stores on September 1, 1962. The release timing was influenced by the fact that a slimmed-down version of the show would be debuted at Monterey, and the label wanted to capitalize on the publicity.[21] By June 20, Columbia had issued some prerelease copies of songs from the album of *The Real Ambassadors*, as noted in a letter to Ralph J. Gleason from Brubeck's attorney, Michael J. Maloney. The letter referred to the advance copies and also mentioned the possibilities offered for a staging at Monterey that year.[22] These advance 45-rpm discs were spread to key jazz DJs so that Columbia might gauge the level of interest in some of the songs from the show. At the same time, Iola Brubeck was facing the challenges of staging the musical on a bare stage, outdoors, with minimal lighting, no actors, dancers, or chorus, and little, if any, rehearsal. By now, Iola had decided that the only possible way to present *The Real Ambassadors* was a concert reading of excerpts from the musical, rather than a full-blown musical theater staging. As a seasoned radio producer, she quickly realized that she would have to translate the original concept to a concert version, stripped of stagecraft, makeup, costuming, dance numbers, chorus, etc.

Since the media coverage over the previous years had referred to *The Real Ambassadors* as a Broadway musical, Iola also needed to make sure that expectations by audience members and jazz critics were recalibrated to the much less ambitious concert version. In the reduced version, cast members would perform the songs live onstage using lyric sheets and printed music.

She wrote to Jimmy Lyons on June 30, 1962, to inform him that she would be sending him a complete set of the musical's lyrics, to make lyric cards for the staging. She wrote that she had not contacted any of the other performers yet, so she could "only pray they are learning their parts." She pleaded that Lyons dispel any notion of a staged musical being presented:

> Please, Jim, be careful in your announcements regarding the show that you make it extremely clear that this is a concert version, or excerpts from the score—not a fully mounted production! If the rumor persists everyone will expect to see a Broadway show which, of course, they will not—and cannot. With such short rehearsal time it will be a miracle to get through it! Do not build it up as the big event![23]

She ends the letter with another concern, asking whether or not the contract to secure the services of Lambert, Hendricks & Ross had been signed. Evidently, word of Ross's pending departure from the group may not have been widely publicized, a fact supported by Bavan's recollection that the trio was still billed as "Lambert, Hendricks & Ross" at a number of her early gigs with the group.

In determining how the Brubecks would replace the dancers, sets, lighting, backdrops, ballet sequences, and miscellaneous character parts required to bring the musical, as originally conceived, to life, Dave Brubeck reflected on the process they followed:

> I recall that Iola went out to a little hut by the stream to escape the usual hubbub of the farmhouse and get to work writing a narrative that should tie the music together. When the LP was made, we thought in terms of a good recording sequence more than a story outline. Now she had to think in terms of making the story match the sequence on the recording. Once the narrative was written, my brother Howard was called in to prepare books containing music and cues for each participant.[24]

Cathy Yaghsizian recalled that some of the outbuildings near their Weston, Connecticut, home were little more than eight-by-ten-foot chicken coops when they arrived. "Our neighbor, Sandy Jackson, acted as a handyman for all the houses on our lane. He converted some of those little outbuildings into what might generously be termed guest cottages. They were habitable for guests who came up for the weekend," she remembered. "You could sleep in them."[25] It was in one of these guest cottages that Iola worked to conceive the narrator's parts that would stitch the songs and plot for the show together. Cathy also recalled that her uncle Howard Brubeck came to spend the summer of 1962 in Weston, bringing his whole family, so that the Brubeck children also had their cousins to play with all summer while Howard helped Dave and Iola prepare the music and performance books for Monterey.[26] Cathy stated:

> I have a vivid memory of the whole manuscript for *The Real Ambassadors* being spread all across the living room floor that summer. There was sheet music along with typed-up manuscripts. Everyone trying to match things up . . . "does this section go here or there?" as they got all the music organized.[27]

Additional obstacles emerged and had to be overcome before the musicians would rendezvous in San Francisco one week before the show's premiere to rehearse. The first was Armstrong's wife, Lucille. When she had learned that Louis was to learn eight new songs to perform at Monterey from *The Real Ambassadors*, she placed a call to Iola Brubeck and explained that there was "no way" Louis could do this. She told Iola that he might be able to sing one or two songs with Dave's group from the show, but that to attempt to do the entire show was out of the question.

When Iola did not agree and declined to call the rest of the cast to cancel the performance, Lucille then asked Joe Glaser to intervene. In a letter dated August 20, 1962, Joe Glaser explained to the Brubecks that he had just learned that in addition to playing his regular set with his All-Stars at the Sunday night finale to the Monterey Jazz Festival, the band was expected to take part in the staging of *The Real Ambassadors* earlier that same evening, performing eight numbers from the Columbia album. "I do hope this was a mistake, in view of the fact that you and I decided that it would be silly for you and Louis to try and do more than one or two [numbers from the musical] at the most." Such language was typical Glaser and reflects his bare-knuckles approach to negotiation. His statement "you and I decided that it would be silly" belittled the nearly five-year effort that the Brubecks had made to stage the show.

Glaser instructed Brubeck to "advise [Jimmy Lyons] immediately you will not be prepared to do so." Glaser then stipulated that neither he nor the agent who executed the booking agreement on behalf of ABC had ever "at any time advised Jimmy that you and Louis would be in a position to do the album at the Monterey Jazz Festival."[28] As a point of fact, the contract that Glaser's staff had signed on behalf of Armstrong was perfectly legal and binding. The

Preliminary Schedule for Sunday, September 23, 1962, Monterey Jazz Festival	
7:15 p.m.	Dizzy Gillespie Orchestra
8:25	Entre'acte
8:35	Real Ambassadors
9:55	Entre'acte
10:15	Louis Armstrong and His All-Stars
End Show	

Table 2—Preliminary typewritten schedule for Sunday night performances at the fifth Monterey Jazz Festival in 1962. This undated schedule was most likely sent by Jimmy Lyons to the Brubecks to confirm the timing for their set (Brubeck Collection, 1.d.15.8).

contract defined Armstrong's engagement as "One Concert between 9 PM and Midnight" on Sunday, September 23, 1962, though it was not specifically identified as *The Real Ambassadors*.[29] The preliminary schedule, as shown in table 2 , for Sunday night's concerts abided by the spirit of the contract that Glaser's representative had signed, if not precisely the letter of that agreement. The entire evening's presentations on the main stage could arguably be viewed as "one concert," and Armstrong would start not long before 9:00 p.m. and end well before midnight, less than the three-hour window stipulated in the agreement.

Glaser's August 20 letter was a broadside designed to stop the staging of the show dead in its tracks. After the bluster regarding how his staff was finessed by Lyons into agreeing to Armstrong's two different performances, the manager shifted gears, trying a second line of reasoning to stop the performance. He intimated that presenting *The Real Ambassadors* at Monterey might be to Brubeck's disadvantage, especially as it could be a flop, with so little preparation time possible. Glaser, instead, offered a mollifying alternative:

[We will] do everything we possibly can to arrange many concerts and promotional dates for you, Louis and Carmen McRae, so you can make yourselves plenty of bucks with the understanding that it will be presented in the proper way. I do hope you agree with the way I feel about you and Louis Armstrong appearing at the Monterey Jazz Festival.[30]

The letter and its two-pronged attack on the premiere devastated the Brubecks. It seemed that the musical's much-anticipated debut might be halted by the one-two punch of Lucille's concerns for her aging mate and Glaser's anger at having been outmaneuvered by Lyons. However, with their goal nearly in their grasp, Dave and Iola were determined that the show could still be saved, and with less than thirty days until its scheduled premiere, a solution was forged.

Fortunately, both Brubeck and Armstrong had been booked under the auspices of George Wein at the first Ohio Valley Jazz Festival, held that weekend, August 24–26, 1962.[31] Brubeck and Armstrong scheduled their own "summit meeting" that Friday night after their respective festival performances, meeting and going over arrangements and songs with Armstrong, trombonist Trummy Young, and the other All-Stars, with Brubeck on piano. Once Armstrong understood that he and his band would be reading the same charts used for the recordings onstage and that he wouldn't have to memorize any of his parts, his apparent concerns were allayed.[32] Despite Lucille's and Glaser's objections, Brubeck and Armstrong had found a way to proceed. Satchmo was back on board.[33]

Brubeck later learned from Trummy Young what had been the source of Lucille Armstrong's anxiety. Armstrong had lost his music from the recording sessions and was painstakingly trying to memorize his parts by listening over and over to the home recordings that the Brubecks had sent him. He had been sitting in his office for hours also laboring to retype all the lyrics. Brubeck commented, "No doubt Lucille was simply trying to protect him" by demanding they cancel the show.[34]

With the clock ticking, the Brubecks called Jimmy Lyons and explained that once the confusion had been resolved, Satchmo was willing to forge ahead. Jimmy Lyons shared the news with Ralph Gleason. On September 2, 1962, Gleason reported the story of the problem and its timely resolution in an article, "Here's One Good Reason Why Promoters Get Grey Hairs," in the *San Francisco Chronicle*. Gleason explained, "It seems that Armstrong had never realized that this would not be a costumed, full-scale production but merely excerpts," with each performer's parts right in front of them on music stands for the performance. Gleason wrote that Armstrong responded, "You mean I don't have to memorize all that stuff?" When told it would all be on the music stands, Armstrong smiled and added, "I can do that—all right."[35]

With the show now back on and its star enthusiastically endorsing its performance, Iola Brubeck continued making her production notes in a standard stenographer's notebook, recording her ideas for costumes, props, stage blocking, lighting cues, and other production requirements. She would join the musicians onstage, acting as the narrator to provide the audience with the overarching story line of the touring jazz ambassadors. She would sketch out the personality traits of the two leads, Armstrong's "Pops" and

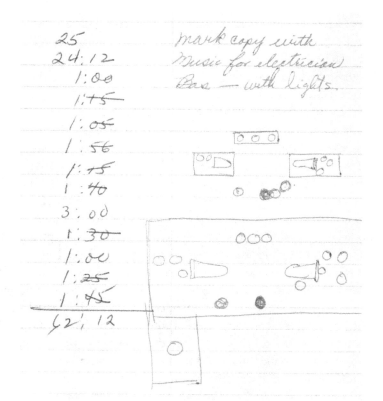

A sheet from Iola Brubeck's stenographer pad, summer 1962. The column on the left shows her timing of the pieces that would make up the concert version performed at Monterey, to confirm the running time would be approximately one hour. On the upper right is a reminder to mark a copy of the script with lighting cues for Paul Vieregge, Monterey stage and production manager. Below that, two stage plots show the vocal trio on a raised platform at the center rear of the stage, with Brubeck and his sidemen situated house left, and Armstrong's All-Stars positioned house right. In the bottom sketch, which most closely resembles the final stage plot, Armstrong's and McRae's positions are marked, and to the lower left, on a wing built off the front of the stage, is the platform from which Iola would introduce and narrate the show at its premiere. The actual location of her wing stage was to the left of the stage and not in front of it, as shown in this sketch. Brubeck Collection, Holt-Atherton Special Collections, University of the Pacific Library, © Dave Brubeck.

McRae's "Rhonda," to give the audience enough context to see the love interest embodied in a number of the songs from the show. Iola also envisioned the vocal trio playing multiple roles, dressed in black robes as priests for hymn-like songs such as "They Say I Look Like God." At other times, she envisioned them costumed in top hats and black waistcoats in the roles of the official US ambassadors, then later dressed in colorful robes and hats as the citizens of Talgalla, the fictional African nation that is the setting for much of the show. In her notes, she asks whether there might be some way to find

and cast Nigerian folk dancers to appear, an option that did not come to fruition for the premiere, but would be followed in the 2013 revival in Detroit.[36]

This notebook also contains an early sketch for the stage placement of the
cast, with Brubeck and Kyle facing each other across their pianos, the respective rhythm sections further behind the pianists, the vocal trio positioned
stage center on a riser, and Pops and Rhonda sharing the front and center
of the stage. The narrator would be on a separate stage, similar to a wing,
slightly removed from the onstage action to provide needed distance from
the main protagonists. Next to the stage plot were Iola's calculations about
how long the show might run based on the musical and narrative elements
making up the Monterey production. She planned to keep the show's total
time to just over one hour, including the newly written narration.

Meanwhile, Howard Brubeck worked to complete the transcriptions of the
show for the forthcoming Hansen piano-vocal print edition, which relied on
the actual performances from the 1961 recordings as its basis. Concurrently,
he created a performance binder for each of the show's fourteen performers
to use for the upcoming concert performance and rehearsals.[37] In each binder
would be that player's score, interspersed with a copy of the narrator's script
so that each entrance and cue would be evident. The books would be used in
the only rehearsal, so individual performers could make notes in their own
hand and refer to them during the performance at Monterey.

On September 1, 1962, when *The Real Ambassadors'* red, white, and blue–
covered album arrived in record stores, Dave and Iola Brubeck were part
of a collection of musicians, journalists, and festival personnel who were
moving collectively to prepare for one of the most consequential premieres
in the history of the Monterey Jazz Festival.

CHAPTER 14

A NIGHT TO REMEMBER

Activity was building rapidly toward the show's premiere. On September 14, Iola Brubeck sent Jimmy Lyons a sketch for the stage setup, which Lyons passed on to his stage manager, Paul Vieregge. In the letter, Iola provides detailed instructions on lighting intensities and placements, requests a follow spot for Armstrong, and suggests that McRae be positioned slightly closer to Brubeck's trio, with Armstrong placed nearer his own band to facilitate soloing with them.[1]

The jazz-savvy Northern California audience was well apprised of the music and its message, as Ralph J. Gleason had been penning a series of advance stories in the *San Francisco Chronicle* extolling the qualities of the show in August and September 1962. One week before the premiere, on September 16, the paper's Sunday-edition weekend entertainment section, dubbed "This World," featured the musical and an illustration of Brubeck on its cover and a major story inside. The centerpiece of the insert was Gleason's lengthy feature advance story, titled "Louis Represents the Human Race: A 'Domestic Peace Corps' Will Gather at Monterey." The article outlined the story of the musical and, quoting liberally from the show's lyrics and album liner notes, attempted to attract jazz fans and the general public to the musical's ambitious message. Gleason made plain that in his estimation, jazz was the perfect vehicle to address both the central role the music was then playing in improving US relations abroad while also addressing social issues at home.

"In my humble way, I'm the USA."—Louis Armstrong in *The Real Ambassadors*

That magnetic attractiveness of American jazz, which has resulted in its being better received abroad than at home in many cases, has been attributed by some observers to the concept expressed in Louis' line quoted above.

Jazz—to those outside the U.S.—seems to have become a distillation of that great American dream whose revolutionary approach shook up and inspired the entire world in the Eighteenth Century and continues to do so, though less dramatically, today. The great qualities of unorthodoxy and equality; the virtues of improvisation and the potential for everyone to be his own Horatio Alger, however battered and shell-torn by our own inadequacies and others' momentary strength . . . continue to wave before the world the hope of a kind of human freedom otherwise unknown. Jazz encompasses all of this ethic.

Within its own small world, it practices what the rest only preach and exemplifies what all could be by the example of the few. In a way, this is the virtue of the jazz festival . . . the jazz musicians who play there and the audience they gather become a sort of domestic peace corps.

The Real Ambassadors is no Pollyanna production. There are irony and social comment in it as well as a deep religious feeling about jazz as an instrument of truth and sanity and peace.

Louis sings, "In my humble way, I'm the USA, though I represent the Government, the Government don't represent some policies I'm for. Oh, we learned to be concerned about the constitutionality, in our Nation segregation isn't a legality. Soon our only differences will be in personality. That's what I stand for." And of course, that is exactly what all of the real jazz, the real ambassadors and the real Americans stand for as well and this concept is one of the things that makes jazz music—American jazz music—the beginning of a new international language in the best image of that American revolution which inspired the world.

Do not pass this up as mere programming . . . This is a message that reaches far out beyond the music itself, though stemming from it. All of us can learn from this remarkable amalgam of music, social thought, religion and joy. "They say I look like God," Louis sings in humbleness. "Could God be black?" Could be.[2]

While Gleason, as cofounder of Monterey, would benefit from a well-attended festival, his enthusiasm is obvious in the depth and level of engagement of his discussion in this and other articles and reviews on the musical published before and after its Monterey performance.

The next day, on Monday, September 17, 1962, the musicians converged on the St. Francis Hotel in San Francisco for their one rehearsal. Yolande Bavan recalled that when she met Iola for the first time at the September 17

The cast of *The Real Ambassadors* at their daylong rehearsal, Monday, September 17, 1962, at San Francisco's St. Francis Hotel. Back row, *left to right*, Howard Brubeck, Danny Barcelona, Eugene Wright, Joe Morello, Billy Cronk, Dave Lambert, Yolande Bavan, Jon Hendricks, and Iola Brubeck; front row, *left to right*, Trummy Young, Carmen McRae, Louis Armstrong, and Dave Brubeck. Not shown, clarinetist Joe Darensbourg. Photo by V. M. Hanks. Brubeck Collection, Holt-Atherton Special Collections, University of the Pacific Library, © Dave Brubeck.

rehearsal, she was "an amazing presence, not just because of her height—but she exuded a sense of movement—while keeping her feet very firmly planted on the ground. She had passion."[3] At the outset, Iola explained the staging to the cast, noting that she would be on an adjacent and separate stage in the role of narrator. Photos documenting this rehearsal reveal both the *esprit de corps* that was emerging as well as the intensity that the cast brought to their daylong study and preparation for the premiere. The superb musicianship of the cast, along with the timely coaching of Howard, Iola, and Dave Brubeck, resulted in a most productive day. Brubeck drummer Joe Morello recalled the integral role Howard Brubeck played in the show's preparation and performance: "He was a great musician and prepared the books for each of us to use, then joined us to play the chimes during the performance."[4]

This rehearsal further validated jazz as an international melting pot and demonstrated the scope of the many interlocking relationships that had been established by American jazz ambassadors throughout the 1950s. As Yolande Bavan walked into the rehearsal and was introduced to the musicians, Louis Armstrong smiled, turned to his wife Lucille, and said, "Hey mama, I know

A candid shot from the same day, showing the musicians with their noses buried in their respective performance binders, which had been prepared by Howard Brubeck. He is sitting in the right background and looking toward Louis Armstrong. Armstrong's clarinetist, Joe Darensbourg, who was cropped out of the cast photo, is shown to the left, sitting in front of Iola Brubeck and to the left of trombonist Trummy Young. Photo by V. M. Hanks. Brubeck Collection, Holt-Atherton Special Collections, University of the Pacific Library, © Dave Brubeck.

dat face," as he gazed at Bavan. She responded, "Louis, I met you in Australia when I was seventeen and I was singing with Graeme Bell." As it turned out, Louis and Trummy Young had sat in with Bell's Dixieland group when the All-Stars were touring Australia in the mid-1950s.

Bavan recalled how, as the rehearsal progressed for *The Real Ambassadors'* premiere, Armstrong impressed everyone with his mastery of the music, showing just how seriously he took the role of Pops and that his repeated listening to the Brubeck home recordings had been an effective review method. "He knew the score cold," she remembered.[5] Armstrong also served from the outset as a source of energy to the rest of the performers as they worked through the one-hour concert score. Bavan added, "You only had to look at his face, the way he was beaming, to get a boost. He'd look over every so often, smile at me, and say 'Hey, mama.'"[6]

She also recalled how Carmen McRae and Trummy Young expounded to her during breaks in the rehearsal about the racial tensions in America and the struggles that people of color, even artists of their stature, faced in

America. These conversations further opened Bavan's eyes to the pervasive and hypocritical impact of segregation practices on the music and entertainment industry of 1962. Bavan learned that prior to her joining the trio, Lambert, Hendricks & Ross had been prevented from making television appearances on every major variety and talk show, such as *The Today Show*, *The Tonight Show*, *Merv Griffin*, and *David Frost*, simply because the trio was integrated. "The only exception," she recalled, "was Steve Allen, who had them on and later had us on his show in spite of the limitations."[7] After Bavan's performances as a member of Lambert, Hendricks & Bavan, the trio and their backing musicians were regularly denied rooms since they were integrated. She recalled one instance where the group arrived at their hotel after a performance in South Carolina, and Bavan and Lambert were offered rooms, while Jon Hendricks and their backing trio were told they would have to find other accommodations. Dave Lambert simply said, "We're not staying here; we'll find another place to sleep." That ended up requiring a ninety-minute drive before they were finally able to rest for the night, Bavan recalled.[8] The fact that such experiences were commonplace helped the cast of *The Real Ambassadors* to bring a sharpened awareness to the show's messages.

Concurrently, plans for the Monterey staging were moving forward. Paul Vieregge was the stage manager for the Monterey Jazz Festival from its inception, continuing in that role for the next forty-two years until 2000. Vieregge had concerns that related to three areas necessary to stage *The Real Ambassadors* successfully: constructing an adequate stage, providing rudimentary theatrical lighting (including a follow spot for Pops), and meeting the costuming requests that Iola Brubeck had made to Jimmy Lyons for Pops and the Greek chorus.

Vieregge recalled that in 1962, the fairgrounds' arena was in the process of being built. The State Fair Board had allocated money to build grandstands surrounding the horse arena, but due to a strike by the builders union, the work would not be completed in time for the festival. In fact, he remembered, the large roof sections were laid out in the center of the arena, making that area unusable. Paul's solution was to construct a smaller temporary enclosure at the east end of the fairgrounds, where a stage would be built just for that year's festival. When Jimmy Lyons related the plans Iola was making for the show to be staged, which included her role as narrator, Paul realized that he and his crew would also have to improvise the auxiliary stage where Iola would stand apart from the main characters in her role as narrator. Thus, the first problem of where to stage the show would be solved.

Since Armstrong was the lead character, Vieregge decided to visit him at his San Francisco hotel to discuss the lighting and staging. Armstrong surprised Vieregge by greeting him in undershorts, wearing his Star of David around his neck. He came to his hotel room door, smiled, and quipped to Vieregge, "What? You didn't know I was a Jewish jig?" Vieregge explained to the veteran showman how he planned to set up and light the performers, with his band and Brubeck's facing one another on opposite wings of the main stage. Satchmo would be closer to his band and Carmen would be nearer to Brubeck's, as they were respectively accompanied by each ensemble for their individual numbers. With respect to the lighting, Vieregge explained that with a follow spot, they could mark his on- and offstage entrances. In reference to Iola's costuming notes, Vieregge asked if Armstrong would agree with the suggestion that Pops use a costume of tuxedo, top hat, and attaché case for his entrance onstage as an ambassador. Armstrong said that would be fine. At the meeting's conclusion, Vieregge said that Satchmo "understood what would be expected of him during the performance."[9]

Upon his return to Monterey, Vieregge secured the necessary props and costumes, including the top hat and attaché case. "One of the festival board members was in a community theater group and borrowed the robes with cowls from their wardrobe closet," he recalled. They would serve as the necessary monks' robes to costume Lambert, Hendricks & Bavan. "When they were in their roles as the [Talgallan] people or the Greek chorus, they would have the cowls back, but when they performed the chant-like role of the priests, they pulled up the cowls," Vieregge recalled.

The final challenges to staging the show would have to solved during the festival itself, because the main stage, lighting standards, and necessary infrastructure were all being set up using temporary resources just days before the festival commenced. Because of the temporary stage and the lighting requirements for the headlining artists on Saturday and Sunday nights, the only available time to position the lighting as requested by Iola was 8:00 Sunday morning. "Lighting director Dick West rearranged the lighting, and visually we created two stages, adjacent to one another, so Iola could be on the second one as narrator," Vieregge stated. "We could black out the main stage for key narration passages."[10]

Back at Monterey, early on Sunday afternoon, the cast met on the stage to work out entrances and cues, confirm focus and placement for lights, and ensure that sight lines would be adequate for the performance, since Brubeck would be cueing vocalists for their various entries. They used the stage directions provided by the Brubecks, with the follow spot in place and enough lighting instruments to provide a sense of motion onstage, illuminating or blacking out various characters according to the script. Vocalist, townsperson, and member of the Greek chorus Yolande Bavan recalled, "There was movement among the cast, otherwise it would appear to be just a band playing."[11] So for their duets with Armstrong, Iola Brubeck directed McRae or Trummy Young to share center stage with the star. Brubeck remembered, "That hasty so-called rehearsal was absolute chaos, spent on working out lighting cues and entrances . . . no time to think about the actual music, only logistics." Adding to his concerns, the camaraderie and cooperation from the daylong rehearsal earlier in the week seemed to have disappeared.

> Lambert, Hendricks, and Bavan objected to their robes as too hot and too itchy. Armstrong refused to make his first entrance with top hat and attaché case as we had arranged. Iola's parents, brother, and family had driven down from Stockton and as they sat in seats out front, observing what was happening onstage with the rehearsal, were convinced that the show was destined for disaster.[12]

Satchmo's refusal to use the props was actually a practical joke played on Dave—one that he didn't get—as Louis had already agreed to use them in his earlier meeting with Vieregge. Clearly, Brubeck was nervous that the couple's first large-scale musical collaboration might fall flat on its face, and Glaser's warnings must have been playing at the back of his mind. Adding to the strain, the music itself was very demanding, especially the fast-paced double-time lyrics sung by the trio, Armstrong's stanzas with lots of multisyllabic words in "The Real Ambassador" and "King for a Day," and the complex, dense harmonies sung throughout the piece by Lambert, Hendricks & Bavan. Yolande Bavan remembered, "It was a bit overwhelming because this music wasn't easy to sing. Some of it is [quite] dissonant. It was a bit scary."[13]

As he left the stage from the walkthrough, Brubeck was approached by a television crew that was filming selected performances at the festival. They asked if he wanted to film the show for a fee of $750. Brubeck knew any filming of Armstrong would require Glaser's permission, so he quickly placed a call to New York. Predictably, Glaser refused to allow the filming to proceed, telling Brubeck, "Dave, wait until we're in New York where we can do it right. Those people out there are a bunch of amateurs."[14] Considered from a strictly business point of view, Glaser's advice made sense, as Armstrong had been the subject of an immensely popular 1957 CBS Television special entitled *Satchmo the Great*, and both Brubeck and Armstrong had frequently appeared on national television. They hardly needed exposure from a local television station. Glaser had only to pick up the phone to speak directly to decision-makers at the three major television networks, as Armstrong was a regular on evening shows across the broadcast dial. Additionally, Glaser

WORLD PREMIERE OF DAVE AND IOLA BRUBECK'S
original musical production

"THE REAL AMBASSADORS"

starring

LOUIS ARMSTRONG   CARMEN McRAE   DAVE BRUBECK

LAMBERT, HENDRICKS & YOLANDE

The theme of "The Real Ambassadors" is contained in the title. Louis Armstrong, Brubeck, Dizzy Gillespie — all of whom have made extensive and highly acclaimed overseas tours under the auspices of the U. S. Department of State — are the "real ambassadors" representing America to foreign peoples. And since jazz has become an international language and a force for world understanding, it may well be that the very phrase "foreign people" will one day become happily archaic.

On closing night of the Monterey Jazz Festival, Sunday, September 23 (at 7:15 p.m. sharp), one of the most ambitious and unusual programs ever presented on any festival stage will be given its first public performance.

Excerpts from the original musical production "The Real Ambassadors," with music by Dave Brubeck and lyrics by Iola (Mrs. Dave) Brubeck will be presented. Heading the cast will be Louis Armstrong, Dave Brubeck, Carmen McRae and the Lambert, Hendricks and Yolande Trio.

The official program book for the fifth Monterey Jazz Festival devoted two pages to introducing *The Real Ambassadors* to the audience. The uncredited copy cites the all-important backstage meeting between Brubeck and Armstrong at the Cincinnati Jazz Festival, at which they resolved any misunderstanding about the upcoming concert performance. Brubeck Collection, Holt-Atherton Special Collections, University of the Pacific Library.

was calculating the moneymaking opportunities that any television production might generate, and the need for a national network and sponsors to be profitable, rather than the potential historical significance the filming of *The Real Ambassadors* Monterey performance might someday have.

Brubeck had to drop the lost opportunity and quickly refocus on the evening's performance, which he would lead from his place at the piano. Having gone back to their hotel to rest and change into their performance attire, Dave and Iola were trying to drive up to the backstage area on the fairgrounds when their car was blocked by an unruly crowd of unticketed hangers-on whom Dave described as "beatniks." "They had had too much to drink and were making remarks about us as we passed. They were not

The internationalism of jazz serves as a unifying theme of the new Brubeck musical, and for the 1962 Monterey Jazz Festival as well. Lalo Schifrin's "New Continent" which has its world premiere on opening night, and Dizzy Gillespie's "The Relatives of Jazz," on Sunday afternoon both have as their subject the universality of jazz. The appearance of Israel's Yaffa Yarkoni, Ceylon's Yolande Bavan, Brazil's Bola Sete, Argentina's Lalo Schifrin, (and Cheraw, South Carolina's Dizzy Gillespie!) make this Festival a truly international spectacle.

Known primarily as a pianist and leader of the poll-winning Dave Brubeck Quartet, the scholarly, serious Brubeck is coming to be recognized as an important jazz composer. Many of his songs, like "The Duke" and "In Your Own Sweet Way," are becoming modern jazz standards, having been incorporated into the repertoire of Miles Davis, Gil Evans and other major figures in the jazz world.

Iola Brubeck, a gifted actress, poet, writer and mother of the five Brubeck children, has written all of the lyrics to Dave's songs.

Recorded in its entirety by Columbia Records (the Festival can only present excerpts) "The Real Ambassadors" includes the following songs:
EVERYBODY'S COMIN'
CULTURAL EXCHANGE
GOOD REVIEWS
REMEMBER WHO YOU ARE
MY ONE BAD HABIT
SUMMER SONG
KING FOR A DAY
BLOW SATCHMO
THE REAL AMBASSADORS
IN THE LURCH
ONE MOMENT WORTH YEARS
THEY SAY I LOOK LIKE GOD
SINCE LOVE HAD ITS WAY
I DIDN'T KNOW UNTIL YOU TOLD ME
SWING BELLS

In Cincinatti a few weeks ago, Dave and Louis got together for a little advance rehearsal for their Monterey appearance. If the audience has half as many kicks as they did, "The Real Ambassadors" will be remembered as a high point during the five year history of the Monterey Jazz Festival.

A. *Louis Armstrong*

B. *Louis Armstrong with Lambert, Hendricks, Ross rehearsing.*

C. *Carmen McRae*

D. *Dave and Iola Brubeck and family*

E. *Dave Brubeck*

F. *L. Paul Desmond, alto sax; Ctr., Dave Brubeck, piano; R., Eugene Wright, bass, at Monterey.*

G. *Dave Brubeck and Paul Desmond rehearsing at Monterey 1958.*

Photo by JERRY STOLL

interested in the music inside the arena, but were simply there to carouse, bang on bongos, and amuse themselves," Dave said.[15]

Fortunately, Jimmy Lyons anticipated such a situation and had assigned plainclothes, off-duty police to clear a path for the couple, who arrived just moments before their announced call time. They met the rest of the cast members, who were also in the appointed stage attire. Yolande Bavan remembered that, as twilight settled over the coastal community, "there was a sunset with a beautiful pinkish sky as we all gathered in the backstage area around a fire pit just before our performance. It was a bit cool outside."[16] At the scheduled time of 8:35 p.m., the cast of *The Real Ambassadors* took the stage.

At the direction of Paul Vieregge, the house went dark as Iola Brubeck, in theatrical makeup and a dark-colored sheath dress topped with an elegant white silk- and gold-embroidered stole, stepped onto her dais before being illuminated by a sole spotlight.[17] She had an imposing presence onstage, due in part to her height of nearly six feet and her bearing and presence, which she had mastered in her earlier years onstage. Drawing on her experiences as

SUNDAY EVENING, SEPT. 23
Early Starting Time
at 7:15 P.M. Sharp

1. DIZZY GILLESPIE and the
MONTEREY BRASS
ENSEMBLE

Trummy Young
Joe Darensbourg
Billy Cronk
Danny Barcelona
Joe Morello
Eugene Wright

2. JEANNE LEE and
RAN BLAKE
Entr'acte
In keeping with the Monterey Jazz Festival's policy of
introducing new talent, this unusual duo is making its
West coast debut at the Festival.

3. "THE REAL
AMBASSADORS" (excerpts)
An original musical production with music and lyrics
by Dave and Iola Brubeck, featuring . . .
    Louis Armstrong
    Carmen McRae
    Dave Brubeck
    Lambert, Hendricks and
        Yolande
        with . . .
            Billy Kyle

4. JEANNE LEE and
RAN BLAKE
Entr'acte

5. LOUIS ARMSTRONG
AND HIS ALL-STARS
With . . .
    Jewel Brown, vocal
    Trummy Young, trombone and vocal
    Joe Darensbourg, clarinet
    Billy Kyle, piano
    Bill Cronk, bass
    Danny Barcelona, drums
And . . .
    LOUIS ARMSTRONG

The lineup from Sunday night, September 23, 1962, which presented the debut performance of
The Real Ambassadors between sets by Dizzy Gillespie leading the Monterey Brass Ensemble and
Louis Armstrong and His All-Stars to close out the night. Brubeck Collection, Holt-Atherton Special
Collections, University of the Pacific Library.

a network radio performer in the 1940s, she created a "theater of the mind"
to open the performance, drawing the audience of six thousand into the
musical's plot with these precisely enunciated words:

> *The Real Ambassadors* is not a musical drama in the usual sense. The
> drama lies in the sudden "coming to life" of words and notes written
> on pieces of paper, propped on music stands before our players. Sets
> and costumes are far more fantastic than any of us could ever see on
> stage, because they exist only in our imaginations. We must paint a

view of the world from an airplane window, build an African village with a church and a palace and people in its streets.

I have said our presentation is not a drama, nor is it a play, except in the sense that to play is to pretend. Nor is our offering really a concert, only in the very special sense of concert—many voices raised as one.[18]

With that, the musicians launched into the first song, "Everybody's Comin'," which in turn musically introduces each of the performers. From the song's first notes, it was clear that the performers were ready to rise to the occasion. Dave Brubeck vividly recalled Armstrong's stage entrance:

> Precisely on cue out walked Louis Armstrong greeted to great applause from the audience. He was wearing the top hat and carrying the attaché case. As he walked by me seated at the piano he said, "Am I hammin' it up enough to suit you, Pops?" And then a big smile as he turned that radiant face to the audience, who immediately responded with a roar to the Louis Armstrong they loved.[19]

Standing directly behind Armstrong, Yolande Bavan had a perfect view. "There was something almost divine about his performance . . . unique and charismatic," she said. From that moment on, Bavan recalled that the audience was clearly united with the performers. Interspersed between many of the songs, Iola Brubeck, described by one reviewer as "looking like the Delphic oracle," performed the role of the narrator, explaining the locations and situations that the characters were experiencing, thereby joining the journey of discovery that the players had embarked upon. Paul Vieregge, who observed the performance from the wings as stage manager, stated, "Dave Brubeck crossed a bridge with the [socially conscious] message in this musical. It showed the love and respect that he had for Louis Armstrong. Those feelings were palpable on the stage that night."[20]

Carmen McRae not only proved the ideal musical partner for Armstrong, but also brought a sense of glamour and vulnerability to the role of Rhonda. Visually, she was clothed in an elegant, full-length glittering formal evening gown, topped by a silver mink stole and an assortment of expensive-looking jewelry. Rhonda embodied the glamorous ideal of a jazz vocalist of the first order. When asked whether she had made any costume suggestions to McRae, Iola said:

> I don't recall advising Carmen what to wear. I think she instinctively decided on that "glam" attire. The only stage instruction I can remember

giving her was for her to light a cigarette or be holding a cigarette when she began "My One Bad Habit." The lyrics start off, "I neither drink, nor smoke, nor swear."[21]

The show's premiere seems to have been blessed by one fortuitous coincidence after another. Brubeck recalled:

> Now, before an audience, the great professionalism of the cast members went into action. With the audience response, some kind of magical inspiration started to make the performance come alive. When an airplane flew over the fairgrounds, Iola incorporated it as part of the script, and the distant banging of the [beatniks'] bongos gave an authentic atmosphere for the mythical African setting. As our confidence grew, so did the interpretation of the musical material. I've never seen a group of "pros" react so positively and beautifully together. I can't recall any hesitation or weak moments in the entire performance. We were flying on pure inspiration.[22]

Vocalist Yolande Bavan was situated on the riser directly behind Satchmo and so had a perfect view of the audience's reaction to his performance of the new work.

> During the performance, it was such an unknown quantity to hear an opera written by Iola and Dave Brubeck, and a jazz opera at that. People were crying in the audience at certain moments because it was just, what can I say? I cried onstage because it was . . . because it . . . *was.* [*Pauses to compose herself before continuing; emphasis in the original.*] I cried with the audience, even being a part of it. And singing it was just so deeply felt and totally moving . . . totally moving.[23]

Bavan also recalled that by performing the musical she and the other cast members were able to transcend the feelings of helplessness for those facing racism that many had been feeling prior to joining the project. As a result, the performers gained a real sense of agency. In essence, *The Real Ambassadors* was a musical answer to those politicians and citizens who continued to advocate for the status quo. Bavan believed that segregation would only be abolished if individuals, including artists, took a stand and convinced others to join them.

A reading of the many glowing reviews that followed the premiere demonstrates beyond any doubt that the musical's messages hit home. Critic

The Real Ambassadors premiere at Monterey. Pictured, *left to right*, are Iola Brubeck (lower left background), Louis Armstrong, Dave Brubeck, and Trummy Young (partially obscured). Photo by Jerry Stoll. Brubeck Collection, Holt-Atherton Special Collections, University of the Pacific Library, © Dave Brubeck.

Ralph Gleason summarized the overall impact that the show made on the packed house:

> Louis's golden horn blew the notes out in the cold night air, and his rough voice turned sweet to sing the lyrics that told of love and human dignity, and hope and inspiration. It was one of the most deeply moving

Howard Brubeck, Dave's older brother, served as musical director for *The Real Ambassadors*. Here he's pictured backstage, rehearsing with Louis Armstrong before the premiere. Photo by Jerry Stoll. Brubeck Collection, Holt-Atherton Special Collections, University of the Pacific Library, © Dave Brubeck.

moments of Monterey's history when Louis sang the lines, "They say I look like God / Could God be black?" and preached a sermon on integration.[24]

Other critics chimed in with similar praise. Jerry Coker of the *Monterey Peninsula Herald* noted, "The strength of this show lay in the narrative and lyrics by Mrs. Dave Brubeck . . . who shows herself to be a satirist of real

Louis Armstrong's stage entrance in the character of Pops, with his ambassadorial top hat and tuxedo. His appearance onstage elicited a thunderous roar of appreciation from the six thousand fans who packed the arena. Brubeck Collection, Holt-Atherton Special Collections, University of the Pacific Library, © Dave Brubeck.

depth." He added, "Satchmo, playing himself, was not in any way diminished. His glow radiated over the whole fast-moving, intricate proceedings, lending warmth and credibility. He was in top form, vocally and instrumentally."[25] Jose Stell of the *San Jose Mercury News* agreed, reporting that

Monterey was "Louisville" for a day. The durable Satchmo spread his usual delicious greeting as the top layer of the five-concert cake with his

Dave Brubeck looks on approvingly as Louis Armstrong plays one of his trumpet solos during the premiere of *The Real Ambassadors*. Photo courtesy of the *Monterey Herald* and Monterey Jazz Festival.

role in the piercingly emotional musical, *The Real Ambassadors*, written by Dave and Iola Brubeck. . . . The impetus of jazz as an international language and promoter of world fraternity was never presented with such poignancy.[26]

The *Berkeley Daily Gazette*'s Johnnie Rodrigues noted:

The Real Ambassadors proved a brilliant and dramatic finale, done with tender care, lilt and musicianship. At the conclusion the crowd responded with a roaring standing ovation which brought tears and smiles from all the performers.[27]

Drummer Joe Morello succinctly remembered, "It was ahead of its time, but that night, the [audience] response to *The Real Ambassadors* was strong."[28] Bassist Eugene Wright concurred:

Sometimes in life you get one shot to do something really unique—that was the case with *The Real Ambassadors*. It was a masterpiece and I had a ball playing it. My favorite tune was "One Moment Worth Years." It's

Carmen McRae performing one of her feature numbers, with Louis Armstrong looking on. According to Iola Brubeck, McRae chose her own wardrobe and costume jewelry to reflect the flamboyant character of Rhonda Brown. Photo by Jerry Stoll. Brubeck Collection, Holt-Atherton Special Collections, University of the Pacific Library, © Dave Brubeck.

too bad we were not able to continue to perform it, as it would have opened the door then to a whole lot more possibilities.[29]

Bavan, too, recalled the audience's immediate response to the performers at the show's conclusion:

They were ecstatic. I mean they just stood up *en masse*! I don't think they'd ever seen anything like that. And no one could escape Mr. Armstrong's vibration. You cannot. Even today, if I'm down, I just play any of his songs . . . and I just smile.[30]

Critic Charles M. Weisenberg appreciated the live performance, comparing it to the album of excerpts, stating:

The enthusiastic reception of the work . . . may enhance the chances of a Broadway presentation. Mrs. Brubeck read a narrative story line that gave the music a dramatic unity missing on the record album.

Louis Armstrong, playing Brubeck's music, sounded inspired. Lambert, Hendricks & Bavan were the surprise of the show, turning in an astounding performance that exceed anything they have previously done.[31]

He also was one of the critics that voiced some negative commentary, complaining that "the work itself is rather uneven, particularly the lyrics," suggesting that this might be because the show was written five years before. Of course, no one other than the performers knew that there had only been a single rehearsal before the complex performance was given. *DownBeat* agreed with Weisenberg about to the musical's lyrical naivete, while still praising the overall performance as "the festival's crowning point." They argued that even if some parts of the story and lyrics were naive, that shouldn't diminish the importance of the new work. *DownBeat*'s Don DeMicheal astutely suggested:

> Whether this sentiment [that this country's jazz performers are its best and "real" ambassadors], as well as the whole production is naïve is unimportant, for without naïveté, the work would lose all charm, its most important characteristic.[32]

Art is not mandated to only reflect the realities of life as it really is. Artists can and should engage the imagination, and DeMicheal saw the parallels drawn by the Brubecks, through the songs and narration in the show, to the persistent struggle for equality. DeMicheal also praised Iola Brubeck for her role in the performance. "Her narrative, well-written and delivered with wit, warmth, and dignity, held everything together and made clear the plot."[33] Reflecting back on the acclaim that her mother earned onstage as narrator, Cathy Yaghsizian said, "The role allowed her to tap into all of her stage and dramatic training."[34]

Gleason, who at this time had some of his columns syndicated nationally, wrote an additional follow-up review in which he used the sub headline "The New Armstrong," citing the fact that since his 1948 formation of the All-Stars, the trumpeter had ignored repeated requests to explore new material, play with different musicians, or vary his tried-and-true set list. Gleason stated:

> This year Armstrong, while he concluded the festival with his usual night club concert set, went onstage earlier in *The Real Ambassadors* in which he danced, sang and played an entirely new repertoire. It was a triumph for Monterey, as well as a personal triumph for Armstrong....

For his performance, Armstrong received a deserved ovation. The delicate problem of handling racial and religious issues in a song ["They
Say I Look Like God"] took a real ambassadorial touch and Armstrong
certainly had it. The evening added to the statures of Armstrong and
Brubeck.[35]

Similarly, DeMicheal's plaudits continued on to Armstrong's work with new
material, echoing Gleason that at this stage of Satchmo's career this was
indeed a rarity. Carmen McRae's sophisticated reading as Rhonda was judged
"superb" by *DownBeat*, while Lambert, Hendricks & Bavan's performance in
The Real Ambassadors came off "better in the Brubeck production than in
their own Saturday night performance." He concluded that although *The Real
Ambassadors* might or might not find its way to Broadway, it would make
an excellent concert package for touring. Finally, DeMicheal commented
that Armstrong's own set, which concluded the festival, was noteworthy, as
Armstrong himself "felt like playing, and his lip never failed him."[36] For both
the veteran trumpeter and his audience, it was truly a night for the ages.

That *The Real Ambassadors* premiered at that moment in time, while the
civil rights struggle was near its apex, very likely influenced reviewers, just
as it did the members of the audience, who overwhelmingly applauded the
troupe for its performance. Many were undoubtedly sympathetic to the cause
championed by Dr. Martin Luther King Jr. and the host of other African
American leaders fighting for equality. Still, the singular nature of the work
itself—which brought together two different styles of jazz, a multiracial cast,
and the concept of America's jazz ambassadors speaking truth to power at
the intersection of the Cold War and the civil rights movement—made its
premiere an important moment in the history of jazz and America.

CHAPTER 15

RECEPTION AND REACTIONS

While the critics applauded *The Real Ambassadors'* 1962 performance and its enthusiastic reception by the Monterey audience, what did individual audience members think about the performance and its message of racial equality?

Ron Cooper was a twenty-one-year-old festivalgoer who recalled:

There was a strong emotional reaction by the audience, in part due to the years of oppression that black musicians had faced. The whole format (of a stage play) wasn't really expected but it came off very well. It let people know that the art form of jazz communicated universally.[1]

At the time of the festival, Don Hoffman, then thirty-two, had just been hired as the program director for KMBY, an FM radio station that programmed jazz. He first heard Brubeck perform with his quartet in 1953 at San Francisco's Black Hawk Club, and recalled:

I was fortunate enough to get a ticket to the festival, the first of many that I've gone to and one of the best, I might add. *The Real Ambassadors* was the jewel in the crown of that year's festival; to see Satchmo and Dave Brubeck perform together was a really big deal.

Remembering the emotions that the performers showed when performing the work's varied songs, Hoffman said, "As the show progressed, the audience was emotional, too. The music had quite an impact on the crowd that night."

Another audience member was fourteen-year-old jazz fan Jon Ratner, who was attending his second Monterey Jazz festival with his family. In a 2012 interview, he reflected:

Looking back today, it's very hard to remember the mindset of 1962, which was at the outset of the civil rights movement. It was still a time of referring to "colored people" and "Negros." No use of the term "black people" yet. The idea that Louis could sing about how a black man was representing the American government, and just how ironic that was, was obvious to everyone in the audience.

With regard to the emotions swirling about the stage that evening, he observed:

> I wasn't close enough to the stage to see if Armstrong had tears, but I could tell he was emotionally moved, both by the material he was doing and the response from the audience. And it wasn't just Louis. It was also the other performers, who appeared to understand the significance of what they were doing.

Mary Ellen Harris was in her thirties in 1962 and had attended each of the first four festivals leading up to that year's. An African American, she was aware of the continued problems the Dave Brubeck Quartet had performing in the US as a mixed-race group.

> What a show, what a show *The Real Ambassadors* was! I think some of the experiences leading up to its creation were that Brubeck's group could perform anywhere in California then, but they weren't allowed to play many places in the South due to having a black bassist, Eugene Wright. Integrated bands just weren't allowed in public down there.

Harris was also keenly aware of Armstrong's plight, being the nation's most loved musical ambassador but still having to routinely face discrimination across America. She believes that this was why the Brubecks chose him as their star.

> Outside of this country he was revered, spreading the gospel of jazz, while here at home he couldn't even use a public restroom. Dave and Iola were addressing racism head on in the musical, and it hit home with us in the audience—I looked around, and at times, the audience was crying . . . and it was beautiful, absolutely beautiful, because it showed how music can touch the heart so deeply.

Vera Algoet, a singer who was twelve years old in 1962, grew up in a family where jazz was king. Like Ratner, she was attending her second Monterey Jazz Festival in 1962 with her father. She recalled:

My brother, who was an even bigger jazz fan than I, couldn't attend, so I got to go in his place. My dad and I drove down there in his little black-and-white 1956 Austin-Healy and had this amazing experience. I think we purchased *The Real Ambassadors* album right there at the venue and proceeded to wear it out after we got back home. . . . I feel so lucky to have been there—the performance was . . . it was a transcendent experience for me. It really was. I'm just amazed that it didn't ever happen again. But thinking back now, you couldn't really replace Louis Armstrong or Carmen McRae.

Algoet recalled that the vocal trio of Lambert, Hendricks & Bavan was particularly memorable. "[It] blew me away, you know, with the speed of their singing," she said. She also remembered that Iola Brubeck's voice as narrator was "a ghostly presence overlaying the whole dramatic production. She wasn't a character on the main stage, but was sort of outside [the main stage]." Asked whether or not she felt that the themes of the musical were still relevant today, she answered:

Yes, I was thrilled to find the reissued version on iTunes, and I've been listening to the music again lately. The message that people-to-people contact between different cultures is so important—that's what the arts can do. And personally, I listened to Armstrong singing "They Say I Look Like God" last night and I had tears pouring down my face. You can play it for people today, and it is still so moving. . . . I was at a voice lesson not long ago and my teacher, who is 85 years old, asked me to just sing any song to start the lesson so I sang "In the lurch, caught standing in the shadow of the church . . . " and she said, "Oh, that's a great song!"—she had never heard it before. And I can still remember the words to nearly every song [from *The Real Ambassadors*] by heart.[2]

Freelance drama critic Larry Taylor attended the show and mentioned it in commentary he wrote following the festival. As a drama critic, he was much more aware of the key elements a musical must have in order to be successful. Like the veteran Broadway producers who had pointed out problems with *The Real Ambassadors*' story line, Taylor also felt it wasn't ready for a Broadway treatment. Reflecting back fifty years after the performance, he said:

We had read about [*The Real Ambassadors* in the press] and understood the concept. Artists like Armstrong and Dizzy Gillespie had been around the world as ambassadors of jazz. It seemed natural that the

Brubecks would take the concept and do something with it. I recall they had aspirations to take it to Broadway, which never happened, but they did record an album that I purchased, and I like it. However, I didn't think the book was strong enough, even though people were very interested in the concept of going overseas with jazz, there has to be a very strong book with conflict and tension. The story seemed a little contrived at the time with mistaken identities and all that. The music was good, but the book was lacking for a Broadway show.

His reservations about the book, which had been brought up by every established Broadway producer who had evaluated the materials, demonstrate that at its best, the show's music provided an effective platform for the Brubecks and the cast to comment on the role of the jazz ambassadors and the disconnect between America's reliance on its largely African American jazz artists and the realities that they faced daily at home. The plot and story line in which the show's songs resided, however, were lacking the structure and dramatic integrity needed for an evening's entertainment in a theater. Simply stated, *The Real Ambassadors* wasn't ready to be presented as a staged musical.[3] Regardless, Taylor felt that "the high level of expectation among the crowd was largely met because the music was good and the artists performed well, so I think that for its performance at Monterey it was a success." Still, the songs and the overarching message of music's ability to bring people together clearly affected the Monterey audience and demonstrated that the underlying ideas resonated with the jazz-savvy crowd at the festival. The show was also very well received by the African American jazz ambassadors in the house that night, especially Dizzy Gillespie, who, like the Brubecks, took every opportunity to speak out publicly about civil rights.

Backstage, immediately after the performance, a host of other musicians gathered to offer congratulations. One backstage photo taken just after the performance shows a glowing Iola surrounded by that year's Monterey Jazz Festival music director, Benny Carter, and Trummy Young, looking over the score to the musical together.[4] Backstage became an impromptu party. "They were all there . . . Dizzy was there, as usual clowning around, wearing one of his 'Dizzy for Prez' T-shirts," recalled Yolande Bavan.[5]

Dave Brubeck remembered the aftermath of the show's premiere:

We took many bows. By the time we finally retreated to a tent backstage, we were surrounded by friends and fellow musicians. I remember Dizzy Gillespie giving Iola a hug and saying, "I didn't recognize you!" and to me, "Man, I couldn't believe what I was hearing" . . . all of us had tears of joy.[6]

Immediately after the performance, the cast was inundated backstage by other musicians, who wished to congratulate them on their triumph. Pictured here, *left to right*, are Benny Carter, the interim music director for the 1962 Monterey Jazz Festival, Iola Brubeck in her stage costume, and Trummy Young. Brubeck Collection, Holt-Atherton Special Collections, University of the Pacific Library, © Dave Brubeck.

The validation from not only the Black cast members but also Gillespie and other Black musicians who saw the performance showed that the musical reflected their shared experiences. Howard Brubeck, whose musical contributions had been vital to both the album recording and the Monterey performance, sent a short note to Dave and Iola, written as he was waiting for a flight to take him back to his family in Los Angeles. An excerpt reads:

> I tried to read the Gleason review over the phone to Bessie [their mother], but it was too much for me. I know you will understand when I say there are no words which will adequately express my thoughts and feelings toward this work and each of you. It is one of the greatest moments of my life to be a small part of this work.[7]

Dave and Iola Brubeck also felt the residual glow of the tremendous reception that the musical had received from the audience, the critics, and their musical peers. Shortly after the premiere, they had wooden plaques made for each cast member as thank-you gifts. Each bore an engraved brass plate with an inscription that read, "To The Real Ambassadors from Dave & Iola

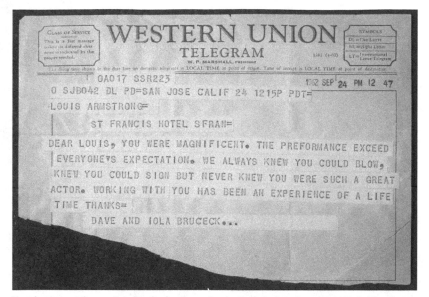

The telegram sent the morning after the show's premiere by the Brubecks to Armstrong at his San Francisco hotel, congratulating him on his musical and dramatic triumph starring in *The Real Ambassadors*. Courtesy of the Louis Armstrong House Museum, Jack Bradley Collection.

Brubeck."[8] The couple also thanked Armstrong via telegram the morning after the premiere, summarizing their view on the veteran performer's contribution to the show's success:

> Dear Louis: You were magnificent. The preformance exceed [*sic*] everyone's expectation. We always knew you could blow; knew you could sign [*sic*] but never knew you were such a great actor. Working with you has been an experience of a life time. Thanks, Dave and Iola Brubeck.[9]

Critic Ralph Gleason agreed, and he penned five columns, one for each day during the week after the festival, recapping the full range of music performed at Monterey that year, including in each a mention of *The Real Ambassadors* to remind his readers of the impact the cast had made with their socially conscious message.

The premiere of *The Real Ambassadors* was a watershed moment in Dave and Iola Brubeck's seventy-year musical and artistic partnership—a partnership that would result in numerous large-scale works for jazz combo, orchestra, and chorus. It was their first major work and was praised as providing a timely, honest take on the social, political, and cultural moment they inhabited. While there may have been criticism of the work's occasional naivete or the book's unsuitability for Broadway, on balance the premiere was a significant victory. Iola's best friend, actress Barbara Baxley, flew to Monterey for the performance, and upon her return to Weston, Connecticut, where she had a small house as a getaway from Manhattan, Baxley recounted to Cathy (Brubeck) Yaghsizian the premiere's tremendous success. She singled out Iola's striking appearance and stellar performance, and Cathy recalls her stating, "'Your mom, she looked so beautiful that night and she performed so well . . . I was so proud of her.' She told me Mom was wearing a long blue dress and how gorgeous she looked out on the stage that night."[10]

The Monterey audience response, along with the overwhelmingly positive reviews, invigorated the couple and fueled their ambitions to bring the musical to the widest possible audience as soon as possible. Writing to one of her close friends, Mary Jeanne Sauerwein, Iola said that she would soon be sending her a copy of *The Real Ambassadors* soundtrack album. Unfortunately, Mary Jeanne had missed the Monterey performance due to illness. Iola wrote, "Naturally, we missed you at Monterey. . . . I'm sorry you were ill and could not see our 'triumph' because it really was just that."[11] Her appraisal of the show mirrored the assessment of Monterey Jazz Festival cofounder Jimmy Lyons, who concluded late in 1962, "*The Real Ambassadors*' production was the most important thing the Festival had done."[12]

As the euphoria from the Monterey performance subsided, Iola and Dave Brubeck found out that there was in fact interest in taking the concert version of the show on the road. Critics had already suggested that a touring package with the original cast might be put together as an alternative way to disseminate the musical. The Brubecks were in full support of such a plan and started working to that end. At the same time, while Glaser refused to bankroll the video recording of the premiere, he had offered to investigate a television production, though surviving correspondence suggests no concrete evidence that either of these possibilities was pursued beyond the "what if" phase.

Although initially he and his staff had helped Dave meet with Satchmo and Broadway producers, Glaser shifted gears as the musical came closer to taking the stage, repeatedly lobbying to delay or block its realization. The soundtrack recording was a notable exception. Glaser backed it because it only required a few days of Armstrong's time (when he would be off the road), it provided an advance payment, and it had the potential to bring in future record royalties. The fact that *The Real Ambassadors* did see the stage lights at Monterey is a testament to the persistence of Jimmy Lyons, the Brubecks, the entire cast, and the Monterey stage crew, who worked overtime to prepare and present its stunning debut. As correspondence shows, Glaser always tried to keep his options open.

The everyday reality of life for Brubeck and his quartet meant that they were immediately back on the road after Monterey, driving from city to city, zigzagging across the Midwest. A letter from ABC's Paul Bannister dated October 4, 1962, two weeks after the show's premiere, cites a phone call with Dave Brubeck cut short because the group needed to get back in their cars to drive to Platteville, Wisconsin, to arrive in time for that day's college concert. The same letter references upcoming one-night performances in Norman, Oklahoma, Topeka, Kansas, and Dubuque, Iowa. Associated Booking was keeping the group on tour, continuing to earn money for all parties involved.[13]

The Brubecks, however, had not given up on the touring-package idea for *The Real Ambassadors*. They had instructed their attorney Michael Maloney to follow up on interest from a promoter identified as Bob Phillips and to investigate the feasibility of putting together a tour. Maloney first reached out to Joe Glaser, and it appeared that a touring package was something Glaser was willing to consider.

In a reply to Maloney dated October 5, 1962, Glaser states first that any such package must be based on an equal partnership between Brubeck and Armstrong. Maloney had evidently suggested that the ensemble might earn a $7,500 guarantee per night, against a percentage of the ticket sales. Glaser pointed out that on the so-called off nights—Monday, Tuesday, and Wednesday—it would be difficult to secure such a guarantee, and he stated that on those nights "the package may have to work for . . . as low as $5,000 a day." Interestingly, he also states, "It can be easily verified that Louis receives minimum guarantees of $2,500 to $5,000 per night on each and every performance he plays, except there are times when I allow him to appear for considerably less when he is working for friends."[14]

Such variation is attributable to fluctuations in the size of the venue and market, the night of the week, and other factors. In the letter, Glaser then outlines a prospective business partnership for a *Real Ambassadors* touring package with Armstrong and Brubeck being equal partners in the venture. He proposed a simple set of operating principles:

> I would be very happy to have a deal worked out where Dave and Louis would enter into a partnership deal—by that I mean an equal partnership, with the understanding they would buy Carmen McRae for a certain amount of money, guaranteeing her a minimum amount of 4 or 5 days a week and pay her transportation or the transportation for her group—or if a certain [greater] amount of money was paid her, she would have to pay her own transportation as it would be

understood that Louis would pay all his transportation for his entire company, such as baggage, etc. and Dave would do likewise—and that all other money would be split equally.[15]

In such a scenario, once Carmen McRae and her expenses were covered, the two bandleaders would split the remaining revenues, paying their respective band members and other tour-related expenses.

Glaser told Maloney that he was not going to share this offer yet with Dave directly, instead relying on Maloney to explore it with him. Glaser ended his proposal by stating, "I am sure you folks realize that Louis is entitled to be an equal partner in any package show he works in, and of course, he has worked in packages with Benny Goodman and other artists and he has always shared the wealth."[16]

Glaser's sincerity appears genuine, and the positive reviews at Monterey must have had the veteran manager seeing dollar signs if the same kind of response could be expected from a tour of the one-hour concert version. Still, the finances to keep a troupe of thirteen performers on the road, plus the two-thirds lower earning potential for off-night engagements Glaser mentioned, would have made the financial prospects for such a package tour somewhat risky. It would have likely taken booking the performance four or five nights a week to have a shot at being profitable. Despite factors in its favor, it still seemed risky, and the package tour idea never advanced further than the memo outlining Glaser's proposed partnership deal. With each of the headline artists already booked months in advance, McRae, Brubeck, and Armstrong all remained out on the road independently earning higher fees as individual headliners. This netted individual musicians more income—and Glaser's Associated Booking much greater agency commissions—than a potential *Real Ambassadors* package tour. With Glaser's absolute control of when, where, and with whom Armstrong would appear, the chances of booking such a tour package seemed distant at best. With little or no financial impetus to explore creating a package to market to clubs and concert promoters, ultimately Glaser and the Brubecks dropped the idea of touring with the show from their future plans.

While further stage presentation of the musical was derailed, Howard Brubeck was working apace on the folio version of *The Real Ambassadors*, soon to be released by Hansen Publications. A letter dated October 9, 1962, sent to Dave and Iola accompanied the corrected piano-vocal arrangements for each of the fifteen songs that had appeared on the Columbia LP as well as onstage at Monterey.[17] The same day, Howard Brubeck forwarded the manuscripts to Hansen with the suggestions that the publisher include the narration used at Monterey (but not on the Columbia recording) in the piano-vocal folio edition, and also that a second edition should be considered, this one a performing version of *The Real Ambassadors* with instrumental and vocal arrangements.[18] The folio was published in 1963 and included the narrator's parts as well as some production and staging advice from the Brubecks. The second edition, with detailed instrumental and vocal arrangements to match the recording, was never produced.

Dave Brubeck thought that he might keep public attention on the musical by recording a live LP featuring some of the show's music during his November 1962 tour in Great Britain. Michael Maloney outlined Brubeck's idea in a November 2, 1962, letter to Teo Macero, Brubeck's Columbia producer. "Tentatively called *Real Ambassadors in London*, there is more than enough material presently being performed by the Quartet to make a whole LP with an overseas flavor."[19] Evidently, the idea went no further—again. One other tantalizing idea to produce another version of the show survives in a short quote by Iola Brubeck, given during an interview while she was on a tour with the quartet to Australia in December 1962. After referencing just how close the Brubecks had come to staging the show in England under the guidance of Harold Davison, she dropped that "a major movie producer was working on an idea of filming it in Africa."[20]

Nonetheless, Brubeck public relations efforts continued getting press notices, as the very next day, the *Santa Barbara News-Press* printed a headline stating that the "Real Ambassadors May Go on Tour."[21] Although entertainment writer Bert Willard did not name any sources, he suggested that it might end up being produced under the auspices of the State Department, with performances in Europe, Asia, and South America, closing his article by writing that "there is a chance that it may be produced as a motion picture or TV spectacular!" Like the earlier piece by Dorothy Kilgallen, such possibilities leaked to and reported by the press put additional wind in the Brubecks' sails. Dave, usually an affable interviewee, must have spoken with Willard and voiced his dreams of how the show might be further disseminated to a broader audience than the crowd at Monterey, and possibly whispered about the filmmaker's interest, but no other written records have surfaced to provide further details of any specific plans that would have led to either of these options being realized.

As Brubeck's fame had grown, Jim Bancroft and his associates had ably helped him identify and develop additional sources of income beyond live appearance fees and record royalties. First, Bancroft had advised Brubeck to establish his own publishing company, in order to hang on to the publisher's share of his mechanical royalties as well as the public performance royalties that had been paid by Broadcast Music Inc., Brubeck's performing rights society, to Blackwood Music, a Columbia subsidiary, over the first few albums Dave recorded for Columbia. Bancroft recalled:

> Dave had signed the standard contract with Columbia and also with Blackwood Music, whereby they got the half that went to the publisher and he kept the half that belonged to the composer. Now we think of publishing companies as publishers of sheet music. Blackwood Music did not do that. They just sat there with a cash register and collected the publisher's half of the composer's royalty. It seemed to me that this was a waste of Dave's intellectual property. He owned it [exclusively] until he did something that deprived him of ownership [signing with Blackwood Music]. Fairly early in our days together, with Dave and Iola's consent and active participation, we set up a company called Derry Music Company, and that succeeded to the role that Blackwood Music might have had if we didn't set up Derry. . . . Columbia was not happy with this arrangement, because otherwise the money would have gone to them.[22]

In the same interview, Bancroft reported that Brubeck was one of a handful of artists who successfully negotiated retaining his ownership rights in the master recordings he was making for Columbia, returning to him five years after a master recording was created.

As Brubeck's career progressed, Derry Music's music licensing fees, publishing income, and public performance royalties would provide a steady, significant part of the artist's income stream, earning revenue whether or not he was out on the road. Later, Bancroft advised the Brubecks to start Kadan, Ltd., a production company set up to provide the services of the Dave Brubeck Quartet, and to also print and sell programs or other merchandise at Brubeck's concerts to further expand his ancillary earnings. Doing so provided business and tax advantages to Brubeck at a time when his earnings had increased substantially from his early days playing at Oakland's Burma Lounge to make rent money.

In 1962, a Kadan-produced Dave Brubeck Quartet concert program included a statement that *The Real Ambassadors* had not yet been produced on a theatrical stage because of the hot-button nature of its anti-segregation message. A two-page spread of photos is devoted to the soundtrack album recording, noting:

> Originally planned for a Brubeck-written Broadway show, *World Takes a Holiday*, the music is out on these recordings because the show has been labeled "controversial" by usual Broadway sources.[23]

This statement hardly fits with the facts, as none of the actual Broadway producers, including Paul Gregory, Leland Hayward, Marshall Jamison, or Josh Logan mentioned concerns about the pro-integration message in the show. It was only Columbia president Goddard Lieberson who objected strongly to the mixed-race cast and some of the lyrics. Lieberson's position as head of Columbia gave him complete control over Brubeck's recordings, and hearing the mandate to drop the interracial cast must have dismayed the Brubecks greatly. Scapegoating unnamed power brokers on Broadway may have been a convenient way for the Brubecks to avoid having to answer with the actual reasons. *The Real Ambassadors* wasn't going to be back onstage anytime soon, simply because it didn't make good business sense to remove multiple headlining artists from circulation to develop a fully staged version of the musical. And while a touring package would have been relatively easy to sell, the reduction in gross earnings to all parties would have been substantial for each musician and for ABC. Glaser's lack of genuine support for the project, the risk for any backers to underwrite the substantial development costs for a staged production, and the resistance to the show's existing book, which needed major revisions per the advice that the Brubecks had received—these were the real reasons the show could not go on. Casting blame on anonymous bad guys may have seemed the best out available, because at the time it would have been unseemly for the Brubecks to mention to their fans the complex roadblocks to realizing their dream beyond its Monterey premiere.

Blaming its controversial content didn't make sense, as the Brubecks had cited contemporary dramatic productions dealing with the issues of race and power, including the aforementioned *A Raisin in the Sun* and *The Blacks*, both of which had played successfully to New York theater audiences, albeit with all-Black casting. Paul Gregory, the first Broadway producer to encourage the Brubecks upon previewing the musical in 1957, debunked the myth fully. In a 2008 interview, Gregory clearly recalled the 1957 meeting with the Brubecks in which they discussed how to realize its production. He confirmed that from his point of view "the elements were all there for a production, except the schedules of the performers. Race wasn't the issue."[24]

Even the wildly successful 1949 Broadway musical *South Pacific* by Rodgers and Hammerstein and its hit 1958 film adaptation had addressed racial bias as a central theme of the work. The prejudice that characters Nellie Bly and Lt. Cable each grapple with throughout the musical and film adaptation demonstrated clearly that such topics were not off-limits by any means, contrary to what the Brubecks had argued. The Rodgers and Hammerstein song "Carefully Taught," sung by Cable, tried to explain how such prejudice was bred into many Americans of that era. By comparison, the social commentary in *The Real Ambassadors* was much more subtle, other than Armstrong's moving performance of "They Say I Look Like God."

In the weeks following the soundtrack album's release, reviewers began to write about the record, offering a variety of opinions. In general, most critics and jazz aficionados praised the ambitious album, but one European critic argued that the entire project was a misfire. While the music itself is mentioned in these reviews, notably, every critic speaks to the show's themes as being as important, or more so, than the music itself.

The two most substantial reviews were in the US: Dan Morgenstern writing in *Jazz* and Leonard Feather for *DownBeat*. Feather begins his five-star review by commenting, "No jazz album released in the last year has made a more immediate impression of freshness, vitality and reality than *The Real Ambassadors*." He attributes its newness and success to its embodying "the essence of jazz in its most timeless and generally acceptable form." He explains the use of jazz as a primary tool of the State Department's cultural exchange program, the worldwide popularity enjoyed by the music, and the "message of racial unity that is inherent in its nature." He praises each of the featured performers, especially the "pleasure and relief to find [Armstrong] tackling some new and ideally suited material instead of repeating the same tired old jazz festival standards." After bemoaning the then largely negative contextualization of jazz in film, which played up the unwholesome aspects of the lives of jazz musicians, he celebrates *The Real Ambassadors* as a welcome change. He applauds the lyrics and its message, stating:

> I don't know how much of the credit goes to which Brubeck for the lyrics, but the skill with which he and/or she balanced all the required elements is an object lesson for songwriters. *The Real Ambassadors* offers patriotism without chauvinism, dignity without stuffiness, humor without bitterness, music without pretentiousness. It is a much truer reflection of our society than *Porgy and Bess* ever was, and as such deserves to be presented not only on Broadway but all over the world as well.

Feather concludes his glowing review by arguing, "There has never before been anything quite like . . . the precedent setting . . . *Real Ambassadors* in the history of jazz."[25]

Morgenstern's review addresses more directly the objectives of the musical:

> In essence, the "message" of *The Real Ambassadors* is that jazz represents certain artistic and social beliefs which are identical with the ethos of true democracy. It is a plea for freedom and for the realization, long overdue, of full equality and human rights. The serious overtones are handled with considerable dignity, but are never allowed to become self-consciously rhetorical or cloying. The music swings throughout.[26]

Morgenstern had been one of the friends who had stopped by the studio before the September 1961 recording sessions were closed to nonperformers. This is where he witnessed the noteworthy spirit of collaboration, discovery, and cocreation evident in the recordings. He acknowledges the tremendous response to the musical when it premiered at Monterey, stating, "The first public performance of this musical production written for Louis Armstrong by Dave Brubeck, and his wife, Iola, was a huge success at the last Monterey Jazz Festival, and this album shows why." Citing the *esprit de corps* that shone through on the recording, Morgenstern writes, "Everybody rises to the occasion. . . . Louis' presence seems to have inspired all those around him." He gives accolades to Carmen McRae, "peerless," and Trummy Young, "featured with such impact as to have merited co-billing as a principal." Lambert, Hendricks & Ross "work so well together that one couldn't imagine anyone else" in their role. He closes his review by offering:

> This production could well become a classic. We hope *The Real Ambassadors* will be done again and again, on Broadway as well as in Festival. The record is a musical document of lasting value. And, among other things, it should once and for all silence all the innuendo about Louis Armstrong, the real ambassador and king of jazz. Don't miss this joyous experience.[27]

Writing in the *Sacramento Bee*, W. C. Glackin applauded Dave Brubeck's "melodic writing style as one of the outstanding facts of the recording" and wrote that overall, the album is "realized with humor and sentiment, satire and style, and some clever and pretty songs delivered here, for the most part, in a highly engaging way." He complained that Lambert, Hendricks & Ross were "a little unintelligible now and then, but [supply] a valuable tone of exhilaration to the record."[28]

At least two reviewers, however, were critical of the album, claiming that it was not the milestone musical event that other critics had claimed. English critic Peter Clayton opened his biting review of the album with, "This is a very strange record, but not by any means a very good one." Clayton was a British jazz critic, BBC jazz broadcaster, and author who worked for a time in various capacities for Decca Records.[29] This review was published in *Jazz News*, the newsletter of the National Jazz Federation. Clayton served as an editor for the publication around this time. He perceptively points out the irony of the album's titular jazz ambassadors carrying "the still unfulfilled American Dream to various less fortunate spots around the globe," suggesting that an element of cultural superiority lurked in the musical's basic idea: American musicians bringing jazz to African nations, from which much of the essential DNA of what would become jazz was drawn. As *DownBeat*'s Don DeMicheal had mentioned when reviewing the Monterey premiere, Clayton also viewed this as a form of naivete in the work. Clayton also complained that Armstrong's performance came across as artificial, exhibiting "terrible stiffness of voice." He opined that the rhyme schemes of the "occasionally witty but very brittle lyrics" formed an impediment to Satchmo's vocal ability, and he likened Armstrong's performance to "Noel Coward played by Steptoe & Son."[30] While Satchmo's struggle with the often complex lyrical patterns and rhyme schemes in "The Real Ambassador" was a matter of record, in Clayton's dismissal of the record, he entirely overlooked Armstrong's more natural reading of "King for a Day," his tender delivery of the ballad "Summer Song," and his moving interpretation of "They Say I Look Like God." He also appears to have been the only reviewer to question whether or not the jazz ambassadors could authentically claim to represent the freedoms that America's democracy promised when those who were African Americans, like Armstrong, could not use a public restroom or secure a hotel room in some parts of the US.

For the biblical passages sung by the Greek chorus during "They Say I Look Like God," Clayton described the result as "embarrassing," drawing readers' attention to what he identified as a more authentic reading of Christian ideals and Black culture, *Black Nativity*, a 1961 off-Broadway production by Langston Hughes. The show retells the Nativity story with an all-Black cast and musical numbers, including well-known Christmas carols, sung in gospel style.[31] Carmen McRae's contributions are described as "ill at ease," and Armstrong's trumpet contributions are described as being played "into a thick woolen sock." It's possible that the earnestness that runs through the show simply rubbed Clayton the wrong way, as he closed his review by saying, "the pity about this is that it should have been so good, and I sincerely wish it

had been a success" [emphasis in original]. While today's listeners and critics have come to appreciate genre-bending collaborations of artists who inhabit very different musical spaces, the blending of Armstrong's Dixieland-based signature sounds with the Brubecks' music, lyrics, and plotline simply didn't add up for Clayton.

Domestically, in their December 1962 issue, *HiFi/Stereo Review* magazine published an review by Joe Goldberg, who praised the stereo audio recording quality (records were still being mixed and released in both mono and stereo versions at this time) of *The Real Ambassadors* LP, but harshly criticized the Brubecks for the naivete and earnestness in the show's lyrics and tongue-in-cheek colloquialisms.

> The theme is the tribulations of jazz musicians on tour for the State Department. Like the special material of collegiate musicals, many of the lyrics are built around parochial concerns. Typical line: "O Satchmo, can it really be that you've set all people free?" Perhaps fortunately, Lambert, Hendricks and Ross mask many lines by singing too fast to be understood.
>
> The Brubecks, who are talented, and genuine in their devotion to the ideological content of the show—integration, world peace—have not mastered the wit and style that would lift such views from the limbo of banal preachment and corny jokes. According to the liner, only half the score is here, but the listener is not likely to mourn the amputation."[32]

For Goldberg, the album's concept was a dud, and its realization sophomoric. Iola had written in the LP liner notes, "Louis embodies in magnificent proportions all the elements of jazz we wanted others to understand. . . . Anyone who has been caught in Louis' spell can really believe that if he were to blast three times 'round, the walls of hate would come tumbling down!"[33] In that statement, she made clear her own belief that Armstrong's role as an ambassador of peace and unity was a viable one. However, it's clear that Goldberg was unmoved by either the use of irony in the show's musical numbers cited earlier, or the sincere beliefs that the Brubecks stated over and over in the media: that equal rights were a cause worth fighting for, in their case, through presenting Armstrong as the most powerful musical voice for tearing down the segregation that plagued America.

Moving beyond the jazz writers, on a more grassroots level, a few members of the listening public were moved by the music in the same way as the audience at Monterey. Mrs. Bette Davidson wrote a letter to Iola and Dave Brubeck citing "the astounding spiritual impact [she] experienced in listening to *The Real Ambassadors*." She went on to say that, based on what she had read in the album's liner notes, since the musical was as yet unproduced, and since it appeared to her that the musical's obvious conclusion in addressing segregation was that "something's gotta give," she enclosed a check for $100 to help put "a drop of oil in the machinery for getting it produced."[34] The head of the Brubeck Fan Club in Prestwich, Lancashire (England), wrote that many of the club's members had penned personal letters to Dave and Iola about *The Real Ambassadors*, thanking them for creating this "fabulous record."[35]

Even though reviews were predominantly positive, sales of the album were disappointing. The soundtrack to *The Real Ambassadors* was a commercial failure on LP when compared to other releases from the same era by Brubeck or Armstrong. A sales summary of the mono and stereo versions of the soundtrack LP shows that only 5,942 albums eventually sold through. Expectations for sales by Columbia, based on past sales by both Armstrong and Brubeck, were much higher, with one projection of possible sales of eighty thousand albums referenced in an internal Columbia memo in May 1962.[36] That record buyers were perplexed by the ambitious Armstrong-Brubeck pairing was further evidenced when more than eleven thousand albums were returned unsold from retailers across the US in the three years following its original release on September 1, 1962—a number that represented two returns for every unit sold.[37]

Its tepid sales resulted from two factors. The first was that without the aid of Iola Brubeck's unifying narration, the songs on the album appear to be unconnected.[38] While an attempt was made in the lengthy liner notes accompanying the album to explain the concepts upon which the show was based, not every fan would read those notes, and radio listeners, unaware of the proper context, must have been mystified by the lyrics to many of the songs. Second, stylistically, the album didn't stick to either Armstrong's Dixieland-influenced, traditional jazz repertoire, or Brubeck's more modern, West Coast jazz style enough to satisfy either artist's loyal fans.

In the 1960s, record labels would provide free promotional copies of newly released records to garner airplay, leading to sales. The actual recipients were the program directors and key disc jockeys who were viewed as tastemakers. A label representative would personally visit important stations to drop off new records and make a play to have one or more added to the station's rotation. Columbia had sent out some advance 45s earlier, but they had not proven popular with radio programmers, and as a result, *The Real Ambassadors* soundtrack, which apparently received some marketing in record trade magazines such as *Billboard*, did not earn any significant airplay.[39]

To better explain the album's concept, early in 1963, the Brubecks decided to mount their own guerilla marketing campaign to persuade disc jockeys to spin the record. They drafted an open letter to radio DJs and program directors asking for their help in presenting the musical and its concept and context to their listeners. Included in each station's mailing was a copy of Iola's narration parts from the Monterey performance. Correspondence documents that the Brubecks secured the agreement of Columbia Records to provide radio stations with the album, script, and pitch letter to help build grassroots support for the project and hopefully sell more records.[40] This campaign echoed the strategy that the couple had employed in the early 1950s to help establish the college concert tour circuit for the Dave Brubeck Quartet and the dozens of other groups who followed in their footsteps.

Dave included a personalized letter for each DJ in which he pointed out that critics had praised Iola's narration as both a unifying element for the story and also one of the high points of the production. He gave permission for the on-air talent to "adapt to your own use with my permission," challenging "those rare individuals who can program an [entire] hour . . . [to] premier for your listeners the entire story [by reading excerpts from the narration interspersed] with music. If you do not have a full hour, the script can still be helpful in giving you the setting for each tune."[41] The Brubecks hoped that by sharing the story line with listeners they might gain further attention for the work and its message. Unfortunately, there is no evidence that a substantial number of stations took them up on their idea to promote the soundtrack album in this innovative manner.

Nonetheless, even though record sales and radio airplay were far below expectations, *The Real Ambassadors* helped to advance the national conversation on human rights and racial equality. Although such benefit was distinctly noncommercial, the show's message of tolerance and change provided inspiration. As the glow from the 1962 performance faded and Brubeck and Armstrong both moved on to release newer records, the prospects for another performance of *The Real Ambassadors* dimmed, although its plea for equality was carried on by other jazz artists.

Dizzy Gillespie had been an outspoken advocate for supporting the civil rights movement, and like Brubeck, he often led an integrated band. Gillespie was one of the highest-profile artists to continue to challenge racism, using the stage as a pulpit. One example was his campaign to take the Oval Office. As had been the case the previous years, Gillespie was one of the stars of the 1963 Monterey Jazz Festival. Throughout the festival, he seemed to be everywhere—backstage and often onstage—sharing his double-entendre-laden "Diz for President" campaign with the largely supportive audience. At Monterey he was famously hawking his bumper stickers and self-described "Equality Buttons," both emblazoned with "Diz for Prez" on them throughout the weekend, and he told the audience that the proceeds from the sales were going directly to the Congress on Racial Equality (CORE), the Southern Christian Leadership Conference (SCLC), and to support Dr. Martin Luther King Jr.'s efforts. To add verisimilitude to the campaign, Jon Hendricks hopped onto the stage during Gillespie's set to sing the official campaign song, "Vote Diz," with the trumpeter's band. Sung to the tune of the Gillespie standard "Salt Peanuts," the lyric proclaimed:

> Your politics ought to be a groovier thing / Vote Dizzy! Vote Dizzy! So get a good president who's willing to swing / Vote Dizzy! Vote Dizzy!

Paralleling the concept from *The Real Ambassadors*' "King for a Day," during which global leaders are drafted into a swinging band, Gillespie told his fans and the media that if elected, he'd form a swinging cabinet made up of a who's who of jazz stars: Duke Ellington as secretary of state, Malcolm X as attorney general, Charles Mingus as secretary of peace, Mary Lou Williams as ambassador to the Vatican, and Louis Armstrong as secretary of agriculture (an inside joke referencing Satchmo's love of marijuana). He also claimed he would change the name of the president's residence from the White House to the Blues House. In private, when hanging out with other musicians, Dizzy took a more militant tone than he did with the media, stating that when elected, he would change the title of the president's residence to the "Black House."[42] While audience members and the press were entertained by Gillespie's efforts, his continued statements drew attention to the fact that in 1963 it would be implausible for any person of color to be seriously considered for the office by a major political party.

Gillespie's on- and offstage banter was ironic until it came time for him to lay out what the proceeds from his buttons and bumper stickers would be supporting. He made a point to stop during each set during the 1963 Monterey Jazz Festival to explain in a serious tone that the money raised from sales of the merchandise was vitally needed. He said, "There are certain things that some of us consider more important than music . . . things like human dignity, for instance."[43]

As the calendar moved from 1963 to 1964, it began to feel to Iola and Dave that *The Real Ambassadors* premiere at Monterey had been a once-in-a-lifetime event. As producer Paul Gregory had stated, the show's stars were fully engaged with their individual recording and touring careers, and the projected financial incentives were not sufficient to justify reassembling the cast. For all practical purposes, *The Real Ambassadors* had been placed on a shelf while each of the cast members returned to performing their regular concert repertoire.

Meanwhile, the Dave Brubeck Quartet was riding the wave of one of the most commercially successful jazz albums of all time, *Time Out*. Lifted by the hit single "Take Five," which became a million-seller, the album itself would go on to become the first jazz record to sell one million units. Using the same characteristics of his earliest popular recordings, "Take Five" juxtaposed an offbeat foundation, its rolling 5/4 meter, with an unforgettable melody conceived by Paul Desmond. This composition and the Brubeck-penned "Blue Rondo à la Turk" would become iconic parts of Brubeck's live performances for the remainder of his career. The group regularly performed instrumental versions of some of the repertoire modified for *The Real Ambassadors*, notably "The Duke," "Everybody's Jumpin'," and "Two-Part Contention." However, the group's bread and butter was still the improvisational ballet performed nightly by saxophonist Paul Desmond and Brubeck, underpinned by the tasteful rhythm section of Joe Morello on drums and Eugene Wright on bass. The group's few forays into accompanying singers were notable but rare in their catalog of record releases. Known by jazz fans as the "classic Dave Brubeck Quartet" due to their ten-year run (1958–67) of hundreds of sold-out concerts and a string of hit albums, the quartet's international celebrity overtook their vision of presenting *The Real Ambassadors* to the broader public.

While Dave Brubeck's attention was no longer directly focused on *The Real Ambassadors* in 1964, music from the show would soon reappear in two contrasting settings that year. The first would be in response to a momentous event on the US popular music charts, which occurred at the height of the so-called British Invasion, when the Beatles owned the American airwaves and hit parade. The second was due to the efforts of a group of high school students and their teachers in a small logging community in central Oregon. Concurrently, one of America's most acclaimed Black playwrights would approach the Brubecks to explore the possibility of adapting the story of *The Real Ambassadors* for television.

On May 9, 1964, Louis Armstrong once again made front-page news, this time for a musical accomplishment that would in large part redefine his later career: his version of "Hello, Dolly!" hit the number-one slot on the *Billboard* pop chart. This was no small feat, as this hit unseated the Beatles' record-setting 14-week stay at the number-one slot. "Hello, Dolly!" becoming a worldwide hit was unexpected, most of all by Armstrong himself. According to Armstrong biographer Ricky Riccardi, the song was originally recorded on December 3, 1963, at the insistence of Joe Glaser, as a favor for one of the manager's friends, Jack Lee. Armstrong had been hired to record a single to promote the musical *Hello Dolly!*, which was set to open on Broadway in January 1964. The All-Stars recorded "Got a Lot of Livin' to Do" (from the musical *Bye Bye Birdie*) and "Hello, Dolly!" in a brief session in New York for Kapp Records. After "Hello, Dolly!" was recorded, Riccardi relates that Armstrong said, "I don't like that. Can't something just be done with this record to pep it up a little or something?" As the band was leaving for its next string of one-night engagements, trombonist Trummy Young suggested that the record producer, Mickey Kapp, call a local banjo player to play on the tune. The famous banjo introduction was added, after which Kapp overdubbed some strings. The Broadway production of *Hello, Dolly!* opened on January 16, 1964, with Carol Channing in the lead role, and Kapp immediately released the All-Stars' recording of the show's most memorable tune, but with the intention of that tune serving as the B side to the better-known "Got a Lot of Livin' to Do."

The session was all but forgotten by Armstrong and the All-Stars until a few weeks after the record's release. While the band was crisscrossing the Midwest by bus, audience members starting calling out "Hello, Dolly!" during Armstrong's February 1964 sets. Armstrong and the All-Stars were flummoxed by the request, having forgotten their recording session two months prior. The demands became so insistent that bassist Arvell Shaw told Louis, "Well you remember that date we did a few months ago in New York? One of the tunes was called 'Hello Dolly!'; it's from a Broadway show." Armstrong requested that a copy of the record be flown out to the band's next stop. The band refreshed their memory of the tune, and that night when they launched into the introduction, "people were already clapping, they knew what it was," according to All-Star drummer Danny Barcelona. Remembering the night they first played the song onstage, All-Star clarinetist Joe Darensbourg said that Louis "had to take about eight curtain calls, so he knew right off he had a hit. They wouldn't let him off the stage."[44]

That the sixty-three-year-old jazzman was able to knock the Beatles off the top of the charts showed just how much Satchmo's unique vocal stylings still resonated with the listening public. Popular tastes had shifted dramatically in the music world with the onset of the British Invasion, the period from 1963 to 1967 when UK pop groups dominated the US sales and airplay charts.[45] During the British Invasion, British bands including the Beatles, the Rolling Stones, the Animals, the Kinks, Herman's Hermits, and the Dave Clark

Five were ascendant, alongside a few notable US exceptions, including the rapidly growing roster of Motown artists producing top-ten hits. American teens swooned over the British groups, with the boys wanting to emulate the musicians and the girls falling in love with the well-dressed UK invaders. Among the British Invasion groups, the Beatles were the most commercially successful, as on April 4, 1964, they became the first and only pop group to occupy the top five chart positions on the *Billboard* Top-100 Chart. In order from the top spot down, "Can't Buy Me Love," "Twist and Shout," "She Loves You," "I Want to Hold Your Hand," and "Please, Please Me" further cemented the Beatles as household names across America. Coming up with an artist and a song to dethrone the Beatles occupied the mind of every American label, and it was Louis Armstrong who did it.

"Hello, Dolly!" became the best-selling single of Armstrong's career. It also further increased the demand for Armstrong and his All-Stars, making any thought of staging *The Real Ambassadors* less likely. The association of Armstrong with the *Hello, Dolly!* musical was so strong that people who had bought tickets to the Broadway show demanded—and received—refunds when they discovered that Satchmo was not in the Broadway cast.[46] Notably, every label that had unreleased recordings by Armstrong in their vaults rushed out many singles to try to ride the coattails of this landmark success. Columbia was no exception, earmarking the unreleased *Real Ambassadors'* track "Nomad" as its choice for a single. Released April 1964 in the US, UK, Netherlands, and Italy, and backed with Armstrong's meditative reading of the Brubecks' "Summer Song," the record resulted in neither noteworthy sales nor renewed interest in putting *The Real Ambassadors* back on a course toward production.[47] Although Satchmo could knock the Beatles out of the number-one chart position, his renditions of two of the songs from the show failed to catch either the public's or radio programmers' ears.

The only promising inquiry that came in was in mid-1964, when Robert Nemiroff, the producing partner and ex-husband of playwright Lorraine Hansberry, inquired about a possible collaboration on the musical. Hansberry's groundbreaking 1959 play, *A Raisin in the Sun*, had become a significant hit with critics and audiences. The Brubecks had referenced it frequently in dialogue with potential backers as proving that the topic of segregation wasn't taboo on Broadway. The *New York Times* applauded Hansberry's work, stating that it "changed American theater forever."[48] The play ran for 530 performances on Broadway and was the first Broadway drama to be written by a Black woman, as well as the first directed by a Black man, Lloyd Richards. The plot addressed the dynamics within one Black family trying to better their lot in life, as they experienced intolerance over their decision to move into an all-white subdivision. Richards recalled that "it was the first [Broadway] play that black audiences were drawn to."⁴⁹

The Brubecks were enthusiastic about the opportunity to collaborate, since the messages in *The Real Ambassadors* and *A Raisin in the Sun* were closely aligned. Iola believed that the inquiry might be a preview of a potentially fruitful meeting of the minds between the Brubecks, Hansberry, and Nemiroff.⁵⁰ In a series of telephone calls, Robert Nemiroff expressed his and his ex-wife's interest in a possible collaboration to adapt *The Real Ambassadors* into a one-hour television special to pitch to one of the major television networks. Sadly, Lorraine Hansberry's rapidly deteriorating health created a gap in the discussions, and the young playwright fought a losing battle with cancer, passing away in January 1965 at the age of thirty-four. Nemiroff restarted the dialogue later that year, as a memorandum from Iola Brubeck to then-Brubeck attorney Michael Maloney documented. Iola wrote, "Bob Nemiroff phoned [again] about the possibility of presenting *The Real Ambassadors* to a network as an hour special. Nothing certain, but he is working on it and wanted to see if we were still interested—which we are."⁵¹ No further record of any correspondence exists between the Brubecks and Nemiroff, leading to the conclusion that the networks weren't interested in such a production.

At the same time as the Nemiroff-Brubeck dialogue was underway, a group of teenage actors, musicians, and dancers took on the challenge of staging the musical in the small town of Lebanon, Oregon. A copy of *The Real Ambassadors* LP had been purchased by a young bass player, Paul Melott, who had just begun his music studies at the University of Oregon. Paul was intrigued by the recording and its message of equality. Paul's sister, Colleen Melott Dimmitt, was at that time the choral director at Lebanon Union High School in Lebanon, Oregon, a logging community of six thousand, eighty miles southeast of Portland. Paul called his sister and asked if she might consider using *The Real Ambassadors* as the spring musical for the high school. Dimmit wrote a letter to the Brubecks seeking permission, and they enthusiastically approved. Iola put together a package and sent a few copies of the original script from Monterey directly to her, and Dimmit then purchased copies of the Hansen piano-vocal edition prepared by Howard Brubeck so students could learn the score, plotline, and dialogue.⁵²

The students learned all the songs included in the printed edition note by note—no small task for a group of thirteen- to seventeen-year-olds, as even the original professional cast who recorded the album and premiered it at Monterey had commented that many of the songs were difficult to perform. Dimmit enlisted the support of five additional faculty members to assist with the staging. Three of the physical education teachers helped to choreograph and incorporate four dance numbers into the show, and two art faculty members guided their students to build scenery, construct staging, and help with lighting. In so doing, the number of students in the cast and production staff expanded to seventy-five.[53] This staging was the closest version to the Brubecks' original vision ever realized. The dancers wore costumes representative of the cultures they portrayed. "We even found someone to play the bagpipes for the Highland fling dance routine," Dimmitt laughed.[54]

Dimmitt recalled that the students responded strongly to the musical's social justice message and made the decision to appear in blackface—something that was still socially acceptable, even though a campaign by the NAACP had been educating Hollywood and Broadway that using white performers in blackface was no longer acceptable.[55] Still, popular television shows like *Amos 'n' Andy* (1951–53, first run; 1954–66, syndicated reruns) and the character of the valet Rochester on the *Jack Benny Show* (1950–65) perpetuated certain racial stereotypes. Even though Hollywood and Broadway had mostly eliminated blackface by the 1960s, Dimmitt's students felt that performing in blackface made their presentation more authentic:

> The students just accepted the premise of the jazz ambassadors being Black and representing their country . . . so it made sense for the students playing the lead roles to appear in blackface, in order to properly represent the original casting by the Brubecks. No one questioned the decision . . . in 1964 Lebanon was a community removed from racial strife.[56]

The original program cover for the Lebanon High School performance included a graphic modeled on the Hansen edition cover art, depicting a Black person and a white person's right hands joined in friendship on top of a red, white, and blue crest to symbolize racial equality as being an aspirational American value.[57]

So while the professional opportunities tested by Columbia Records' release of two singles from *The Real Ambassadors* and the potential one-hour television adaptation with Lorraine Hansberry and Bob Nemiroff failed to reignite interest in the show, a group of dedicated teenagers in a small Oregon logging community embraced the music and the message that Iola and Dave Brubeck had crafted and made it their own, reflecting the timeliness and musicality of the work. *The Real Ambassadors'* story didn't end in rural Oregon, however. Instead, a long pause ensued until it was rediscovered nearly three decades later as a forgotten gem in the extensive Brubeck catalog.

The concept of developing larger-scale works and imbuing them with some form of social or spiritual commentary appealed to both Dave and Iola Brubeck. In a 2009 interview, they agreed that this was due in part to the impact that seeing the audience reaction to *The Real Ambassadors'* Monterey premiere had on them.[58] With the tremendous successes of *Time Out* and subsequent Columbia LPs, the Brubecks realized they were at a moment when Dave could shift gears in his career. He was ready to concentrate on creating more serious, long-form contemporary works for larger ensembles and choirs while reducing the amount of time he spent on the road.

As a result, the members of the classic version of the Dave Brubeck Quartet—saxophonist Paul Desmond, bassist Eugene Wright, and drummer Joe Morello—were informed by Brubeck at the end of 1966 that he would be disbanding the group at the end of 1967. For more than fifteen years, touring had been Dave Brubeck's way of life, and it had taken its toll. Biographer Fred Hall recounted Brubeck's heavy touring schedule from 1951 to 1967:

> In many instances, it meant doing two programs a day, getting to the next stop, setting up and playing that night, then packing it up and going to another city for the same routine. Dave hated it. It meant being away from Iola, a growing family, and the home he loved. To Dave, that was the heaviest price to pay for the career that was ascending steadily toward its zenith.[59]

The classic Brubeck Quartet played its final overseas engagement on November 13, 1967, in Paris. The group's final stateside concert was given in Pittsburgh on December 26, 1967. One more factor pushing Brubeck to disband the classic quartet was that Paul Desmond's drinking had become so problematic that he started missing concert appearances due to being too drunk to function. A clearly distraught Iola wrote to Jack Higgins, one of Harold Davison's agents, in advance of the quartet's fall 1967 tour of the UK and Europe that "[Paul] missed two engagements . . . he hadn't sobered up enough to know what day it was."[60] Clearly, something had to change, and Brubeck knew that he was also primed to move on to new challenges that would follow in the footsteps of *The Real Ambassadors*. In addition to planning to spend more time at home with his family, Brubeck was also ready to dedicate a substantial portion of his energy to composing contemporary music that would blend his jazz roots with classical forms. His first large-scale composition had already been in development during the final year of the quartet's touring.

It was a biblically inspired oratorio, *The Light in the Wilderness*. As she had for *The Real Ambassadors*, Iola worked in tandem with Dave and adapted Bible passages for its libretto. She drew on the sections that serve as the core of Christian faith: Christ's forty days in the desert and resultant temptation by Satan, the Sermon on the Mount, the selection of the disciples, and God's commandment to love your enemies as you love your friends. The seventy-minute work called for a full orchestra, a mixed chorus of one hundred voices, organ, and Indian and Middle Eastern instruments. After its well-received February 1968 premiere by the Cincinnati Symphony under the direction of Erich Kunzel, the work caught the ear of orchestral conductors far and wide. *The Light in the Wilderness* would reportedly go on to log more than one hundred performances in the next four years across the US, Europe, and Australia. Brubeck found a new musical métier in which he would be able to successfully compose, perform, and record a series of ambitious large-scale musical works that combined chorus, orchestra, and jazz ensemble. The struggle for human rights, equality, and the environment would all be a source of inspiration for these and other works the couple would create together.

Brubeck remained in demand as a performer, resulting in a limited return to touring and recording with a new Dave Brubeck Quartet in 1968. Fred Hall explains that George Wein was planning a festival in Mexico, and the promoter would not agree to back the show unless Brubeck would perform. Wein put a finer point on the matter when he told Brubeck, "I need you, Dave, in Mexico. They won't take the festival unless you come. You're gonna put a lot of guys out of work unless you sign on!" Since Wein had been a tireless promoter of Brubeck, often booking him to perform on his various Newport Jazz Festival tour packages that traveled worldwide, Brubeck felt an obligation to help. Wein had already booked baritone saxophonist Gerry Mulligan and suggested that he and Dave anchor the quartet. Dave had been impressed by the chops of bassist Jack Six, and Wein's wife, Joyce, recommended British drummer Alan Dawson to round out the group.[61] Six and Dawson became longtime members of the new Dave Brubeck Quartet. Alto saxophonist Bobby Militello came onboard in 1981, after Mulligan and clarinetist Bill Smith (who had been part of Brubeck's postwar experimental octet in the San Francisco Bay Area) had each served a stint on reeds.[62]

Dave Brubeck now had the best of both worlds: he reserved the time and energy to focus on his contemporary compositions while Iola helped to manage his career with the help of attorney James Bancroft and his associates. Iola had managed Dave's business affairs and finances exclusively, aside from the period 1956–59 when Mort Lewis served as manager. When Lewis resigned to manage musical acts including the Brothers Four and Simon & Garfunkel, Iola resumed charge of the family business. The couple insisted on a greatly reduced touring and performance schedule for the new quartet, allowing Dave adequate time for his family and for music creation.

In 1975, Dave met Russell Gloyd while performing with the Dallas Symphony. Gloyd was serving as manager of operations for the orchestra and coordinated all the details of Brubeck's collaboration with the symphony. The two musicians clicked. In 1976 when Dave returned to Texas for another performance, he asked Russell to come on board as a multifunctional manager-conductor-producer for his musical projects. He served as a critical intermediary to the orchestras, concert promoters, musicians, and record labels, all of whom engaged in presenting the Brubecks' contemporary classical and jazz efforts.[63] Gloyd would hold this position for thirty-six years, until Brubeck's 2012 passing, touring the world again and again with the Brubecks.

The Brubecks' commitment to human rights continued to be a hallmark of their careers. While *The Real Ambassadors* gathered dust in the Brubecks' music library, three Brubeck children, Darius on keyboards, Chris on electric bass and trombone, and Dan on drums, performed and toured with their father during the 1970s. The all-Brubeck group was billed as the New Brubeck Quartet, and as such agreed to a 1976 tour of South Africa, then facing a long-standing cultural boycott by international artists due to the its system of racial discrimination, called apartheid.[64] It had been eighteen years since the classic Dave Brubeck Quartet had to turn down a lucrative offer to play a week's worth of concerts in South Africa, since Dave insisted on playing with an integrated band and would not hire a white substitute for bassist Eugene Wright. This time around, Dave and Iola agreed to travel to South Africa even though it was still under apartheid rule, since they were able to include a contractual stipulation that the group's performances would be given to integrated audiences. In this way, they hoped to draw attention once again to the absurdity of segregation policies such as apartheid. Darius Brubeck recalled:

> Dave also insisted on adding a local, black bass player so that Chris could be featured on trombone on certain numbers and a local black opening act that would appear at every concert before the New Brubeck Quartet took the stage. I don't think the promoters, Wright & Benn, had any problems with this and they booked the venues that were licensed for black and white audiences as a special exception for international shows. However, such a provision did not guarantee that black and

white jazz fans would actually be in the same room at the same time as we all later found out.[65]

All went according to plan during the group's first concerts in Johannesburg, and Black South African bassist Victor Ntoni performed with the group to integrated houses there.[66] The Malombo Jazzmen, a famous local Black group, was the opening act. However, when the entourage arrived in Capetown, problems started to emerge. First, the group learned they would have to play some concerts to white audiences and others to Black audiences. In an article titled "Angry Brubeck Slams Apartheid," journalist Aggrey Klaaste reported:

> Dave Brubeck, the American jazz pianist, is a disenchanted man. The reason? The segregated shows he has to perform in Johannesburg. Brubeck feels he has been let down by his backers who did not give him a full picture of South African entertainment . . . he said he was under the impression he would be performing to multiracial audiences.[67]

Sounding remarkably like some of the interviews Brubeck had given in 1960 as he and Iola were immersed in creating *The Real Ambassadors*, he is quoted in that article saying, "The real law all over the world should be that we are all equal. If we can play to mixed audiences in this country, I can assure you that all my friends would want to come here."[68]

Things got worse when Iola received a call at their hotel from an anonymous man threatening violence if the group performed there onstage with Black musicians. The caller was a right-wing supporter of apartheid, not a South African who supported the cultural boycott. Such a call was intended to intimidate the Brubecks into canceling the rest of their tour, since Dave's requirements for a mixed-race group to perform for integrated audiences flew in the face of South Africa's strict apartheid restrictions. Dave recalled:

> It wasn't so easy in South Africa. But, it was a signed contract that the audience would be integrated. And, the first night we were there [in Johannesburg], Iola got a call from an organization saying, "We're going to gradually murder or kill your husband or your sons if you play tonight."
>
> Iola said that was the first time she ever got cold feet and couldn't get warm—hearing this conversation, and knowing that I was going to play. And, I told our sons, "Don't stand too close together. If we take a bow, just spread out . . ." The police came and searched the building with dogs. They were scattered through the crowd. On each side of the

curtain were detectives to pull the curtain in, and their eyes were on that crowd all night. The caller had told Iola, "If we don't shoot one of them or murder one tonight, we'll get them tomorrow night."

My contract required the concert would be integrated and that I would have a South African bass player, Victor Ntoni. And, I said to him, "You don't have to go on and go through this. But we'll go on." And he said, "No way. I'm going out there with you." So, I played a duet with just Victor. And, he said, "You know, my brother was killed in Soweto, and I know certain things they'll do. But, they won't do anything. They'll be afraid to do anything to you. So, don't be afraid."[69]

Victor Ntoni's courage in performing regardless of the death threats is an example of just how much Black South Africans desired an end to apartheid.[70] When the group got to the final stop of their three-week tour of South Africa, the authorities in Durban informed them that they could perform for white-only audiences and that no audience integration was possible. This proved to be a deal-breaker for the group, who decided not to bow to such pressure. Rather than play for an all-white audience, the group decided to cancel the final concerts in Durban and depart South Africa. Brubeck's frustration was evident as he spoke to a local reporter for the *Durban Times* just before the group was leaving:

I blame myself entirely, when I signed the contract I was aware that I wasn't to appear in front to totally integrated audiences, but I was told it would be in front of the most integrated audiences possible.[71]

Brubeck said that it was one of the few times when he had signed an agreement without knowing exactly what was in it. He continued, "We didn't get any money" for the canceled shows, "but I think I did the right thing."[72] Throughout the group's tour, because the ensemble included a Black South African musician, media reporting on the controversy surrounding the tour served the same purpose as *The Real Ambassadors*: it drew attention to issues of inequality and the absurd limits segregation placed on people.

Having endured death threats and government restrictions, the Brubecks had done their best to chip away at the power that apartheid held over South Africa at that time. The seeds planted during their 1976 South African tour would bear fruit a few years later. The Brubecks' oldest son, Darius, had married a South African, Cathy. In 1982, the couple traveled to South Africa to visit Cathy's family. While there, he called an acquaintance, who was head of the music department at the University of Natal (now the University of

KwaZulu-Natal). Darius was invited to apply for a position there as a lecturer in music theory, which he was offered with an implicit understanding that once he joined the faculty, the two would expand the music department's jazz curriculum. Darius accepted the position, and in 1983, he and his wife relocated to Durban, where the university is situated. By 1984, he had helped to found the first university jazz studies program in Africa.[73] He worked hard to make jazz education accessible to college-age students, as well as deeply motivated older students, some of whom were working musicians who could benefit from learning theory and receiving more formal music training. In 1989, as a result of the high-profile international acclaim accorded to the Jazzanians, a multiracial student ensemble from the program, Darius and Cathy persuaded the university to create the Centre for Jazz and Popular Music, which further transformed the cultural landscape into a true multicultural quilt more representative of Africa's rich heritage.[74]

CHAPTER 16

REDISCOVERING
THE REAL AMBASSADORS

While Darius was blazing new trails helping to establish jazz in South Africa's higher education system, *The Real Ambassadors* remained largely forgotten, until the compact disc boom of the early 1990s. During that time, in a rush to capitalize on the new format, record labels dug through their vaults to reissue recordings for listeners eager to upgrade their music collections. Columbia Records hired producer John Snyder to put together a reissue of the 1962 *Real Ambassadors* soundtrack album. The 1994 compact disc release featured four additional cuts that were not on the original album, offering fans a complete set of all the songs recorded in the September–December 1961 sessions, including Armstrong's spoken-word rendition of "Lonesome." Satchmo's poignant reading of Iola's text echoed that moment in December 1958 when he had performed the lyric for Brubeck. The recording demonstrates Armstrong's dramatic talents:

> All of my life, I've been lonely.
> I'll go way back in my past.
> I'll tell you about Lonesome,
> How the winters last and last.
> I know the loneliest autumns,
> Watching the leaves slowly turn,
> Sad as the tag end of summer,
> When dreams with the leaves will burn.
> I've stood alone in springtime,
> High up on a hill,
> Cried in the rain in springtime,
> Cause no one's there to share the thrill.
> There a certain glory in summer,
> Quiet contagious joy.

There is a silent story in summer,
That calls the mind of a young boy.
You fell in love in summer,
Then grew up far too fast.
Still he returns each summer,
To visit in the past.
The past.
The past.

The recording is unlike anything else in Armstrong's massive catalog: he played the song's melody on trumpet, accompanied by Brubeck, then over-dubbed the lyrics as a recitation, rather than singing the melody.[1] One can hear the emotions developed over a lifetime by Satchmo as a touring Black artist who had experienced so many forms of discrimination yet still hung on to a joy for his life as a musician and optimist. Armstrong biographer Ricky Riccardi sums up the chilling effect:

> Though "Summer Song" is about as melancholy as a song can be, "Lonesome" really has some deep, low notes. Perhaps Brubeck toyed with the idea of using his Quartet to back Pops on this one, but in the end, someone had the great idea of having Pops play the melody on the trumpet while overdubbing his monologue on top of it. The result is almost an Armstrong sensory overload . . . he's coming at you from all angles! Having him just speak the words without alluding to anything that remotely resembles a melody gives the song a chilling quality . . . the words of "Lonesome" should be written down for it truly is much more a poem than a song.
>
> It's a completely straight-faced performance, though he manages a slight chuckle after mentioning the "young boy." His voice goes way down for the final repetitions of "the past." He sounds tired and scarred, but it's just the true sign of Armstrong's acting ability. He was marvel-ous at conveying drama and "Lonesome" is one of his finest moments.[2]

Reflecting on this performance, one can imagine the dimension Armstrong would have brought to a fully realized musical theater production of *The Real Ambassadors*.

The reissue also included Carmen McRae's alternate reading of "Summer Song," an abbreviated version clocking in at nearly a minute less than Arm-strong's performance, in which he repeats the bridge and a verse. McRae's reading is more delicate and understated, and it showcases how she could

infuse lyrics with extra meaning through her gift for phrasing and inflec-
tion. The other previously unreleased tracks included the 45-rpm version of
"Nomad," whose lyrics depict Dave Brubeck's experience while staying in
Kabul, Afghanistan, on his 1958 State Department–sponsored tour. He heard
the muffled beat of drums and a lone flute as nomadic shepherds drove their
herds through the city on their way to the mountains. Brubeck described it as
the "weirdest sound I ever heard."[3] Joe Morello lays down a Latin-style beat
using his toms, and clarinetist Joe Darensbourg conjures up visuals of a snake
charmer with his harmonic minor introduction, leading into Armstrong's
bouncy interpretation. An instrumental version of the song had appeared
on the quartet's 1958 release, *Jazz Impressions of Eurasia.*

The fourth and final addition on the 1994 reissue was "You Swing, Baby,"
a duet featuring McRae and Armstrong set to the melody of Brubeck's well-
known standard "The Duke." The timing and playful exchange between the
two singers show off their natural chemistry. Satchmo takes two verses on
trumpet, staying close to the melody while adding a few flourishes. The song
concludes with the following passage:

> **Pops**: When you send me, I stay gone. People ask me "what I'm on."
> **Rhonda**: To quote a phrase from ol' Satchmo, if ya' gotta ask, then
>   you'll never know!
> **Pops**: [ad lib—"I'm in love"]
> **Pops**: You swing, baby, you swing for me. I vote you soul mate of the
>   century.
> **Rhonda**: Alone I sing a melody . . .
> **Pops**: But it takes two for harmony.
> **Together**: Singing, swinging, our lives complete . . . as long as you're in
>   rhythm with the consummate beat. Living, loving, the human race
>   . . . this makes this crazy, mixed up world a swinging place.

In this lyric, Iola cleverly included Armstrong's oft-cited rejoinder to the
question he had often been asked: "What is jazz?" His famous answer was
always, "If you gotta ask, then you'll never know." The fun Carmen and Louis
were having on this recording is palpable, so it was a loss that the song never
made it into the Monterey performance.

While the addition of these four numbers to the Brubeck catalog was
noteworthy, it was of greater import that the CD reissue brought the musical
back into the consciousness of the jazz community. A new generation of jazz
musicians too young to know about its historic 1958 performance recognized
that the work was truly groundbreaking, and its message of tolerance and

equality still resounded more than a half century after its creation. Writing about the CD reissue for AllMusic.com, critic Scott Yanow awarded it a four-star rating and characterized the work as "a largely upbeat play full of anti-racism songs that celebrated human understanding." He cautions listeners who are familiar with the cast members not to come to the disc with too many expectations, as "Paul Desmond is nowhere to be found, Louis Armstrong does not play that much trumpet here, and Lambert Hendricks and Ross essentially function as background singers." He does praise the duets between McRae and Armstrong as making a potent team, concluding by offering that the disc reveals "many touching and surprising moments."[4]

The CD sold a total of 5,189 copies in the two-year period following its 1994 rerelease, nearly as many as the original album, and reported a negligible fifty-nine copies returned to Columbia for credit, only 1 percent of albums shipped.[5]

In 1999, Dave and Iola Brubeck decided to partner with their alma mater, the University of the Pacific, to found the Brubeck Institute. The purpose of the institute would be to foster the next generation of jazz artists through a one- or two-year scholarship program in jazz performance, the establishment of the Brubeck Collection (one of the world's largest archives dedicated to a single jazz artist), a Summer Jazz Colony to bring together gifted high school–aged jazz musicians from all over the world to study and perform for a week under the direction of established jazz pedagogues, and the annual Brubeck Festival. The festival combined performances by world-renowned artists such as Wynton Marsalis and the Lincoln Center Jazz Orchestra, Regina Carter, the Clayton-Hamilton Big Band, Pete Escovedo, Al Jarreau, and dozens of other noted artists, including a number of memorable performances by Brubeck and his quartet. Music from *The Real Ambassadors* was prominently featured in the 2007 festival's programming, which was billed as "Words and Music," with the Saturday night concert focused on the vocal repertoire cowritten by Dave and Iola Brubeck and featuring Roberta Gambarini singing with the Dave Brubeck Quartet. The institute has also sponsored talks and presentations by jazz scholars and journalists about the important role that jazz plays in the fabric of American culture and society.[6]

As the fortieth anniversary of the show's premiere approached in 2002, Tim Jackson, who had succeeded Jimmy Lyons as the Monterey Jazz Festival's general manager, suggested a historical salute to *The Real Ambassadors*. With Brubeck producer Russell Gloyd helping to prepare newly updated arrangements, a five-song suite was prepared, to include some of the show's most notable pieces, designed to introduce the characters of Pops and Rhonda to a twenty-first-century audience. The Dave Brubeck Quartet first played a six-song set, partway through which bassist Christian McBride stepped in for regular Brubeck bassist Michael Moore and Chris Brubeck came on to add his trombone to the mix. Brubeck drummer Alan Dawson and alto sax player Bobby Militello also performed in the ensemble.[7]

Midway through the set, actor and director Clint Eastwood came onstage to introduce Dave and Iola Brubeck, mentioning that the couple had just celebrated their sixtieth wedding anniversary. Eastwood then turned the microphone over to Iola. She began by stating that their performance would be "an homage to those original ambassadors who were here in Monterey forty years ago."[8] She introduced the vocal trio of Fred White, Lynne Fiddmont-Lindsey, and Lamont Van Hook, then set the music in motion with this cue:

> *The Real Ambassadors* is a story of a jazz musician on a State Department tour whose plane lands in an African village, and when the character played by Louis Armstrong is mistaken for an official US diplomat, the question is asked, "Who's the real ambassador?"[9]

At that moment, the voice of Louis Armstrong soared over the capacity audience as the band launched into the first verse of "The Real Ambassador," with Louis's originally recorded voice added to the mix. As the song continued, the audience viewed a montage of photos of Satchmo taken at both the 1962 premiere and the rehearsal the week before it. The audience responded enthusiastically and the effect was electric. Jazz critic Scott Yanow reported, "The most haunting moment in this partial recreation was on one number when the vocal trio sang a chorus and then Satch (from a recording) sang the next one as if he were actually there!"[10]

After this number, Iola continued her remarks, noting that the show had personal songs and ballads that delineated the development of each of the key characters—"Summer Song" for the character of Pops and "My One Bad Habit" for Rhonda, as portrayed by Carmen McRae in the original cast. Vocalist Lizz Wright then stepped onstage to perform Rhonda's signature tune, "My One Bad Habit." Chris Brubeck recalled that "Wright's performance of that song was really magical. Her voice reminded me of young Ella [Fitzgerald] . . . the tune fit her voice like a glove and it went over like gangbusters."[11] Next, Iola told the audience of the original pairing of Armstrong and McRae: "Together, they were an incomparable swinging duo, and this was especially true on their duet, 'You Swing, Baby.'" She invited Byron Stripling, playing the role of Pops, to join Lizz Wright onstage, with special guest Roy Hargrove joining the ensemble to perform on trumpet for that number.

Iola then summarized the joyous reactions to Pops's musical takeover of the African village: "In our story, Louis Armstrong works his magic, causing the entire world to declare a holiday."[12] The band kicked into the finale of "Swing Bells," transitioning into the high-energy "Blow Satchmo." Stripling picked up his trumpet, joining Chris Brubeck, Bobby Militello, and Roy Hargrove to provide a four-horn, wailing New Orleans–inspired musical tapestry, over which the vocal trio performed Iola's biblically infused lyrics. At the song's conclusion, the audience erupted into a lengthy ovation. As it began to subside, a close-up photo of Armstrong was projected, over which he sang the show's closing lines, "Now I leave you / Now I go / Now I guess you know as much as old . . . Satch . . . mo," supported by Christian McBride playing a bowed string bass countermelody.

As Satchmo's voice faded, without missing a beat Dave Brubeck picked up the musical thread and launched into a meditative solo improvisation that served as an elegant and moving coda to Armstrong's memory and the tremendous impact that he and the original cast had forty years ago. As Brubeck concluded this homage, the group immediately launched into the Dave Brubeck Quartet's signature set closer, "Take Five," with Lizz Wright and Byron Stripling trading lines, singing the lyrics Iola had penned for the tune. After the rollicking "Take Five" ended, there was a lengthy ovation from the audience as the artists all took their bows and the curtains were drawn. Yanow confirmed that some of the magic that had occurred at the show's 1962 premiere returned: "Brubeck looked so happy throughout the show (for which Iola had written the lyrics), which concluded with the entire company playing and singing 'Take Five.' As the curtains closed, Dave Brubeck could be seen hugging each of the performers."[13] As the applause continued, the curtains reopened to reveal the show's creators, Dave and Iola Brubeck, together for a final curtain call.[14]

In 2004, a book was published offering an in-depth appraisal of the role and impact of America's jazz ambassadors. Its author, historian Penny Von Eschen, devoted a chapter to *The Real Ambassadors* and its unique position as a complete work devoted to the role of artists in the world of Cold War global politics. Her book *Satchmo Blows Up the World: Jazz Ambassadors Play the Cold War* looked back at the Brubecks' 1958 State Department–sponsored tour and the resultant musical that drew on those travel experiences. She was one of the first scholars to single out the musical as an important work that helped to document jazz and cultural diplomacy history at the time that history was being made. Von Eschen offered in-depth analysis and context for the show's lyrics, set in the Cold War milieu. She argued that the show and its message should be reexamined today and seen as an activist victory for social justice, not simply an attempt to write a hip, jazz-influenced musical. Covering the history of the Eisenhower-initiated jazz ambassador program, Von Eschen skillfully documented how a wide variety of American artists used their cultural and political agency when in foreign nations to espouse their own attitudes and views about civil rights, capitalism, and in a few cases what was wrong in America, even though Uncle Sam was footing the bill for their touring. As a result, jazz fans from Thailand to Turkey got a much more authentic and nuanced perspective on race relations in the US than the more sanitized version being offered by the State Department.

In 2008, the annual Brubeck Festival would stage concerts and events in Stockton, California, and Washington, DC. The 2008 Brubeck Festival was a special celebration of the fiftieth anniversary of Brubeck's lengthy and impactful State Department–sponsored jazz ambassador tour. From March 31 to April 5, the series of concerts in Stockton featured artists whose origins and influences were truly global. The lineup featured Japanese American pianist Hiromi, a South African–born bansuri flute artist of Indian origin, Deepak Ram, and the Pete Escovedo Orchestra performing its signature Latin jazz. It also included a group of college-age jazz all-stars from Russia dubbed the Open World Jazz Octet, representing some of that nation's finest young artists. The visit of the Russian jazz ensemble was funded in part by the National Endowment for the Arts, through a grant supporting cultural exchanges. When the festival relocated to the nation's capital, some of the music from *The Real Ambassadors* was performed by a high school vocal ensemble from Connecticut's Hartford Academy of Arts, who billed themselves as "The Real Ambassadors," under the direction of Diane Mower. Their April 10 performance was at a sold-out Coolidge Auditorium in the Library of Congress and hosted by the National Endowment for the Arts chairman Dana Gioia and James H. Billington, the librarian of Congress.

In an introduction for the program, Brubeck stated, "The effect of our first cultural exchange tour lasted with me for a half century." He continued by quoting Pops's lyrics from the song "The Real Ambassador":

> All I do is play the blues and meet the people face to face,
> I'll explain, and make it plain, I represent the human race,
> And don't pretend no more.

Brubeck also explained that regardless of the social changes needed in the 1950s and '60s, his own role as a jazz ambassador was a pragmatic way to help foster social or political change:

I was aware in 1958 that we were being used in the Cold War propaganda battle, and acutely aware that Eugene [Wright] did not enjoy all the privileges that the rest of our group did in the U.S., particularly in the still segregated South. Yet, Eugene and I agreed that our mission was as President Eisenhower had declared it: "People-to-People." And it was on that level we tried to communicate. We found common interest with musicians from different cultures. In a subtle way, I believe, this kind of exchange with intellectuals and fellow artists can lead to gradual political and social change.[15]

During the festival period, Dave and Iola Brubeck were guests of honor in a series of events held in the nation's capital to recognize the couple as pioneer cultural ambassadors. The Washington events featured panel discussions and presentations that included a full range of State Department personnel, such as three current or former US ambassadors, as well as academics and noted jazz critics, including Dan Morgenstern. Concurrently, the Washington, DC–based Meridian International Center hosted a major gallery exhibit of curated photographs titled *Jam Session: America's Jazz Ambassadors Embrace the World*.[16] It featured dramatic and thought-provoking photographs that showed the jazz ambassadors in a wide variety of settings, such as the wildly cheering standing-room-only audience in an Athens, Greece, concert hall, packed to the rafters for Dizzy Gillespie's 1956 triumph. This was the very first State Department–sponsored jazz ambassador tour, when Dizzy quelled the riots, and which formed the basis for *The Real Ambassadors'* tune "Cultural Exchange." A 1958 candid photo of Dave, Iola, and Michael Brubeck interacting with everyday citizens on the streets of Kraków, Poland, showed them clearly enjoying the people-to-people interactions that were built into the jazz ambassador tours. In another, Duke Ellington is mobbed by Russian fans who sought autographs when he arrived there as a jazz ambassador in 1971. These images showed the fervor with which jazz was embraced by dozens of nations all around the globe.

The Meridian Center also hosted a half-day symposium on April 11, which concluded with a gala reception and a concert by the Andrzej Jagodziński Trio from Poland. The group had been invited to appear as a nod to the strong ties to the Polish jazz community that the Dave Brubeck Quartet had initiated fifty years earlier, further evidence of the lasting benefits from the State Department's investment in the jazz ambassador program.

That same week, secretary of state Condoleeza Rice presented Brubeck with the inaugural Benjamin Franklin Award for public diplomacy. The official State Department notice recognized him for "offering a positive vision of hope, opportunity and freedom through a musical language that is truly American."[17] In her remarks at the presentation ceremonies on April 8, Secretary Rice stated:

> As a little girl I grew up on the sounds of Dave Brubeck because my dad was your biggest fan . . . thank you for your patriotism and your leadership in representing America by introducing the language, the sounds and the spirit of jazz to new generations around the world.[18]

In sum, the events of March to April 2008 helped raise awareness of just how important the collaboration between artists and diplomats had been in helping improve international relations during the Cold War era. *The Real Ambassadors* was frequently brought up in the formal context of the symposia, as well as in informal conversations, renewing interest in what had become a largely overlooked milestone achievement in Brubeck's and Armstrong's lengthy careers.

In summer 2009, I undertook making a facsimile version of the 1962 concert performance in collaboration with Iola and Dave Brubeck, since no recording of the historic 1962 premiere was made.[19] The memory of the film crew standing by to document the Monterey premiere in 1962 was a bittersweet one for the Brubecks. Not being able to afford the $750 to film the Monterey performance remained "one of the biggest regrets of my career," Dave recalled.[20] Since the performance books assembled for Monterey were extant in the Brubeck Collection, the 1961 studio recordings could be reassembled in the same sequence as originally performed in concert on September 23, 1962. Missing was Iola Brubeck's narration and the few incidental lines performed by the Talgallan townspeople.

First, I recorded the narrator's part performed by Iola Brubeck, sitting at home in her living room in Wilton, Connecticut. Next, the narration was married to the newly sequenced songs using the recordings from the Columbia 1962 soundtrack release in the sound studio of the University of the Pacific, the Brubecks' alma mater. A group of University of the Pacific students were enlisted to play the parts of Talgallans so that the entire Monterey performance could be recreated. In this way, a newly assembled facsimile, approved by Dave and Iola Brubeck, became available to students and scholars for study as a part of the Brubeck Collection.[21]

Fast-forward to 2012: as the fiftieth anniversary of the premiere approached, the Brubeck Institute and Monterey Jazz Festival discussed how the anniversary might be celebrated while informing a contemporary audience about the work and its significance in the struggle for racial equality.

In April 2012, the annual Brubeck Festival hosted by the University of the Pacific in Stockton presented a symposium on *The Real Ambassadors* titled "Blow Your Horn—Set Man Free," a title borrowed from the Brubecks' lyrics to the show-stopping number "Blow Satchmo" that is part of the medley of tunes making up the musical's finale. The proceedings included my own introductory presentation explaining the context for the show's premiere at the height of the civil rights struggle, followed by a panel discussion that featured Yolande Bavan, one of the original performers at Monterey, and Armstrong biographer and archivist Ricky Riccardi. Ms. Bavan recounted her experience as a twenty-six-year-old vocalist having but a single day of rehearsal to learn the complex vocal parts before taking the show onstage in front of six thousand people. Panelists also made the point that the show's messages about the agency that jazz musicians developed through their overseas tours, as well as the show's indictment of segregation, should be viewed as bold statements by the Brubecks—statements the panelists suggested were still relevant half a century later.

To celebrate the fiftieth anniversary of the musical's Monterey debut in 2012, a major exhibition was planned collaboratively by the Brubeck Collection archival team at University of the Pacific and the Monterey Jazz Festival. *Remembering The Real Ambassadors* presented a multimedia gallery exhibition that explained to twenty-first-century festival attendees the behind-the-scenes story of how Dave and Iola Brubeck labored for five years to realize the show's premiere at the fifth Monterey Jazz Festival. Cocurated by University of the Pacific's Holt-Atherton Head of Special Collections Michael Wurtz and myself, it included video clips of Dave and Iola talking about *The Real Ambassadors*, as well as original music manuscripts, the 1962 festival program book, and many photos with descriptions of the machinations that the Brubecks, in partnership with Monterey cofounder Jimmy Lyons, had to engage in to bring the show to the stage.[22]

A panel session titled "Reflections on *The Real Ambassadors*" was also convened at the 2012 Monterey proceedings, with Bill Minor, jazz writer and unofficial historian of the Monterey Jazz Festival, as moderator. Yolande Bavan, Ricky Riccardi, and I reconvened to recount the story of the musical's premiere during the days of the civil rights movement. Audio excerpts were played and discussed with the audience during this lively reflection on the piece's place as another in a long line of notable jazz premieres that Monterey Festival founder Jimmy Lyons helped to underwrite.

The third and final initiative undertaken at Monterey was to invite any 2012 festival attendees that had also been at the 1962 premiere to sit for an oral history interview. These interviews were subsequently added to the

Brubeck Collection of the University of the Pacific. At the time the idea was broached with the management of the festival, there was no guarantee that any 1962 audience members would be attending fifty years later, but organizers were fortunate to have five respondents come forward to be interviewed. Their voices added another layer of understanding to just what the musical meant to its audience when it premiered.

A few months after the fiftieth-anniversary recognition at Monterey for *The Real Ambassadors*, another jazz festival across the country decided to recognize the life and legacy of Dave Brubeck through performances of his music and scholarly discussions. As a part of the proceedings scheduled for September 2013, the Detroit Jazz Festival committed to staging the first revival of *The Real Ambassadors* since its premiere half a century before.

The world was stunned to learn of the passing of Dave Brubeck on December 5, 2012, one day short of his ninety-second birthday. The cause of death was heart failure. His son Darius had been taking him to a cardiology appointment at the time of his death. In the wake of Dave Brubeck's passing, musicians and arts presenters began to program a range of concerts centered on honoring his legacy. One of the most ambitious programs to honor the legendary jazz musician was undertaken by artistic director Chris Collins and the team at the Detroit Jazz Festival, which dedicated a significant amount of its 2013 festival resources to honoring the late jazzman. Collins programmed the *Dave Brubeck Tribute Series*, which included commissioning four leading arrangers to create new charts of some of Dave Brubeck's best-known songs that had premiered there; a full concert staging of Brubeck's Mass, *To Hope*, with orchestra, choir, soloists, and jazz quartet; a set dedicated to the late pianist by the Brubeck Brothers Quartet featuring Chris and Dan Brubeck; a panel discussion led by jazz scholar and disc jockey John Penney, discussing *The Real Ambassadors*; a talk by Dr. Simon Rowe, executive director of the Brubeck Institute, and myself, on jazz diplomacy during the Cold War; and importantly, the staging and musical production of the full concert version of *The Real Ambassadors*. Brubeck was also posthumously awarded the Jazz Guardian award, the highest honor offered by the Detroit Jazz Festival.

Detroit jazz pianist, bandleader, and social activist Bill Meyer was drawn to *The Real Ambassadors* in large part due to its socially conscious messages, and he persuaded Collins to support a staged production of the entire musical. Using the original concert notes and performance books from the Brubeck Collection, as well as studying the Hansen-published folio of the musical's songs, Meyer conceived a revised stage version of the concert arrangement for the show and soon was in touch with Russell Gloyd, who proved instrumental in helping Meyer prepare the necessary charts for the performance. Chris Brubeck recounted:

> I spoke with Bill a few times, but when it came to the nuts and bolts of feeding Bill material, it was really Russell who did the work. I can remember Russell listening to the record and writing out the [vocal] harmonies that Lambert, Hendricks & Ross sang. And that was no easy task, since the notes they were singing sometimes came by so fast, it was difficult to pick out exactly what note a particular part should be.[23]

Meyer would serve as music director and producer, and lead the band during the performance. Casting the show presented challenges, as few contemporary artists have the range of playing, singing, and acting abilities of Louis Armstrong. Meyer solved this problem by casting actor Augustus Williamson in the lead role. Instead of using Pops, the original character name from the show, however, Meyer opted to list Williamson's character as Louis Armstrong. Trumpeter Dave Greene played Satchmo's parts from the musical. The role of Carmen McRae was played with élan by Michelle McKinney, who had paired with Williamson to star in a revival of Duke Ellington's *Sophisticated Ladies* prior to costarring in *The Real Ambassadors*. For this performance, Bill Meyer also added four songs not performed in 1962: "Nomad," "Lonesome," "I Didn't Know Until You Told Me," and "Since Love Had Its Way." He also realized that the narrator parts were critical to bringing a modern-day audience along for the show's musical and emotional journey.

Meyer faced the same challenges that Dave and Howard Brubeck had, learning the limits of each singer's range and working closely with them to accurately represent the show's intent. With the assistance of Russell Gloyd and review of earlier scores, Meyer stitched together a cohesive show out of the songs, bridging dialogue spoken by characters throughout the show and the all-important narration, which once again would bring the audience into the world of the traveling jazz musicians as they arrived in Talgalla.

One of the most inspired bits of casting was Meyer's choice of retired judge and civil rights activist Claudia Morcom in the role of the narrator. She had a wealth of experiences that would inform her performance of the part that day, and was also known as a jazz singer in her own right.[24] She understood the courage and bravery required to enlist in the early fight for civil rights, having endured death threats for her civil rights work, as she was one of the few Black female attorneys who took the fight for equal rights to its epicenter, Mississippi, in the early 1960s. The *Detroit Free Press* described her as a leader:

She led the legal assault on racial discrimination in Mississippi. She recruited and coordinated the arrival of lawyers and law students from across the country, filed lawsuits to desegregate public facilities, fought against voter intimidation and defended freedom fighters—all in the face of eminent threats to her life and those she was there to defend.[25]

As a young woman of color and recent law school graduate, Morcom had participated in a June 23, 1963, Freedom March in Detroit, led by Dr. Martin Luther King Jr., after which he previewed his soon-to-be famous "I Have a Dream" speech.[26] The site of the show's performance, in the Hayes Plaza area adjacent to the Detroit River, was just a few hundred yards from Cobo Hall, the first site of King's historic speech. Judge Morcom's authoritative voice set each scene and established the story as it departed from the US to its overseas destinations.

To introduce the audience to the *raison d'être* for the work, volunteers circulated in the crowd before showtime passing out a single-page program. It listed the cast and order of songs performed and also provided commentary from Meyer, in which he drew parallels from the 1950s struggles for equality to the present day. He argued:

> The message [of equality] is as relevant today as it was back then. Inspired by musicians like Louis Armstrong, the story tells of cultural exchange artists hired by the U.S. State Department as "goodwill ambassadors" to represent America during the Cold War. Most of the African American jazz musicians knew by personal experience they were not treated as equals in their own country, the birthplace of jazz, but they felt that the power of music, specifically jazz, could bring about social change and help resolve world tensions. . . . [In the original performance] Armstrong expressed his deep feelings about racial issues and civil rights, preceding the massive civil rights struggles that eventually changed America.[27]

Just before the downbeat, producer and music director Bill Meyer stepped to the microphone to further connect *The Real Ambassadors* and the civil rights movement to that day's audience:

> Fifty years ago, the great Reverend Dr. Martin Luther King Jr. gave a speech remembered as "I Have a Dream." And there was a first time he gave it, and that was here in Detroit . . . [*audience ovation*] he gave it in that building [*pointing to Cobo Hall*], right there in Cobo Hall. We're

here in the shadow of Cobo Hall. Then he gave the speech [again] at the March on Washington. Fifty-two years ago, Dave and Iola Brubeck wrote a jazz musical that shared many of the same dreams: a world where people would be treated with justice and equality. Jazz musicians and jazz lovers have always been ahead of the game and have been willing to accept people on the content of their character instead of the color of their skin.

Dave and Iola had a dream, also. They knew that the arts could be used for social change. They had hoped to perform this on Broadway, but it didn't happen. Instead, they only performed it once, in a shortened version. This is fifty years later now—and we're going to do it again [*audience ovation*]. We want to dedicate this performance to a woman who also had a dream fifty years ago: Iola Brubeck. These are her words in this show and Dave's music, of course. You know, we all still have a lot of work to do to make these dreams come true. The jazz community can lead the way.

And now let's go back to 1961 . . . here's our narrator, the Honorable Judge Claudia Morcom, who was at Cobo Hall fifty years ago to hear Dr. Martin Luther King's speech.[28]

The Detroit audience responded enthusiastically to Meyer with an ovation, and the performance then got underway.

As had been the case at Monterey in 1962, the 2013 Detroit audience was very responsive, interrupting the performance numerous times with ovations for the singers playing the lead roles. The energetic and emotive vocal trio made up of Carl Cafagna, Meri Slaven, and Armond Jackson provided an excellent counterbalance to Williamson and McKinney. Moving from the front of the stage, from time to time the vocal trio went backstage and changed costumes, added props, and in the memorable scene where the traveling jazz ambassadors are circling the airfield of the tiny African nation prior to landing, used a prop painted to look like the windows of an airplane as they ran through their thoughts, singing about their impending arrival in Talgalla. For "They Say I Look Like God," the most moving piece in the musical, they donned purple choir robes and intoned the biblical passages from the book of Genesis that provided the bedrock for Pops's emotional pleas, asking when all mankind might be truly free.

Meyer simultaneously conducted and covered the piano parts that had been created by Dave Brubeck and Billy Kyle for the original, while bassist Ibrahim Jones and drummer Butter Hawkins provided a solid foundation for the varied musical stylings found in the piece. The three-piece horn

The Detroit Jazz Festival's 2013 revival of *The Real Ambassadors* brought the show to life for a new generation of listeners. Musical director Bill Meyer incorporated colorfully costumed extras to play the part of the Talgallan townspeople, as Iola had envisioned in her plans for the original staging of the show. Pictured, *left to right*, are Augustus Williamson as Pops; the vocal trio, made up of Armond Jackson, Meri Slaven, and Carl Cafagna; some of the uncredited Talgallan townspeople in authentic African attire; and, *left rear*, bassist Ibrahim Jones. Photo courtesy of Bill Meyer.

section, David Greene (trumpet), Wendell Harrison (clarinet, sax), and Ed Gooch (trombone), captured the spirit and style of Armstrong's All-Stars for the Detroit audience. Michelle McKinney, working from memory, gave a beautifully nuanced and physical reading to Carmen's part, drawing loud ovations from the crowd for her interpretations of "My One Bad Habit," "In the Lurch," and her duet on "You Swing, Baby" with Pops.

Meyer involved a seven-member troupe of extras to represent the important roles of the Talgallan townspeople. Dressed in festive African garb and wielding rain sticks, shakers, maracas, and other hand percussion, they chanted the lines "Ambassador, ambassador, he's the real ambassador" and made their way onto the stage, across the stage, and finally offstage, dancing, singing, and making merry while drawing strong applause for their reenactment of similar scenes that played out in real life hundreds of times around the world.[29]

The final segment of narration, in which Iola Brubeck envisioned a society that did treat everyone equally, was acted out on the Detroit Jazz Festival stage. Narrator Morcom intoned the notion that freedom and democracy

Jazz at Lincoln Center, under the artistic direction of Wynton Marsalis, staged the New York City debut of *The Real Ambassadors* in April 2014. The performances were staged in the Appel Room overlooking Central Park and the Manhattan skyline. Pictured, *left to right*, are Peter Martin, pianist and music director; Yolande Bavan, narrator; Roberta Gambarini as Rhonda; Robert Hurst, bassist; Brian Owens as Pops; Ty Stephens and Vivian Sessoms, from the vocal trio; Ulysses Owens, drummer; Russell Graham, from the vocal trio; and James Zollar, trumpeter. Photo by Frank Stewart. Courtesy of Jazz at Lincoln Center, © Jazz at Lincoln Center.

were precious, and that the show's hero, Pops, was a symbol of the universal dream of equality for all.

Exactly on cue, a small girl, clad in white and bedecked in flowers, joined the Detroit cast onstage, exactly as Dave and Iola had envisioned it for the Broadway stage. As Pops bent down, she placed a crown on his head to signify the victory of jazz and human dignity in the struggle for human rights that the Brubecks hoped could one day be realized in society. The ensemble then proceeded into the rollicking "Finale" medley that got the whole crowd on its feet. *The Real Ambassadors'* story had come full circle, and the audience roared its approval, demanding numerous curtain calls for the cast members at the conclusion of the triumphant Detroit performance.

From a review afterward, it is clear that Meyer's production of *The Real Ambassadors* rekindled the sensibility and spirit of the original. One need only compare the reviews from 1962 and 2013 to see that even after fifty-one years, the messages of social justice and the notion of using artists as spokespersons for social change still came through loud and clear. In his review for the *Detroit Free Press*, critic Mark Stryker wrote:

The balance of humor and deftly plotted progressivism in Iola Brubeck's libretto has aged well, and I found many passages deeply moving. Dave Brubeck's infectious melodies, and especially the heartfelt ballads like "Summer Song" and the spiritual-like "They Say I Look Like God" (sung with pathos by Williamson), deserve wider circulation.[30]

For Stryker, the show's carefully interwoven music, dialogue, and narration worked effectively to deliver its heartfelt messages more than five decades after its premiere. The Detroit Jazz Festival performance was an overwhelming success, applauded by critics and audience members alike. Stryker also recognized the "heroic" effort of Bill Meyer, who produced and directed the performance, while referencing the fact that it was the first complete reading of the concert work since its 1962 debut. Concurrent with the Detroit Jazz Festival's revival taking the stage, however, another milestone, a New York City debut for *The Real Ambassadors* presented by Wynton Marsalis and Jazz at Lincoln Center, had already moved from the what-if stage to being realized.

While Chris Collins, Bill Meyer, Chris Brubeck, Russell Gloyd, and many others had been hard at work preparing for the Detroit Jazz Festival's September 2013 Dave Brubeck Tribute Series, wheels had already been set in motion for an even larger celebration of Brubeck's life and works to be held in New York City, hosted by Wynton Marsalis and Jazz at Lincoln Center, the world's preeminent jazz-presenting organization. The idea had come to life in 2011 when the Brubeck Institute's Simon Rowe proposed a joint bicoastal jazz festival copresented by the institute and Jazz at Lincoln Center. Marsalis was receptive and talks proceeded at a steady pace.

Even though their paths had crossed dozens of times, Marsalis and Brubeck had never performed together until the 2005 Newport Jazz Festival, when Marsalis sat in with the Dave Brubeck Quartet for two numbers. At the time, Wynton said:

> We've seen each other a lot of times, but it's the first time we had played . . . and it was great. It was warm and down-home and just felt great. I've always loved Dave as a man and a musician . . . he's always just a gentleman, a man with a dignity.[31]

The two kept in touch, and their relationship continued to develop as Wynton, like Dave, began to compose orchestral works. At the 2010 Newport Jazz Festival, promoter George Wein asked Wynton if Dave Brubeck could return the favor and sit in with Marsalis's quintet. He agreed, much to the audience's delight, and Marsalis's band played a New Orleans–style "Happy Birthday" to acknowledge Dave's upcoming ninetieth birthday. Before bringing Brubeck onstage to join his ensemble, Marsalis told the crowd that Brubeck was more than a jazz legend, he was "a man who represented the essence of what it is to be an American."[32]

The 2011 conversations were productive and led to an offer that December for Marsalis to bring his Jazz at Lincoln Center Orchestra to California to headline the sold-out Brubeck Festival in Stockton, California, in March 2012. Engineering the details of bringing Wynton's storied ensemble to the festival had been the work of Brubeck Institute executive director Simon Rowe. In conversations leading up to the 2012 collaboration, Rowe and Marsalis had begun to visualize a partnership that would result in a "coast to coast" future Brubeck Festival with the first part in California and the second part in New York City. From those early conversations, it was clear that both men wished to involve Dave and Iola Brubeck as much as possible in the planning of the bicoastal events.

That October, five months after Wynton's appearance at the Brubeck Festival, Marsalis and Rowe were in the back of a town car from Manhattan on their way to the Brubecks' Wilton, Connecticut, home. There they would hold a jazz summit to brainstorm how the couple's namesake institute could partner with Jazz at Lincoln Center to develop a comprehensive festival celebrating Dave and Iola Brubeck's contributions to jazz and society over their seventy-year partnership. There was a sense of urgency to the visit, as Rowe had learned that the elder Brubeck's health had been declining rapidly in the preceding weeks.

On the ride up from New York City to Connecticut, Marsalis and Rowe, joined by Jason Olaine, Jazz at Lincoln Center's director of programming and touring, discussed possible components of the project: new realizations of some of Dave's notable works; a large-scale exhibit telling the story of the couple's lengthy and productive career, with special notice of their work as advocates for equal rights, the environment, and other social causes; late-night jam sessions to serve as a homecoming for a host of the Brubeck Institute Fellowship program's talented alumni, many of whom were playing in top groups around the world; and possibly, at long last, a New York City premiere for *The Real Ambassadors*. Darius and Chris Brubeck and their spouses, along with the Brubecks' veteran producer and manager, Russell Gloyd, were all present.

The meeting was more than just brainstorming the creative direction for the proposed festival, however. Marsalis wanted to learn all he could about Dave Brubeck, the composer and humanitarian, and asked if he might be shown around the sprawling residence that displayed so much of the history of the couple's prolific seventy-year career. Darius Brubeck obliged and remembered:

> Wynton was fascinated by the house and the things that were in it. He was asking to go into every room so he could capture some mental images of everything. He looked closely at the titles of books on shelves, and at Dave's LP collection. I think in some way Wynton was just filling himself with Dave's presence . . . just getting the vibe of the house and what was in it.[33]

Everyone gathered around the big wooden kitchen table that had been the site of so many family meetings during the five decades since the Brubecks had built their Connecticut dream home in the early 1960s. Rowe recalled:

> Wynton set the tone for the discussion by explaining to the Brubecks that he was determined that Jazz at Lincoln Center would produce a tribute to Dave that would be comparable to one that Wynton would feel was appropriate for his own grandfather. Dave had been in poor health and was quite fragile. Although he was less verbal, he was very expressive throughout the brainstorming session. At key points along the way, he would get excited and almost leap out of his seat with a look of joy on his face. It was clear that many of Wynton's ideas were passing muster with Dave. Iola was serving as translator and was offering input on behalf of herself and Dave. Chris and Darius were also chiming in with ideas. But you could see Dave was following the conversation very closely, as at certain points, he would respond affirmatively. Throughout our time together that evening, it was evident the tremendous level of mutual respect that Dave and Wynton had for one another.[34]

Chris Brubeck added:

> We all saw that the upcoming festival meant a lot to Wynton as he discussed all the possibilities about what parts of Brubeck's extensive catalog of compositions, including choral, orchestral and ballet pieces, might inform the programming. Staging a full orchestra and chorus had to be considered in light of what the potential cost might be. After further discussion, Wynton said, "The one thing I can absolutely guarantee you, Dave, is that I have some of the greatest musicians in the world and they're great arrangers. And we could take some of

your tunes and do fantastic new arrangements." Everyone was enthusiastic about that idea and that turned out to be the dominant idea that emerged that day. As the conversation eventually circled back to what would be manageable . . . the other main idea that made it was that the program should include the New York City debut of *The Real Ambassadors*.[35]

Tish Brubeck described how eloquently Wynton made clear his intention to honor Dave. He said to him that he wanted Dave to "understand just how much he meant to him and that he wanted to honor him from the heart. That was a very touching, sentimental moment."[36]

So it was that just a few weeks before Dave Brubeck's unexpected December 5, 2012, passing, plans were being finalized to allow the *The Real Ambassadors* to make its New York City debut. Darius Brubeck recalled, "From the moment that we all agreed to move forward, Wynton and all the resources of JALC were fully committed. Putting the festival together was completely collaborative." Over the next eighteen months, working closely with the Brubeck family and the Brubeck Institute's Simon Rowe, Marsalis and the Jazz at Lincoln Center team distilled that brainstorming session into action.

According to their plans, the 2014 Brubeck Festival would be broken into two parts. First, from March 27 to 29, Al Jarreau, Eddie Palmieri, and Terri Lyne Carrington would headline the three-night Stockton segment of the festival. Then a week later, the New York segment of the coast-to-coast festival would kick off and run from April 7 to 14. It would be a seven-day, thirty-five-event celebration of the life and work of Dave and Iola Brubeck. All three Jazz at Lincoln Center venues, the Rose Theater, Dizzy's Club Coca-Cola, and the Appel Room, featured music written or inspired by the Brubecks. Members of the Lincoln Center Jazz Orchestra were commissioned to create a number of new arrangements of some of Brubeck's repertoire, showcasing his melodic and rhythmic inventiveness and demonstrating how readily they could be developed into notable new charts for the world-renowned band. Thursday, Friday, and Saturday nights the Lincoln Center Jazz Orchestra played these fresh new takes on classic Brubeck titles to packed houses in the 1,200-seat Rose Theater. Darius, Chris, and Dan Brubeck all performed numerous sets in Dizzy's Club Coca-Cola, with Dan and Chris coleading the Brubeck Brothers Quartet through four shows, and Darius leading four other shows featuring a frequent collaborator, saxophonist Dave O'Higgins, backed by Dan and Chris in the rhythm section. Late-night sets by twenty-two current and former Brubeck Institute Fellows, which sometimes resembled the joyful "basement sessions" referred to in the musical's "King for a Day," rounded out five consecutive evenings of jazz during the New York portion of the festival.

Two more essential components completed the weeklong celebration of the Brubecks' work and lives. A comprehensive 3,800-square-foot exhibit titled *Dave Brubeck: Jazz Ambassador* was created and open to the public for the entire month of April. Admission to the exhibit was free, and thousands of New Yorkers visited the exhibit to learn more about Dave and Iola Brubeck's life in music. Through various sections of the exhibit, filled with photographs, video clips, and historic artifacts such as scores and Brubeck's iconic black-rimmed glasses, the story of Dave and Iola's career was told in seven chapters: Performer, Family Man, Cultural Ambassador, Civil Rights Activist, Big Man on Campus (creating the college jazz concert market nationally), Composer, and Environmentalist. Citing his importance, the program hailed Brubeck as "one of America's most significant musicians to emerge after the Swing Era."[37] Iola Brubeck and her seminal contributions as wife, manager, librettist, lyricist, and confidante during Dave's seventy-plus-year career were also prominently documented.

The final piece of the festival was to present *The Real Ambassadors*. Simon Rowe remembered:

> Presenting *The Real Ambassadors* would serve as one of the linchpins to reflect the depth of Dave and Iola's commitment to social justice issues. Both of them felt strongly that it should be included. Chris and Darius felt the same way. . . . Sadly, Dave passed away eight weeks after that meeting, but Iola was involved and helped to sculpt every last detail of the festival.[38]

More than five decades after they had conceived of the show and dreamed of bringing it to Broadway, *The Real Ambassadors* would finally have its New York City premiere. Detroit pianist and arranger Bill Meyer graciously provided his Detroit Jazz Festival charts to Peter Martin, who served as music director for the Jazz at Lincoln Center production. On hand to help was Dave Brubeck's longtime producer, Russell Gloyd, who served as creative advisor to the New York City production. The entire cast included Brian Owens as Pops; Roberta Gambarini in the role of Rhonda; Russell Graham, Vivian Sessoms, and Ty Stephens as the versatile vocal trio alternating between townspeople, priests, and part of the touring jazz band; James Zollar, trumpet; Robert Hurst, bass; Ulysses Owens, drums; Peter Martin, piano and music director; and Yolande Bavan, narrator.

When the idea first surfaced to recreate the original live performance, everyone realized that the role of narrator, written and performed at Monterey by Iola Brubeck, would once again be a pivotal one. It would be essential to help the audience understand the context for the musical portion of the program. Judge Claudia Morcom had proved to be an inspiring and able narrator for the Detroit production. Yolande Bavan, who helped premiere the work at Monterey, was mentioned as a possible choice for the New York City debut, and Iola Brubeck heartily agreed that Bavan, who since her tenure with Lambert, Hendricks & Bavan had gone on to a distinguished career on stage and screen, would be an ideal choice. She also provided an important emotional link to the spirit of the original cast.

Bavan recalled learning that *The Real Ambassadors* would finally have its debut in New York in May 2013:

> I was having lunch with Simon Rowe after the memorial service, and he mentioned that a festival was being planned by Wynton to celebrate Dave's life and *The Real Ambassadors* was going to be part of the program. Simon mentioned that Iola was involved in the planning and someone would need to play her role as narrator. Since I had been part of the original cast, he asked if I would consider taking on that role, and I said I would be overjoyed to do so.[39]

The songs and order of performance were identical to the score used in Detroit in 2013. However, the setting was quite different, as the show was presented in the Appel Room, a 420-seat theater with full lighting and sound and the dramatic backdrop of a thirty-foot-high glass vista overlooking the lights of New York City's Columbus Square. Four performances were given to standing-room-only audiences whose enthusiasm rivaled the original Monterey audience. They frequently interrupted the performance for sustained applause, not only for the performers themselves but for the humanitarian ideals espoused through the music. Yolande Bavan sat downstage and, using her acting ability, introduced the audience to the plot and led them through the character development that Dave and Iola Brubeck crafted into the musical for its lead characters, Pops and Rhonda. In the program notes, critic Will Friedwald wrote:

> *The Real Ambassadors* is the rare work of art to have grown in stature over the last 50 years. When most of us first hear it, it lays on our ears as an oddity, a true curate's egg of a project. Yet the more one listens,

the more amazing it sounds. Far from being mainly notable as a curios-
ity, *The Real Ambassadors* is now generally regarded as a little-known
gem of an album, a remarkable and one-of-a-kind project—a jazz song
cycle with the flair of Broadway and a sense of social consciousness
unique to any musical medium . . . a work that defies both categorization and time.[40]

Now, more than five decades after its inception, the underlying themes of
the show were proving just how relevant they were for contemporary audiences and performers. The Detroit festival staging more closely adhered to
Iola's original staging intent. It included Talgallan townspeople in colorful
garb dancing and playing percussion, a bespectacled town spokesperson
speaking "mission school English," the use of props as had been done at
Monterey, and a chosen child to represent the hope for the future by crowning Pops as the real ambassador. This contrasted with the Jazz at Lincoln
Center staging, which was a concert performance without the extramusical
elements, instead relying solely on the narration and lyrics to inform the
audience. These two successful approaches confirmed the versatility of both
the songs and the underlying themes voiced by the narrator.

Yolande Bavan remembered, "People were pleasantly surprised by the
music. And a number of persons commented on its social relevance—after
all, we're going through some of the same things as when the show was written, but with a different patina."[41] Darius Brubeck and his wife, Cathy, were
sitting with fellow pianist Bill Charlap at one of the four performances of the
show. After the audience departed, they went down to the stage and joined
some other musicians to mingle with the performers. The post-performance
conversation among the cast gravitated to the spiritual nature of the musical.
Darius stated:

> I got the sense from the cast that this wasn't just work, and it wasn't
> just music. They remarked that there was a spiritual dimension to
> Dave's work. They said, it had the result of elevating them, in terms
> of consciousness.[42]

So the same consciousness-raising effect that the original cast had felt fifty-
two years earlier at the show's premiere was still alive in its insightful words
and memorable tunes.[43]

Sadly, Iola Brubeck was unable to attend the New York City premiere of
The Real Ambassadors. Just thirty days before it was performed, on March 12,
2014, she had passed away at the family home, losing her battle with cancer.

As was later learned, she had been so focused on caring for her husband as his health declined throughout 2012 that she seemed to have had ignored warning signs about her own health. After the pianist's passing in December 2012, she had next thrown herself fully into planning the elaborate public memorial service that took place in May 2013 at the Cathedral Church of St. John the Divine in New York City. The Celebration of the Life and Music of Dave Brubeck featured musical tributes by a who's who of jazz artists and other dignitaries that had been touched or inspired by Dave Brubeck and wanted to bid him a fond musical farewell. After a welcome by Rev. James Kowalski, there were heartfelt opening remarks by Iola Brubeck and Newport Jazz Festival founder and longtime Brubeck collaborator George Wein, both of whom helped the audience understand Brubeck as an individual, family man, and friend. Then the musical portion of the celebration commenced.

The program of all-Brubeck compositions featured all four of Dave and Iola's sons, Darius (piano), Chris (bass and bass trombone), Dan (drums), and Matthew (cello), performing as a group and backing other players: Chick Corea, Jon Faddis, Branford Marsalis, Randy Brecker, Paquito D'Rivera, Renee Rosnes, Bill Charlap, Roy Hargrove, Paul Winter, Deepak Ram, John Salmon, Mark Morganelli, Michael Pedicin Jr., Hilary Kole, Ted Rosenthal, and a number of Brubeck Fellows. At the midpoint, a duet on "King for a Day," one of the signature songs from *The Real Ambassadors*, featured the last surviving member of the classic Dave Brubeck Quartet, Eugene Wright, singing the part of Pops, accompanied by Darius Brubeck on piano.[44] It was another touching moment in tribute to the ideals that Dave and Iola championed throughout their seven-decade career. After a rousing rendition of the Brubeck classic "Blues for Newport," featuring Jon Faddis and Chris Brubeck trading choruses, the celebration drew to a close, although the hundreds in the audience remained long after to share reminiscences about their memories of Brubeck, his life, and his music.

As was shared at the memorial service, Dave Brubeck was more than a gifted musician. He was a father, bandleader, composer, cultural emissary, and lifelong activist. An appreciation for his persistent commitment to speaking out against intolerance and racism, along with his efforts to convince others to take action to change society for the better, was a constant thread throughout the day's remarks, including a heartfelt acknowledgment sent by former president Bill Clinton. Both Dave and Iola Brubeck would have been happy to know that their ideals, which informed their first important joint musical creation, were alive and well in the hearts of the hundreds who celebrated his life that day.

In February 2021, a fifty-five-minute music video debuted on social media titled *The Real Ambassadors in Concert*. It combines performances of new arrangements of selections from the show with archival materials and visits to both the Brubecks' and Louis Armstrong's homes, where the music was originally written and rehearsed in 1961.[45] The production was cosponsored by Brubeck Living Legacy, Louis Armstrong House Museum, and the Forum for Cultural Engagement. The talented cast, consisting of Alphonso Horne (trumpet/vocals), Vuyo Sotashe and Shanel Marie Johns (vocals), Endea Owens (bass), Camille Thurman (vocals/saxophone), Chris Pattishall (piano/arranger), and Jake Goldbas (director/drums), gives a spirited and soulful reading of the material. Chris Brubeck talks about his memories of the musical and performs one of the songs in the Brubeck's Wilton, Connecticut, home. Trumpeter Horne takes on the role of host, explaining the significance of the musical in the context of the struggle for equal rights that continues today. Making such a film available freely over the internet may introduce *The Real Ambassadors* to another generation of listeners.

EPILOGUE

Looking back today as America grapples with the ongoing effects of racially motivated violence and killings, brought into sharper focus by the Black Lives Matter movement, *The Real Ambassadors* can be seen as an important early effort by artists to draw the public's attention to the terrible toll exacted on Blacks by centuries-old systemic racist practices and ideologies.[1] The fact that two of the world's best-known jazz musicians, one Black and one white, joined forces to address segregation, was in itself notable. However, the songs and performance that made up the Monterey premiere were soon overshadowed by the subsequent achievements of each artist. Nonetheless, the journey taken by the show's principals to finally perform it at the height of the civil rights movement shows that artists who take a stand to demand social change can have far-reaching impact, even beyond their own lifetimes. The show also stands as a lasting testament to the power that America's jazz ambassadors wielded during the Cold War, reminding us that artists can be influential purveyors of so-called soft power, cultural influencers whose music can be more appealing and effective than a political manifesto.[2]

As the Brubecks and Armstrong applied their efforts to the show, they found themselves in good company, as *The Real Ambassadors*' genesis, recording, premiere, and immediate impact spanned the years 1956–64. In the wake of the historic 1954 *Brown v. Board of Education* Supreme Court decision, a musical uprising was building momentum that helped galvanize artists and audiences into awareness and action. It took the form of benefit concerts, public statements, and civil rights–inspired compositions and recordings that kept the issue prominently in the limelight. In 1958, a few months after the Little Rock crisis, saxophonist Sonny Rollins released his *Freedom Suite* on Riverside.[3] The nineteen-minute instrumental recording became the title track for a five-song album. Rollins was accompanied by bassist Oscar Pettiford and drummer Max Roach. On the album jacket among the liner notes was a brief statement from the artist. In it, Rollins made the title track's inspiration and purpose unambiguous. He was one among many artists who began to raise their voices to decry racism. Rollins stated:

> America is deeply rooted in Negro culture: its colloquialisms, its humor, its music. How ironic that the Negro, who more than any other people, can claim America's culture as his own, is being persecuted and repressed, that the Negro, who has exemplified the humanities in his very existence, is being rewarded with inhumanity.[4]

Perhaps the most recognized musical composition of the time speaking against intolerance was composer, bassist, and pianist Charles Mingus's "Fables of Faubus," calling out the infamous Arkansas governor who blocked the integration of Little Rock's Central High. The tune first appeared on his groundbreaking 1959 debut Columbia release, *Mingus Ah Um*, an album cited as one of the most significant of its time. While it's hard to single out any one of Mingus's outstanding albums, reflecting back on this particular album's import, critic Steve Huey argued that *Mingus Ah Um* "may well be Mingus' greatest, most emotionally varied set of compositions."[5] Mingus had evidently written the song immediately after the Little Rock incidents and began playing it in concert as early as 1957. For live performance, unlike the Columbia album recording, Mingus and drummer Dannie Richmond sang the lyrics, which called out Faubus and a host of other political leaders, including various senators, by name. Paralleling Louis Armstrong's broadside, Mingus indicted President Eisenhower (for his initial refusal to take action), Jim Crow laws, and the Ku Klux Klan for all standing shoulder to shoulder to block the rights of those Black teens to enter the school.

It's not surprising that "Fables of Faubus" was an instrumental track on *Mingus Ah Um*, as Columbia would have likely seen little benefit, and much greater risk, in providing a platform for Mingus to rail so prominently against racism. However, in 1960, jazz critic Nat Hentoff was set up to run his own short-lived jazz label, Candid Records, as a subsidiary of Cadence Records, an independent label based out of New York City founded by Archie Bleyer, who rose to prominence as radio star Arthur Godfrey's music director.[6] One of Hentoff's earliest releases for Candid was Mingus's 1961 album, *Charles Mingus Presents Charles Mingus*, with the original tune—this time with the vocals—retitled "Original Faubus Fables," likely to avoid any contractual breach with Columbia's stringent rerecording restrictions.[7] Hentoff, a staunch liberal who used his soapbox whenever possible to call for social change, also released another landmark recording a few months before the Mingus album. *We Insist! Max Roach's Freedom Now Suite* was the most complete musical indictment of racism to date. Written by the talented drummer and bandleader, with lyricist Oscar Brown Jr., it featured Abbey Lincoln on vocals and Coleman Hawkins for one number on saxophone. Historian Ingrid Monson stated, "The work is organized as a historical progression through African American history . . . from slavery to emancipation to the contemporary civil rights struggle and African independence in the final movements."[8] Copies of the record were provided to support the fundraising efforts of the various grassroots organizations working for equal rights, and notably, the record was banned in South Africa, which further legitimized it as an important work that directly opposed inequality.[9] Listened to today, the thirty-seven-minute suite still resonates with intensity and relevance. It shifts from gut-wrenching wails that represent the pain and suffering of slaves in America to contrasting soulful and celebratory sections representing the moment that slavery was banned. Its lyrical themes include voting rights, equal pay, and equal treatment under the law for African Americans, issues that are still largely unresolved sixty years later and are being tackled by African Americans and their allies today though the Black Lives Matter movement and other initiatives.

Three other contemporaneous recordings merit mention as links in the chain of musical outpourings during this decade of activism in response to racism and its bitter fruits. Drummer and social activist Art Blakey was in the midst of recording a new album in 1961 when he learned of the violence perpetrated on the integrated bus passengers who volunteered to challenge local Jim Crow laws on interstate transport. These bus trips were dubbed "Freedom Rides" and were initiated by the Congress on Racial Equality (CORE) with the intent of baiting racists into taking action to block the newly ordained requirement that bus depot services be provided equally to white and Black passengers, overturning decades of segregated policy.[10] Blakey walked into the studio and recorded an extended drum solo he named "The Freedom Rider" as an homage to the brave men and women who endured beatings and even the burning of their bus to show the nation that passing a law did little to curb the hatred and violence against integration in the South. Blakey's powerful solo drum performance became the title track of his next Blue Note release.[11] Switching hats back to his role as a jazz critic, Nat Hentoff connected the piece to the drama that was playing out as activists put their lives on the line to root out racists and their institutionalized hatred. Hentoff praised Blakey's work as being an essential part of the musical resistance efforts necessary to foment change. Both the piece itself, as well as Hentoff's review, further elevated the awareness and commitment of artists and jazz audiences to the cause.

Joining the chorus of like-minded artists, saxophonist John Coltrane was also moved to respond through his music to the hatred represented by racism. On November 18, 1963, he recorded "Alabama," an atmospheric, moving tour de force dedicated to the four young girls who were killed in the Ku Klux Klan's September 15, 1963, bombing of the 16th Street Baptist Church in Birmingham, Alabama. Jazz critic Matt Micucci makes the case that Coltrane modeled the song's melodic evolution on the actual speech given by Dr. Martin Luther King Jr. three days after the tragedy, at the church where it happened. Micucci offered, "Like the speech, 'Alabama' shifts its tone from one of mourning to one of renewed determination for the struggle against racially motivated crimes."[12] Coltrane's moving tribute demonstrated that artists were suffering emotionally, along with many other Americans; and music was one of the few tonics to provide some sense of solace or agency during this tumultuous time.

Nina Simone, a noted Black jazz singer and pianist, also reacted to the violence that had been perpetrated on African Americans via her 1964 album, *Nina Simone in Concert*. Recorded live at Carnegie Hall during March and April of 1964, this album marked the beginning of her militant songs attacking racism and inequality. One song, "Mississippi Goddam," was a fierce critique of the hatred and racism that been evidenced through the murder of Medgar Evers and the Birmingham church bombing. In another song on the album, "Old Jim Crow," Simone argued it that was time for the long-standing discriminatory practices to finally end.[13] For the remainder of her career, Simone would be a proponent of Black power and breaking free of the systems she viewed as holding back her fellow African Americans.[14]

The Brubecks aptly framed the duality of the jazz ambassadors' experience in a lyric from the tune "Cultural Exchange," offering the wry assessment that "No commodity is quite so strange / As this thing called cultural exchange." To that point, virtually none of the jazz ambassadors endorsed Jim Crow policies, yet as representatives of the US, they faced constant questioning overseas about America's civil right struggles and the violence being perpetrated on peaceful protesters. In this light, *The Real Ambassadors* remains an essential work in helping us understand the complexity of how on the one hand, jazz functioned as a powerful propaganda platform for the government, while on the other, it afforded the jazz ambassadors and audiences around the globe the chance for meaningful dialogue on- and offstage, as artists used their newfound agency and regularly shared their personal beliefs, which did not align with actual US policies.[15]

After their two-month 1958 State Department tour, Brubeck and his group continued to be a frequent choice for jazz tours representing the US, visiting

Asia, Central and South America, and the Middle East. Throughout much
of the Cold War, America's leaders tapped jazz artists to represent American culture as a counter to Soviet cultural offerings and, more broadly, the
restrictive policies to which Soviet satellite nations were subject. The program
delivered a unique advantage to US diplomats, since no other nation could
marshal such singular cultural ambassadors as Duke Ellington, Louis Armstrong, Dave Brubeck, Dizzy Gillespie, and dozens of other internationally
acclaimed jazz artists. For twenty-two years, dating from Dizzy Gillespie's first
State Department tour in 1956, America continued to invest in application of
the soft power that jazz represented. Trumpeter and bandleader Clark Terry's
four-week tour in 1978 proved to be the final State Department–sponsored
jazz ambassador tour. As had been the case throughout the program's history, artists were still being sent to politically sensitive regions to foster an
improved image for the US. Commenting on Terry's itinerary, historian
Penny Von Eschen observed that

> the tour had a remarkable overlap with the first Middle Eastern and
> Asian tours by Gillespie in 1956 and Brubeck in 1958, serving as an eerie
> reminder that encircling oil fields and shoring up military alliances
> was a fundamental and abiding feature of American foreign policy.[16]

Policy priorities changed around that time, and the cultural exchange programs were moved out of the State Department to be administered by an
organization called Arts America, under the umbrella of the federal Office
of Citizen Exchanges—Cultural Programs. In essence, the initiative was
moved to a lower-level agency and lost a bit of the luster it had enjoyed as
one of the State Department's premiere programs. Still, in reduced form and
content, some type of cultural exchange did continue until the fall of the
Soviet Union, after which the program was eliminated.[17]

However, in the wake of the 9/11 attacks and America's growing involvement in foreign conflicts as a response to those attacks, cultural exchange
initiatives resumed under the direction of the State Department in an effort
to counter the negative perceptions in many nations of the US role in Iraq
and Afghanistan. Commenting on these renewed efforts, Maura Pelly, a State
Department representative in the Cultural Affairs division acknowledged:

> [We're] really committed to using smart diplomacy—using all the
> tools available in reaching people at different levels. Music enables us
> to connect with other cultures. It's something that transcends religion
> and politics and other things that might otherwise divide us.[18]

As was demonstrated in the Cold War, when perceptions need changing abroad, sending American artists out as cultural ambassadors provided clear benefits, especially in countries where sentiment was predominantly anti-American.[19]

This new initiative, dubbed "The Rhythm Road: American Music Abroad," ran from 2005 to 2012, sending a total of 159 musicians making up forty-one ensembles to one hundred countries on five continents over its seven-year run. Jointly administered by the State Department's Bureau of Educational and Cultural Affairs in partnership with Jazz at Lincoln Center, the artists who toured for the program encompassed not only jazz, but also hip-hop, gospel, bluegrass, and blues. The program's design was to bring American culture to places where commercial US artists rarely toured. For instance a 2007 tour by the Ari Roland Jazz Quartet traced the path of the ancient Silk Road in Russia, Kazakhstan, Kyrgyzstan, Tajikistan, and Turkmenistan. Nations with a significant Muslim population were often the destination for the tours, which reportedly totaled 260 performance dates per year by the ten Rhythm Road ensembles chosen annually. Each group spent an average of four weeks abroad and played two final US concerts: one at Dizzy's Club Coca-Cola, a Jazz at Lincoln Center venue, and a second at National Geographic Live! in Washington, DC.[20]

Like their predecessors, these twenty-first-century musical ambassadors found themselves fielding domestic and foreign-policy questions. According to bandleader Ari Roland, "Occasionally, we'd get a question, 'What do you think about the war in Iraq?' we were pretty honest. The State Department told us to be honest."[21] Like the jazz ambassadors of the 1950s, artists touring overseas in the Rhythm Road program had greater agency and influence to represent their personal viewpoints. Interestingly, the State Department's directives on how to respond to such difficult questions had evolved— instead of the strict dictates that the Brubecks and Armstrong had been given—to avoid discussing sensitive topics while touring as a jazz ambassador—Rhythm Road musicians were encouraged to keep it real, favoring authenticity over toeing the company line, as Roland confirmed.

Rhythm Road ensembles also helped break down societal barriers existing in some of the countries they visited. In 2010, the Little Joe McLerran Quartet, a four-piece blues band, was slated to play at the King Fahd Cultural Center in Riyadh, Saudi Arabia. Public concerts are virtually unknown in the kingdom—much less a performance at which men and women might mingle. The quartet's harmonica player, David Berntson, recalled that prior to the date, the group was told there was a 90 percent chance the concert would be canceled. The day of the concert the band was informed they would be allowed to play to an audience segregated by gender, a situation similar to what the earlier jazz ambassadors had faced when they played in the American South, where Blacks were often forced to sit in the balcony or on the other side of a rope dividing a hall. Near the end of the McLerran Quartet's performance, members of the audience of both genders were seen dancing, which Berntson later learned carried great significance in the battle Saudi women have waged for equal rights in their kingdom.[22]

One of the most volatile countries in the Middle East, Syria, was a destination for Rhythm Road artists. In 2010, Brooklyn-based hip-hop ensemble Chen Lo and the Liberation Family were booked to play in Old Town Damascus, Syria. While on the surface, hip-hop might seem very different than Dizzy's bop, Brubeck's cool jazz, and Ellington's sophisticated sounds, Hillary Clinton, then secretary of state, opined about why American music and musicians were a vital part of her foreign diplomacy efforts: "Hip-hop is America, and so is jazz and every other form of music with American roots that tell a story."[23] So enlisting hip-hop artists to help demonstrate how American culture presents the music as both a product and a critic of domestic and world issues is a timely response to the new place America has assumed in the global landscape.

Chen Lo and the Liberation Family performed for a packed house in a restaurant that had been converted into an impromptu venue overnight. The overflow audience comprised mostly younger Syrians. CBS News had a crew there to document the event, and footage clearly shows the audience following the beats and rhymes laid down during the group's set. Afterward, a reporter asked one of the young Syrian women in the audience for her impressions, and if attending the concert influenced her perception about Americans. She replied, "They [the musicians] were very down-to-earth. Nothing like [what] anyone ever says about Americans." When asked if he thought their performance made a difference, front man Chen Lo stated, "No question. Definitely. The impact was felt, I think, both ways. I know I was affected." Such exchanges prove that the modest investment of sending American artists overseas to share their music and art with foreign nationals can have outsized positive benefits to both countries involved in such exchanges.

The Rhythm Road program adopted a more formal framework to guide each ensemble's in-country touring and residencies, adding workshops, classroom visits, master classes, and performances in venues of all sizes. Where the earlier jazz ambassadors had often played to thousands in stadiums, arenas, and massive concert halls, Rhythm Road shows were much more intimate. Berntsen recalled that the emotional high point of his tour was the band's performance for a Saudi special-needs classroom of mixed gender where the kids "boogied with abandon" to the Chuck Berry classic "Promised Land."[24] Some of the Rhythm Road groups even wrote jazz arrangements of well-known folk melodies from their host countries in advance of their tours. As the program's success grew, so did its annual budget—from roughly $750,000 at its start to nearly $1.5 million in its final year of operation. The partnership with Jazz at Lincoln Center concluded at the end of the 2012 season, and the program was brought under the sole control of the State Department and the Rhythm Road moniker was dropped. A brief check of the State Department's current cultural exchange offerings lists the American Music Abroad program, which, beginning with its 2013 season, has continuously sent ten to fifteen ensembles, performing various types of American roots music, to other countries. The fifteen touring bands for 2019 included hip-hop, Hawaiian slack-key guitar, bluegrass, and gospel, demonstrating the diversity of American talent that is still touring the world to create better understanding and goodwill, especially where sentiments may be anti-American due to political or religious ideologies. Dave Brubeck, who was changed as a result of his jazz ambassador tours, offered a strong endorsement for sustaining such programs when he was interviewed by CBS News as part of their reporting on the Syrian tour of Chen Lo and the Liberation Family. He advised, "The more exchanges with artists, all kinds of artists, the better the world would be."[25]

As creative artists and collaborators, Dave and Iola Brubeck's attitudes and objectives were affected both by their experiences abroad as jazz ambassadors and by the contemporary civil rights movement, which they wholeheartedly supported. The couple viewed it as their responsibility to speak out against injustice through the media whenever possible, and increasingly, through music. Brubeck frequently appeared at benefit concerts for various civil rights groups during this time, including the Southern Christian Leadership Conference (SCLC) and the Student Non-Violent Coordinating Committee (SNCC).[26] As Ingrid Monson observed, these and other fundraising events "created social spaces in which musicians and audiences could feel that they were *doing something* to aid the southern struggle" [emphasis in original].[27]

When Brubeck announced in 1967 that the classic Dave Brubeck Quartet would be disbanded, the reasons given were twofold: to reduce the amount of time he was away from his family, and so he could devote substantially more time to writing longer-form works, compositions that would be the direct descendants of *The Real Ambassadors* in addressing societal, environmental, religious, and humanitarian themes. A succession of larger compositions resulted, beginning with the aforementioned 1968 oratorio titled *The Light in the Wilderness: An Oratorio for Today*, and continuing through the 2006 premiere of the *Cannery Row Suite*. The latter work also premiered at the Monterey Jazz Festival forty-four years after *The Real Ambassadors*. Together, Dave and Iola Brubeck collaborated on what stands today as a largely homogenous body of long-form musical works, including *The Gates of Justice* (1969), written largely as a response to the assassination of Dr. Martin Luther King Jr. (whom Brubeck often mentioned in interviews) and the riots of the late 1960s; *Truth Is Fallen* (1972), a response to the student protesters who were killed by troops at Kent State and Mississippi State; *La Fiesta de la Posada*, a celebratory Christmas cantata (1979); *To Hope! A Celebration*, a Mass written for Pope John Paul II and premiered at San Francisco's Candlestick Park in 1987 before an audience of seventy thousand, with the Pope presiding over the service; *Earth Is Our Mother*, a choral work addressing the environment, with lyrics adapted from an 1854 speech attributed to Native American leader Chief Seattle; and *Cannery Row Suite*, the couple's final major collaboration, a jazz operetta built on the indelible characters from John Steinbeck's novel of the same name, who so poignantly portrayed Depression-era life in a California coastal community full of immigrants.[28]

While all the artists who have followed in the footsteps trod by the cast of *The Real Ambassadors* to challenge racism through music are too numerous to detail, three examples merit mention as following a similar path to address America's systemic racial problems. All are long-form compositions featuring jazz orchestras and vocalists. Wynton Marsalis's Pulitzer Prize–winning 1994 oratorio, *Blood on the Fields*, is a major work dedicated to acknowledging the centuries-old pain and suffering caused by slavery that African Americans have been struggling to overcome. Unlike Max Roach's *We Insist!*, which didn't draw substantial mainstream media attention at the time of its creation, *Blood on the Fields* premiered at a sold-out Alice Tully Hall in New York City's Lincoln Center, performed by the world-renowned fifteen-member Jazz at Lincoln Center Orchestra and broadcast live to the nation via NPR. Marsalis chose one of *The Real Ambassadors'* cast members, Jon Hendricks, as a featured vocalist to premiere the work, creating a direct linkage to the Brubecks' musical. Like its predecessor, *Blood on the Fields* acknowledges that delineating the concept and meaning of freedom in America is never a simple equation for any individual, or the nation as a whole, more than four centuries after the first enslaved Americans were brought here.

Marsalis returned to the themes heard on *Blood on the Fields* with 2007's album *From the Plantation to the Penitentiary*, another indictment of American society and its systemic racism that disadvantages people of color. "Obviously spurred on by the war in Iraq, the tragedy of Hurricane Katrina, and what he clearly views as gluttonous, vapid, misogynistic and deeply racist American culture," writes critic Matt Collar, "Marsalis has crafted a bluesy, cerebral, soul-inflicted album reminiscent of work by such iconic artists as Charles Mingus and Nina Simone."[29] On the album, which reached number two on the *Billboard* jazz charts, Marsalis makes the claim that the overwhelming incarceration rates of Black men echoes the destructive system of slavery, which intentionally dissolved family structure for slaves, blocking any opportunity for resistance or resilience for Blacks for hundreds of years. Marsalis stated,

> Why I say from the plantation to the penitentiary is because I see a lot of similarities between the incarceration, the style of it now and the way of enslavement. No, it is not exactly the same, but it is the same in many ways, it generates a lot of income, and it reduces people to less than what they are.[30]

The seven-song, hour-long album features Marsalis as part of a quintet along with several Jazz at Lincoln Center Orchestra stalwarts: Ali Jackson Jr. on drums, Dan Nimmer on piano, Carlos Henriquez on bass, Walter Blanding on saxes, and guest vocalist Jennifer Sanon. One inspiration for the album was the startlingly incompetent 2005 response to Hurricane Katrina, which devastated Marsalis's hometown of New Orleans and surrounding areas and revealed just how weak the safety net was for the poor, largely Black working-class in New Orleans and the Mississippi Gulf Coast. Reflecting on the shock Americans felt as they watched the tragedy in the aftermath of Katrina, Marsalis stated, "People looked at the TV set and saw central government—and let's not forget, local government, which was black—behaving with incompetence and inhumanity. We saw human beings suffering through bureaucratic fumbling, ignorance and stupidity."[31]

The lyrics for the song "Supercapitalism" decry the seemingly out-of-control consumerism that Marsalis observed through a chorus that chants, "There's never enough, there's never enough, there's never enough, it's never enough, there's always some more. Oh, where you hidin' it?" And on the album's closing track, "Where Y'all At?," Marsalis delivers a blistering spoken-word performance that indicts the American citizenry, from its leaders to the people sitting safely at home watching the seemingly never-ending succession of injustices on the nightly news. Marsalis wondered why many were no longer engaging in the forms of direct action that helped ignite the social changes wrought by the 1960s civil rights movement, which he points out was a battle fought by Blacks and whites working together as allies to improve society:

> We supposed to symbolize freedom and pride
> But we got scared after King and the Kennedys died
> We take corruption and graft in stride
> Sittin' around like owls talkin' 'bout "*Who?* Who lied?"[32]

Marsalis's mood on this release is much more strident and direct than what's heard in *The Real Ambassadors*, but it is similarly anchored in the belief that artists have a duty to speak out against human suffering and racial injustice through their most influential platform, their music.[33]

A decade later, Christian McBride's recording *The Movement Revisited: A Musical Portrait of Four Heroes* continued along a similar path walked by the cast of *The Real Ambassadors* and Marsalis's socially conscious albums. McBride was championed early in his career by jazz legends, including bassist Ray Brown and saxophonist Benny Carter. He played his first professional gig at thirteen and found himself invited to study at Juilliard in New York City in 1989. A professional career took precedent as he left Juilliard after one year of formal studies to tour with saxophonist Bobby Watson. From there he has gone on to become one of the preeminent bassists, bandleaders, and public champions for jazz in America, hosting the syndicated weekly radio broadcast *Jazz Night in America*, which airs on National Public Radio. In 1995, he joined other emerging jazz stars, including Roy Hargrove and Joshua Redman, on an album led by Dave Brubeck titled *Young Lions & Old Tigers*.[34] Brubeck and McBride struck up a friendship that led to McBride serving for three years as the first artistic director of the Brubeck Institute after its founding in the early 2000s, during which time the bassist came to understand more about Brubeck's deep commitment to social justice issues.

The Movement Revisited is a sixty-four-minute suite built around the actual words of civil rights icons Rosa Parks, Dr. Martin Luther King Jr., Malcolm X, and Muhammad Ali, voiced by actors and supported by a musical score that cleverly punctuates the narration. AllMusic's Matt Collar praised the album, stating that it is "a powerful and deeply considered work that invokes not just the words, but also the ebullient spirit of the civil rights movement."[35] McBride composed, arranged, and produced the album, which features an eighteen-piece jazz orchestra and Voices of the Flame, a ten-member gospel choir. J. D. Steele collaborated with the bassist to provide the choral arrangements and lead vocals on two pieces. Steele is an accomplished performer,

composer, and arranger whose family ensemble, the Steeles, recorded for
Elektra Records. They also have toured internationally as part of the cast
for the acclaimed Broadway show *The Gospel at Colonus*, starring Morgan
Freeman.

First conceived as a commission from the Portland (Maine) Arts Society in 1998, for McBride's quartet and a choir, the four-movement piece's
premiere was well received that year, which is when Steele and McBride
first worked together. In 2008 while serving as their creative chair for jazz,
McBride was invited by the Los Angeles Philharmonic to reimagine the work
and present it that season in Walt Disney Hall. "I was more than excited to
play the piece the way I'd always dreamed of playing it—with a big band,"
McBride commented.[36] Six months after the performance in Los Angeles,
Barack Obama was elected president of the United States, which McBride
believed was directly related to the work of the four civil rights heroes he
recognizes in *The Movement Revisited*. Two years later, the former director
of the Detroit Jazz Festival, Terri Pontremoli, asked McBride if he would
consider a commission to further expand the piece, in light of Obama's elec-
tion. The newly composed fifth movement, titled "Apotheosis: November 4,
2008," was premiered on February 13, 2010, at the University of Michigan
in Ann Arbor. The suite was recorded at New York City's Avatar Studios in
September 2013, but the release was held up due to the lengthy negotiations
required to secure permissions to use the words of Muhammad Ali and Dr.
King in such a project. Finally, in February 2020, the record was released to
critical acclaim. In an interview with his hometown newspaper, the *Philadelphia Inquirer*, McBride explicitly referenced his own two-decade effort to
memorialize the civil rights struggles of his antecedents:

> There's always a need to know what happened in your past. We some-
> how tend to think that we're making progress when what we're really
> doing is picking up the ball where someone else left off. So a lot of
> what we're fighting for in today's culture are old battles.[37]

McBride clearly respects and builds on the musical efforts of the artists
who came before him to draw attention to the ongoing fight to bring equal
rights, and even more importantly, the systemic limitations placed on African Americans today in the US. What better way to achieve this goal than
through a compelling blend of the narrator's performance of the stirring,
thought-provoking letters and speeches, including Obama's heartfelt 2008
inauguration speech, and the music McBride has written in response to these
fundamental, eloquently expressed truths and ideals. It's no coincidence that

a through line can be traced from the lyrics sung in "Freedom Day," which celebrate Lincoln's Emancipation Proclamation, in Max Roach and Oscar Brown Jr.'s *We Insist!*, through *The Real Ambassadors'* "Blow Satchmo," which exhorted the character of Pops to use his horn to blow down the walls of segregation and set all men free, to Jon Hendricks's character Juba in *Blood on the Fields* declaring that "freedom is no simple thing," to Christian McBride's triumphant conclusion to "Apotheosis: November 4, 2008," where the gospel choir shouts, "Free at last, free at last, thank God Almighty, I'm free at last." Each of these artists used their musical agency to call for or celebrate the notion of freedom that was denied to persons of color in America. As such, jazz has once again confirmed its place as an art form that provides invaluable social commentary in the continuing struggles for equality.[38]

Contemporary composer and singer John Legend has remarked that "part of an artist's job is to imagine a different future."[39] With that expression, he clearly aligned with the Brubecks and Louis Armstrong at the moment they first performed the show.

Real Ambassadors represented Dave and Iola Brubeck's optimistic vision of what might be possible in an ideal world, where love could replace hate and fear. It came to life fueled by its creators' desire to bring about change in the world. Its success was in large part due to Dave and Iola crafting a story and music that operated on multiple levels at a critical juncture in US history. First, there were the jazz ambassadors and their love for sharing their musical gifts with an international, multicultural, and multiracial audience. Iola grounded the show's plot in actual events, including the triumphs of Dizzy Gillespie in Greece, Armstrong in Africa and Europe, and her own experiences on the 1958 State Department tour of the Dave Brubeck Quartet. Second, there was a tender love story expressed in the musical itself, the complicated and evolving relationship between Rhonda and Pops, that showed how patience and sympathy for one's partner could result in a strong and sustaining love. Additionally, the outpouring of love between the Talgallan people and Pops showed how music could be a powerful bridge across perceived chasms of race, social or economic standing, language, political belief systems, and culture.

Working together as creative partners, Dave and Iola Brubeck wrote lyrics that drew upon their deepest feelings. Some of the show's most moving passages exemplify this, including the melancholy "Summer Song," which Armstrong felt fit him to a T; the anguished plea for acceptance voiced in "They Say I Look Like God," which was undergirded by biblical call and response; and the triumphant jubilation expressed in "Blow Satchmo" that envisioned some future date when true freedom would be possible for all

African Americans, and which concluded the work. That tune argued that, like Joshua, Satchmo's trumpet could blast through the centuries-old walls of intolerance that were the source of America's malaise.

Dave Brubeck might have chuckled at the irony in his and Iola's inability to find any sponsor from 1957 to 1962, when he was arguably at the peak of his career, while in the twenty-first century, in the space of a few years, jazz impresarios have returned to the work and skillfully staged it to bring new audiences its compelling, humanistic message. Through the efforts of Chris Collins and the Detroit Jazz Festival, Wynton Marsalis and Jazz at Lincoln Center, and Simon Rowe of the Brubeck Institute, *The Real Ambassadors* has taken audiences of multiple generations on an emotional journey, pondering what will be required for mankind to inhabit a better world.

The Brubecks were trying to point the audience toward what they saw as mankind's Promised Land, a day when men and women of all races could be true equals. It is in this moment of dénouement that the genius and artistry of *The Real Ambassadors* comes fully to light. Standing ovations by audiences in 1962, 2002, 2013, 2014, and 2016 attest to the lasting relevance of the show.[40]

The opening lines of the musical's "Finale" demonstrate the idealistic dream that Dave and Iola Brubeck shared with us:

> Swing bells! Ring bells!
> The great day may now begin.
> Ring out, the news!
> The world can laugh again.
> This day we're free
> We're equal in every way
> Ring bells, swing bells,
> Declare a holiday!

At the time of this writing, it is still a largely unfulfilled dream—whose promise echoes as loudly today as it did during the civil rights movement's apex in the early 1960s. America is once again facing the daunting specter of division and hatred of the other after having elected the nation's first African American president. Perhaps the lessons of the grit, persistence and determination that the composers and cast of *The Real Ambassadors* embodied in their journey to its realization can help guide us toward a more humane future.

ACKNOWLEDGMENTS

Researching and recounting the untold story of *The Real Ambassadors* has provided me with a look at the life and work of a wide range of characters during a tumultuous time in America's history. As was the case with my earlier research into the Dave Brubeck Quartet's 1958 two-week State Department–sponsored tour of Poland, my attention was drawn to the jazz musical by a tiny mention in a Polish jazz magazine, which stated that a jazz musical titled *World Take a Holiday*, written by Dave and Iola Brubeck, was in the works. I had never heard of that composition before and decided that once I concluded my Polish essay, I would investigate the mystery musical.

In the process of documenting the Dave Brubeck Quartet's tour of Poland, I was introduced in 2005 to Dave and Iola Brubeck, who from our first meeting the morning after a gig in Sacramento, California, displayed a generosity of spirit and willingness to answer my many questions. The couple were in their mid-eighties when we began corresponding, and I was pleasantly surprised that both Iola and Dave had exceptionally clear memories of the times I was investigating. I corresponded primarily with Iola via email, and without fail, unless the couple was traveling, I would have a detailed and thoughtful reply within twenty-four hours. Relevant excerpts from Dave's unpublished autobiography, *A Time to Remember*, were another resource that the couple kindly shared with me and which proved invaluable.

The Brubeck children, especially Darius and his wife Cathy, Chris and his wife Tish, Cathy Brubeck Yaghsizian, and Dan Brubeck, were all gracious and kindly agreed to interviews to recount their own memories of the events covered in this work. Additionally, the Brubecks' longtime manager and musical director, Russell Gloyd, arranged my initial meeting with the couple and corresponded with me throughout much of the decade spent on this project. The Brubeck family attorney, Richard Jeweler, truly went above and beyond in providing me with a copy of the 1963 Hansen folio edition of the work, answering myriad questions about the Brubecks' business arrangements, and taking on the task of digging through decades-old statements to provide sales histories of the original release and the later compact disc reissue of the soundtrack album. Without the information and resources shared by Team Brubeck, this story could not have been told. Posthumous thanks are also due to the inimitable George Avakian, who signed Brubeck to Columbia and shared his witty and insightful commentary.

I was fortunate to be able to interview many of the participants in the historic 1962 performance. In addition to Dave and Iola Brubeck, Eugene Wright, Joe Morello, Jon Hendricks, Yolande Bavan, and stage manager Paul Vieregge shared their first-person recollections of the show's premiere. A significant portion of the historical documentation upon which the book rests resides in the Brubeck Collection. It includes extensive correspondence, audio recordings, sheet music, and sketches and other artifacts that helped me to piece together this story. To my knowledge, it represents one of the largest and most comprehensive collections dedicated to a single jazz musician.

As I began this project, the University of the Pacific Holt-Atherton Special Collections team of Shan Sutton, Trish Richards, and Mike Wurtz provided patient and knowledgeable guidance and support for my efforts. When Shan's career led him elsewhere, Mike Wurtz was promoted to lead the Special Collections team and became an essential collaborator in my research. Mike cocurated the fiftieth-anniversary exhibit that was featured at the Monterey Jazz Festival in 2012 and has copresented with me at numerous conferences, sharing how the varied holdings in the Brubeck Collection have been used to better understand the arc of jazz, civil rights, cultural diplomacy, the Cold War, and the struggles of jazz musicians to make a living. No researcher could have a more able and kind collaborator than he. His colleague Nicole Mountjoy graciously and promptly answered dozens of queries about Brubeck Collection assets and offered essential help in digitizing many of the images found in the book.

The sheer quantity of documents in the Brubeck Collection that needed review led me to hire talented undergraduate research assistants over the course of this project: Amy Langford, Nicole Sternagel, and John Langdon. Each was a tremendous help in the process of sifting through the hundreds of letters, telegrams, trip receipts, lyric drafts, lead sheets, and notes found throughout the collection that pertained directly or tangentially to my research. Thanks to each of you for your diligence and persistence. The encouragement and financial support for my research from University of the Pacific allowed me to make various research trips to Connecticut to spend time with the Brubecks and record Iola performing her original narration, and to visit New York City to interview Jon Hendricks and Yolande Bavan and access the assets of the New York Public Library for the Performing Arts. My appreciation also goes out to Ignacio Sanchez-Alonso and John Langdon for handling the oral history recordings of audience members of the 1962 Monterey premiere.

Deans Peter Witte, Daniel Ebbers, Giulio Ongaro, Bill Hipp, and Steve Anderson encouraged my research. Faculty colleagues Sarah Waltz, Patrick Langham, Ruth Brittin, Jim Haffner, Brian Kendrick, Veronica Wells, Michelle Maloney, Greg Rohlf, Jennifer Helgren, Bill Swagerty, Cynthia Dobbs, Joan Lin-Cereghino, Jim Uchizono, and Margaret Roberts all acted at various times as cheerleaders, supporters, chapter readers, or sounding boards. Glenn Pillsbury kindly read one of my first scholarly papers on *The Real Ambassadors* before a presentation at the Society for American Music and offered a much-needed critique and advice on how to best share my research findings. Conservatory staff including Yvette Khan, Kim Girardi, Melissa Riley, Judy Nagai, Simon Rowe, and Katie Neubauer all offered support over the term of this project. Provosts Maria Pallavicini and Phil Gilbertson endorsed my efforts to tell this story as well.

The story within the jazz musical and the tale of its making revolve around its sun, Louis Daniel Armstrong. His life in many ways is an analogue for jazz itself. Its origins are a bit murky, its popularity is undeniable, and its ability to serve as a vessel to communicate deeply and with lasting impact has proven durable and uniquely American. The best way to come to know Louis Armstrong is through his own words and music. He was a prolific author, penning hundreds of letters, recording thousands of hours of unedited conversations, and writing for news outlets and his own autobiographical works. The Louis Armstrong House Museum and Archives at Queens College in New York City provides another rich repository of historical materials for study.

Archivist and Armstrong biographer Ricky Riccardi has been a friend and confidante while serving as a veritable encyclopedia of wisdom and advice in all things Armstrong. His Dippermouth music blog is an astounding collection of writing and research drawing on rare recordings to help us appreciate the breadth and depth of Armstrong's contribution to jazz and American thought. Ricky not only helped me access the varied assets held in the Armstrong and Jack Bradley Collections but also graciously answered the call to partner with me to speak to audiences at Jazz at Lincoln Center, the Monterey Jazz Festival, and the Brubeck Festival. He's also introduced me to many other jazz writers and scholars, which has widened my network greatly. The late Michael Cogswell, former head of the Louis Armstrong House Museum and visionary for its future, supported my early research and also encouraged me greatly. Special thanks are also due to Susan Gedutis

Lindsay, whose thoughtful and experienced eye provided me with a critical, detailed reading of the draft manuscript at a crucial juncture and pointed out many ways to improve the narrative quality, chronology, and overall organization of my manuscript.

Early drafts of various chapters were also read and commented on by Pacific faculty mentioned earlier, as well as Simon Rowe, Kate Post, and Lewis Porter, who each offered suggestions and encouragement. Lewis also kindly invited me to sit in on his lecture on Dave Brubeck when I was visiting the Institute for Jazz Studies at Rutgers, which I greatly appreciated. Stephen A. Crist, another Brubeck scholar, has been a friend and confidante, especially when my enthusiasm flagged at various points in my research journey. Stephen's encouraging pep talks and sharing resources with me have been invaluable—many thanks for your support, Stephen! Jazz scholar Ryan Maloney kindly spent a day accessing and copying the relevant documents in the Teo Macero Collection held at the New York Public Library for the Performing Arts, which proved crucial to telling the story of how Columbia planned and produced the soundtrack album. Thanks so much, Ryan! Growing up in the San Francisco Bay Area, I learned a lot about jazz by listening to KJAZ and its successor, KCSM radio. The passionate and erudite on-air talent of both stations served as my music curators and jazz history instructors, piquing my interest to learn more about America's homegrown art form.

The staff of the Monterey Jazz Festival have been a tremendous help, pulling all the archival materials held in storage from the 1962 festival for me to study, partnering with me to convene the oral history project at the 2012 festival, and providing a platform for me to share my research. Tim Jackson, Colleen Bailey, Timothy Orr, Shawn Anderson, and Rob Klevan have all been incredibly supportive. Jazz writer Bill Minor, an expert in all things pertaining to the Monterey Jazz Festival, kindly shared his own perspectives on the musical and moderated the 2012 panel session there. Thanks are also due to Jake Cohen, Zooey Jones, and Jason Olaine at Jazz at Lincoln Center for providing a photo of the show's New York City premiere.

At University Press of Mississippi, kudos are due to editor Craig Gill for reading the manuscript and championing its publication at the press. His advice and support in refining the manuscript in various ways, especially the last chapter, which places *The Real Ambassadors* into the arc of mid-twentieth-century jazz history, greatly improved the final result. Craig's assistant, Carlton McGrone, has been an indispensable ally in assisting me with the minutiae of digital manuscript and image submissions and an additional critical eye to check each detail. Helping to get the word out about the book was the talented marketing team led by Steve Yates, and including Courtney

McCreary, Joey Brown, and Jordan Nettles. This volume benefited greatly from the deft copyediting of Nicholas Bergin, who helped to fine-tune the final text. Thanks to Pete Halverson for his creative talents in book design. Project manager Shane Gong Stewart shepherded the various processes and information to arrive at the final version you are holding.

Finally, I own an immeasurable amount of gratitude to my wife, Laura Hatschek, for her unflagging support of my research work now and over the previous decades. Fortunately, she loves music, and especially jazz, and has been by my side at some of the festivals where *The Real Ambassadors* has been remembered or performed. My daughters, Elyse and Megan, have also been cheering me on over the years in my passion to write about music history and culture. My own parents, Hans and Helene Hatschek, instilled a love of reading in me from birth, and for that I am grateful.

Dave Brubeck and his music, much like that of Armstrong, are woven into the fabric of American musical consciousness. Over the years as I have given talks or made appearances presenting my research on Brubeck, I have been continually surprised and delighted by audience members who approach me and have a personal anecdote or a signed program, or clarify or correct some fact I have mentioned. Accordingly, the assertions and conclusions I have drawn in this book are entirely my own work, and if there are any errors or inaccuracies, I am solely responsible for them. Similarly, there are no doubt others who have assisted me along the way to completing this book that I have neglected to mention, and my omission of those persons is entirely due to my own forgetfulness—to each of those persons, thanks from the bottom of my heart.

KEITH HATSCHEK
Livermore, California

NOTES

PROLOGUE

1. The Dave Brubeck Quartet's talented alto saxophonist, Paul Desmond, did not contribute to the recording or performance of the musical.

2. Penny Von Eschen, interview with Jerry Jazz Musician website, August 22, 2005, https://jerryjazzmusician.com/2005/08/penny-von-eschen-author-of-satchmo-blows-up-the-world/2/.

3. Fred M. Hall, *It's About Time: The Dave Brubeck Story* (Fayetteville: University of Arkansas Press, 1996), 23–25. Brubeck, a US Army private leading the band, was told to keep the Wolfpack all white by various officers, but he was able to skirt these orders due to the support of a senior officer who loved the band and, instead, ordered Brubeck to use the best musicians available, no matter their race. Trombonist Dick Flowers and emcee Gil White were two of the band's African American members.

4. Philip Clark, *Dave Brubeck: A Life in Time* (Boston: Da Capo Press, 2020), 93–94. In this detailed biography, Clark reports that Ruther played both live dates and recording sessions during this time; however, he traded off with bassist/bassoonist Fred Dutton, in part because Brubeck could not choose between the two players.

5. Jose Stell, "If You Want Your Jazz Festival to Go, Just Book Ol' Satchmo," *San Jose Mercury News*, September 26, 1962. The attendance number quoted here was underestimated, as a post-festival report in the September 24, 1962, *San Francisco Chronicle* (Gleason, "Symbolic Finale at Monterey") confirmed the audience on Sunday was closer to six thousand, setting attendance and revenue records (Brubeck Collection, 1962 Clippings, 1.e.3.14).

CHAPTER 1. MEET THE BRUBECKS

1. By 1956 the Brubeck family included Darius (born 1947), Michael (born 1949, died 2009), Chris (born 1952), Cathy (born 1953), and Dan (1955). In 1961, the Brubeck family grew again with the birth of Matt. State of California, *California Birth Index, 1905–1995* (Sacramento, CA: State of California Department of Health Services, Center for Health Statistics); and "Brubeck, Matt (Matthew)," Jazz.com, accessed January 4, 2021, via Internet Archive, https://web.archive.org/web/20131222083019/http://www.jazz.com/encyclopedia/brubeck-matt-matthew.

2. Hall, *It's About Time*, 23–24.

3. Iola attended first grade in a one-room schoolhouse that included first- through eighth-grade students. Notably, the older students acted as tutors to the younger ones.

4. Susan Matheson wrote an informative master's thesis exploring the life and philosophy of Iola Whitlock Brubeck. Susan Matheson, "In the Stream of Time: Iola Brubeck's Contributions to Jazz" (master's thesis, 1999), Brubeck Collection, University of the Pacific.

5. Noted newsman Walter Cronkite, who served overseas as a correspondent in the Second World War, conducted a one-hour interview with Brubeck that highlighted many of the experiences of his time serving in the Third Army, as well as reminiscences about growing up in California on a ranch. It is available as a bonus disc along with the 2004 musical release *Private Brubeck Remembers* (Telarc CD-83605).

6. Tjader moved from drums to vibraphone after leaving the Dave Brubeck Trio and would go on to lead his own groups and establish himself as an innovative voice in Latin jazz. Grove Music Online, s.v. "Tjader, Cal," by Lise Waxer, accessed June 10, 2019, https://o-www.oxfordmusiconline.com.pacificatclassic.pacific.edu/grovemusic/view/10.1093/gmo/9781561592630.001.0001/omo-9781561592630-e-0000049882?rskey=XOndvY&result=1.

7. *The Dave Brubeck Octet* is an eighteen-song compilation disc released in 1956 that combined recordings the ensemble made primarily in 1946–48, along with a later session from 1950. Although they received little notice when the original recordings were released, the arrangements and compositions marked a fresh new sound that would help create what would be referred to as cool or West Coast jazz. The CD version was reissued by Fantasy Records in 1991 (F-3-329).

8. Ted Gioia, *West Coast Jazz: Modern Jazz in California* (Oakland: University of California Press, 1992), 84–85.

9. Not to be confused with alto saxophonist Jimmy Lyons, who played in Cecil Taylor's ensemble from 1961 until Lyons's passing in 1986.

10. Gioia dedicates a chapter of *West Coast Jazz* to Brubeck's rise, while additional information about the pianist's early career is discussed in Fred Hall's biography, *It's About Time*. Coronet was a Dixieland label based in San Francisco that went bankrupt, and its masters were purchased by the then-fledgling Fantasy Records.

11. Dave Brubeck, interview with Bill Minor, September 17, 1996, Audio 1189, Stanford University Archive of Recorded Sound, Monterey Jazz Collection.

12. *Forty Great Years*, 1997 Monterey Jazz Festival commemorative program, F 10, Brubeck Collection, Brubeck Mentions, 1.e.8.9.

13. Clark, *Dave Brubeck: A Life in Time*, 49. Clark reveals that Lyons owned the Burma Lounge in 1949, concurrent with his regular promotion of Brubeck and his music on his radio broadcasts. See also Monterey Jazz Festival panel discussion, "Conversation with Dave Brubeck and Herb Wong," September 18, 1996, Item 1337 (video), Stanford University Archive of Recorded Sound, Monterey Jazz Collection.

14. Gioia, *West Coast Jazz*, 86. Brubeck's compositional approach was deeply influenced by his postwar studies with French classical composer Darius Milhaud at Mills College in Oakland, California.

15. Gioia, *West Coast Jazz*, 87.

16. Philip Elwood, liner notes to *Stardust*, Fantasy 24728, Brubeck Collection, Business Correspondence, 1.d.33.

17. Desmond's brilliant but somewhat turbulent life has been detailed in the excellent book *Take Five: The Public and Private Lives of Paul Desmond* by jazz journalist Doug Ramsey (Seattle: Parkside Publications, 2005).

18. Keith Hatschek, "Jazz at the College of Pacific—Celebrating a Landmark Recording," *Rifftides*, December 13, 2013, https://www.artsjournal.com/rifftides/2013/12/guest-column -a-brubeck-anniversary-2.html. This is an appreciation of the musical gems found on the December 13, 1953, live recording that was recorded and released as the third in a series of live dates by the group. The close interplay between Desmond and Brubeck is readily apparent throughout this album (Fantasy OJCCD-047-2).

19. Clark, *Dave Brubeck: A Life in Time*, 74. The club operated at the corner of Turk and Hyde Streets in downtown San Francisco from 1949 to 1963. Clark points out that the club's name was in fact two words—Black Hawk—but that it was referred to throughout its life interchangeably as Blackhawk or Black Hawk, including on album artwork of live recordings done at the famous nightspot.

20. Philip Elwood, liner notes to *Stardust*.

21. Dave and Iola Brubeck, interview with the author, July 22, 2009, Brubeck residence, Wilton, Connecticut.

22. "Conversation with Dave Brubeck and Herb Wong," (Monterey Jazz Festival panel discussion, September 18, 1996), Item 1337 (video), Stanford University Archive of Recorded Sound, Monterey Jazz Collection.

23. Ramsey, *Take Five*, 154.

24. Gioia, *West Coast Jazz*, 97.

25. Clark, *Dave Brubeck: A Life in Time*, 61.

26. Hall, *It's About Time*, 54–55.

27. Keith Hatschek and Veronica A. Wells, *Historical Dictionary of the American Music Industry* (Lanham, MD: Rowman and Littlefield, 2018), 47, s.v. "Avakian, George."

28. Stuart A. Kallen, *The History of Jazz* (New York: Lucent Publishing, 2002), 66.

29. George Avakian, correspondence with the author, May 3, 2010.

30. Hall, *It's About Time*, 83.

31. Robert Rice, "The Clean Up Man," *New Yorker*, June 3, 1961.

32. Virginia Lee Warren, "For the Brubeck Family, the Stress Is on Togetherness," *New York Times*, September 11, 1972.

33. Cathy Brubeck Yaghsizian, interview with the author, December 8, 2018.

34. Darius Brubeck, interview with the author, December 15, 2018.

35. Barbara Baxley (1923–1990) was a classmate and very close friend of Iola Brubeck at College of the Pacific. She went on to success on Broadway and television, being nominated for a Tony Award for her performance in Tennessee Williams's *Period of Adjustment*. She was also in the cast of Neil Simon's acclaimed comedy *Plaza Suite*. Later in her career she received critical acclaim for her film roles as Sally Fields's mother in *Norma Rae* and the feisty Lady Pearl in Robert Altman's *Nashville*. Susan Boyer, "Barbara Baxley: Biography," IMDb, accessed January 4, 2021, https://www.imdb.com/name/nm0062642/bio?ref_=nm_ov_bio_sm.

36. Chris and Tish Brubeck, interview with the author, December 3, 2018.

37. Iola Brubeck, interview with Mike Lawless, "The Dave Brubeck Show," WJZZ, September 8, 1961, audio tape, Brubeck Collection. While Iola recalled Central Park as the setting for the 1956 Basie/Joe Williams Concert, a search of contemporary sources reveals that the concert most likely occurred at Randall's Island Stadium. In an ad featured in the July 29, 1956, *New York Times*, the "First Annual New York Jazz Festival" listed Basie and Williams headlining the Friday, August 24, show, with none other than the Dave Brubeck Quartet performing the next night, Saturday, August 25, 1956. Hence, it's likely that the Brubecks would have had comp tickets to the performances.

CHAPTER 2. WORDS AND MUSIC

1. For example, Armstrong's band had been banned from playing throughout the South due to having an integrated lineup. Most famously, the All-Stars were forbidden from playing in Armstrong's own hometown of New Orleans. Iola included reference to the places Armstrong wasn't welcome with his integrated group in the script, when an offstage voice calls out, "Look here, what we need is a good will tour of Mississippi!!" They are answered by a second voice, suggesting, "Forget Moscow, when do we play New Orleans?" In just two lines, the Brubecks provided the audience with references to the racism Satchmo faced in America, as well as the State Department's plans to send jazz ambassadors around the world, even to the Soviet Union. *The Real Ambassadors*, Hansen piano-vocal folio (1963), 21.

2. *World Take a Holiday* story synopsis (1957), Brubeck Collection, 1.d.13.

3. Iola Brubeck, "Memo re: *World Take a Holiday* Synopsis—First Western Bank," Brubeck Collection, 1957 Correspondence.

4. The one-hour concert version of the show did not allow for the characters of Saul and Ellie to be included.

5. *World Take a Holiday* story synopsis.

6. To avoid confusion, the musical itself will regularly be referred to as *The Real Ambassadors* throughout this work. The original title, *World Take a Holiday*, will only be used when a specific reference to its original title was made or used by the Brubecks or others during its development. The final name was not confirmed until a title was needed by Columbia Records in the summer of 1962, just before releasing the soundtrack album on September 1 of that year.

7. Arthur North, "Back By Request," *New York Daily News Sunday News*, April 1, 1962, Brubeck Collection, Clippings, 1962.

8. Darius Brubeck, interview with the author, December 15, 2018.

9. *The Real Ambassadors*, piano-vocal folio, 9. All excerpts from the musical throughout are kindly provided by permission of Derry Music, Brubeck's publishing company.

10. Penny Von Eschen, *Satchmo Blows Up the World: Jazz Ambassadors Play the Cold War* (Cambridge, MA: Harvard University Press, 2006), 34. This is an indispensable work for understanding how the jazz ambassadors impacted the Cold War culture wars.

11. Von Eschen, *Satchmo Blows Up the World*, 39.

12. *The Real Ambassadors*, piano-vocal folio, 10.

13. Leonard Feather, "Jazz: Goodwill Ambassador Overseas—Fighter Against Jim Crow in the U.S." *Billboard*, May 4, 1974, N-40.

14. *The Real Ambassadors*, piano-vocal folio, 21–23.

15. A fascinating account of the complicated behind-the-scenes machinations required to pull off Brubeck's 1958 State Department–sponsored world tour is detailed in Stephen A. Crist's essay "Jazz as Democracy? Dave Brubeck and Cold War Politics," *Journal of the American Musicological Society* 26, no. 2 (Spring 2009): 133–74.

16. *The Real Ambassadors*, piano-vocal folio, 21.

17. *The Real Ambassadors*, piano-vocal folio, 47–50.

18. "The Real Ambassador" lyrics, n.d., Brubeck Collection, 1.d.13.

19. "Holiday" lyric worksheets, n.d., Brubeck Collection, 1.d.13.

20. *The Real Ambassadors*, piano-vocal folio, iii.

21. Dave and Iola Brubeck, interview with the author, July 22, 2009. Also reported in the *Montreal Gazette*, July 8, 2013, in an anecdote attributed to Chris Brubeck as he introduced the song at a concert (https://montrealgazette.com/entertainment/music/montreal -international-jazz-festival-2013-the-brubeck-brothers-quartet-at-theatre-jean-duceppe -of-place-des-arts-july-7).

22. *The Real Ambassadors*, piano-vocal folio, 24–32.

23. "World Take a Holiday" lead sheet, n.d., Brubeck Collection, 3.a.8.14.

24. Iola would not complete the final narrator's script until the summer of 1962, just before the show's premiere at the Monterey Jazz Festival.

CHAPTER 3. BECOMING JAZZ AMBASSADORS

1. Felix Belair, "United States Has Secret Sonic Weapon—Jazz," *New York Times*, November 6, 1955, 1.

2. ANTA was the arts-presenting organization charged by the US State Department with coordinating cultural exchange tours by US performing artists to foreign countries. While on tour, the performers were directly supported by the United States Information Agency and local embassy staff, including the cultural attaché.

3. Crist, "Jazz as Democracy," 138–39.

4. Grove Music Online, s.v. "Wright, Eugene," by Brenda Pennell, 2003, updated by Barry Kernfeld, accessed May 27, 2020, https://0-www.oxfordmusiconline.com.pacificat classic.pacific.edu/grovemusic/view/10.1093/gmo/9781561592630.001.0001/omo-97815615926 30-e-2000492100.

5. Brubeck's 1958 State Department–sponsored tour has been analyzed in a number of works: the previously cited Stephen Crist essay, "Jazz as Democracy? Dave Brubeck and Cold War Politics"; a chapter in Von Eschen's *Satchmo Blows Up the World*, which follows Brubeck's tour and situates the musical as an important part of the struggle for equality in America; and finally, Keith Hatschek, "The Impact of American Jazz Diplomacy in Poland During the Cold War Era," *Jazz Perspectives* 4, no. 3 (December 2010): 253–300, which examines Brubeck's two-week residency, concerts, and people-to-people interactions in Poland, narrowing the lens more than the two other scholars.

6. Avakian worked at Columbia until March 1958, when he left to go to Los Angeles and help found Warner Brothers Records. The Brubecks maintained their relationship with him in the role of an informal advisor.

7. Paul Gregory, interview with American Legends, American Legends, accessed May 5, 2019, https://www.americanlegends.com/interviews/paul_gregory.html. Among the few sources on Gregory, this interview with the director and producer includes a detailed biography as a preface to an interview that primarily covers his role in producing the hit 1955 motion picture *Night of the Hunter*.

8. This amount of income would represent more than $2.3 million in 2021 revenue. NB: All current dollar amount estimates are based on the US Bureau of Labor Statistics CPI Inflation Calculator (as of June 2021), found at https://www.bls.gov/data/inflation_calculator.htm.

9. Paul Gregory, interview with American Legends.

10. Iola Brubeck, email to the author, May 3, 2010.

11. Dave Brubeck, letter to George Avakian, December 13, 1957, Brubeck Collection, Business Correspondence, 1.a.3.21.

12. George Avakian, correspondence with the author, April 30, 2010.

13. Dave Brubeck, letter to Howard Brubeck, January 26, 1958, Brubeck Collection, 1.a.2.36. Many of these letters are addressed to "Pete" or "Peter" Brubeck, which was Howard Brubeck's family nickname, as well as Dave's father's name.

14. Crist, "Jazz as Democracy," 149.

15. Hatschek, "The Impact of American Jazz Diplomacy in Poland During the Cold War Era." This essay includes more detailed descriptions of the Brubeck entourage's people-to-people interactions, as well as the US-Poland "Jazz-Lift" efforts, which provided a consistent stream of donated jazz recordings to Polish jazz circles after the 1958 tour. A parallel effort to the Brubecks' Polish music donations may be found in a contemporary article by Mildred Schroeder, "Russians Offered Visits for Peace Plan," *San Francisco Chronicle*, September 27, 1962. In it she cites the gifts of recordings from the Monterey Jazz Festival destined for the Moscow Jazz Club.

16. Crist, "Jazz as Democracy," 148–50.

17. Hatschek, "The Impact of American Jazz Diplomacy," 278.

18. During a 2007 research trip by the author to Poland to interview local jazz musicians and fans who attended the quartet's 1958 shows, a personal copy of the original twelve-page program book was donated by Kris Wilski to the Brubeck Collection.

19. Eugene Wright, interview with the author, October 28, 2008.

20. Dave and Iola Brubeck, interview with Caroline C. Crawford, 1999 and 2001, in *A Long Partnership in Music*, (Berkeley, CA: Bancroft Library, 2006), 63.

21. Ralph J. Gleason, "Mrs. Dave Brubeck Discussed Jazz Abroad," *DownBeat*, July 10, 1958, Brubeck Collection, 1958 Clippings.

22. Hatschek, "The Impact of American Jazz Diplomacy," 292.

23. Gleason, "Mrs. Dave Brubeck Discussed Jazz Abroad." Russ Wilson of the *Oakland Tribune* also reported on Iola's observations upon her return in an April 6, 1958, column titled "Goodwill Envoys Home from Trip Behind Iron Curtain," Brubeck Collection, 1958 Clippings.

24. Hatschek, "The Impact of American Jazz Diplomacy," 278.

25. Dave Brubeck, letter to Ernie Farmer, Shawnee Press, May 27, 1958, Brubeck Collection, Business Correspondence, 1.a.2.36.

26. Dave Brubeck, "The Beat Heard 'Round the World," *New York Times*, June 15, 1958. Millstein is not cited as a co-author even though a telegram dated June 3, 1958, from Dave Brubeck to Lewis Bergman of the *New York Times* asked that the article include the byline "By Dave Brubeck as told to Gilbert Millstein." The *Times* opted to only cite Dave Brubeck. Letter from Dave Brubeck to Lewis Bergman, *New York Times*, June 3, 1958, MS4, Brubeck Collection, Business Correspondence, 1.a.2.36.

27. Brubeck, "The Beat Heard 'Round the World."

28. Brubeck, "The Beat Heard 'Round the World."

29. Brubeck, "The Beat Heard 'Round the World."

CHAPTER 4. FINDING A PRODUCER

1. The visit is cited in a letter from Dave to Howard Brubeck dated May 29, 1958 (Brubeck Collection, Personal Correspondence, 1.a.2.36). At the end of it, the strain of the four-month tour can be seen, as Brubeck wrote, "Eventually, I intend to get away from this constant touring and develop our growing stockpile of music; and if we can just see this first show [*World Take a Holiday*] in production, I will be encouraged to develop this field of writing." The steady stream of one-nighters not only kept Brubeck away from home, it also precluded developing his interest in starting to compose long-form music.

2. Gary Marmorstein, *The Label: The Story of Columbia Records* (New York: Avalon Publishing, 2007), 269.

3. Dave and Iola Brubeck, interview with the author, July 22, 2009.

4. Correspondence mentions Lieberson's introduction to Logan, while it also appears that agents in the Associated Booking offices introduced Logan to Dave and Iola, according to other letters from this period.

5. Logan's papers are held at the Library of Congress, http://memory.loc.gov/service/mss/eadxmlmss/eadpdfmss/uploaded_pdf/ead_pdf_batch_17_July_2009/ms997002.pdf.

6. Typewritten correspondence from Dave Brubeck was regularly authored jointly with Iola Brubeck, as she handled virtually all formal correspondence on behalf of her husband. In separate interviews with the author, longtime Brubeck attorney James Bancroft, as well as the Brubecks themselves, confirmed this fact.

7. Paul Finkelman and Cary Wintz, *Encyclopedia of the Harlem Renaissance* (New York: Routledge, 2004), 581. The authors point out the irony that even though the wildly popular Connie's Inn was located in the heart of Harlem, only white patrons were allowed to attend shows there put on by exclusively Black casts. See also Terry Teachout, *Pops: A Life of Louis Armstrong* (Boston: Houghton Mifflin Harcourt, 2009), 136. In this comprehensive biography, Teachout refers to that fact and also cites that club owners Connie and George Immerman were backed, as was the Broadway version of the review, by mobster Dutch Schultz, who provided the liquor for their popular nightclub during Prohibition.

8. Dave Brubeck, letter to Joe Glaser, November 20, 1958, Brubeck Collection, 1.a.2.36.

9. Ralph Gleason, "You Can't Play Here," *San Francisco Chronicle*, September 21, 1958. For reference, the proposed $17,000 in gigging and travel fees would be valued at $159,821 in 2021.

10. "Why Brubeck's Band Won't Play Georgia," *New York Post*, February 24, 1959, Brubeck Collection, 1.e.1.a.9

11. "Prejudice Losing World for U.S.," *Jet*, April 30, 1959, Brubeck Collection, 1.e.1.a.9.

12. Hall, *It's About Time*, 72. The value of $40,000 dollars in 1960 would equal $356,167 in 2021. The three colleges that did not cancel the group's performances were Vanderbilt University in Nashville, the University of the South in Sewanee, Tennessee, and the University of Jacksonville in Florida, according to an undated clipping titled "Brubeck Sees Bias in the South," Brubeck Collection, 1.d.1.12.

13. Eugene Wright, interview with the author, October 22, 2008.

14. Iola Brubeck, correspondence with the author, December 4, 2011.

CHAPTER 5. JOE GLASER

1. Ricky Riccardi, *Heart Full of Rhythm: The Big Band Years of Louis Armstrong* (New York: Oxford University Press, 2020).

2. Devra Hall and John Levy, *Men, Women and Girl Singers* (Silver Spring, MD: Beckham Publications, 2000), 70.

3. Michael Cogswell, *Louis Armstrong: The Off-Stage Story of Satchmo* (Portland, OR: Collectors Press, 2003), 168.

4. Laurence Bergreen, cited in Simon Hodgson, "A Hell of a Businessman: A Biography of Joe Glaser," *Inside A.C.T.* (blog), January 29, 2016, http://blog.act-sf.org/2016/01/a-hell-of-businessman-biography-of-joe.html.

5. John Levy, who worked frequently as a road manager for Glaser, reported that it was Glaser's mother who owned all or part of the Sunset Cafe, although Capone's involvement was in supplying the liquor and enforcement necessary to keep the club operating during Prohibition. Hall also references jazz musicians Milt Hinton and Harry Gray (of the Musicians Union) telling him that Glaser had close ties to the underworld. Hall and Levy, *Men, Women and Girl Singers*, 36.

6. George Avakian, correspondence with the author, May 3, 2010.

7. Riccardi, *Heart Full of Rhythm*, 164.

8. Mark Meckna, *Louis Armstrong Encyclopedia* (Westport, CT: Greenwood Press, 2004), 34. Bigard is cited as having enhanced the critical reaction to the debut of Armstrong's All-Stars, since his playing, like that of Louis, was infused with authentic New Orleans flavor.

9. Barney Bigard and Barry Martyn, *With Louis and the Duke: The Autobiography of a Jazz Clarinetist* (New York: Oxford University Press, 1985), 31.

10. Teachout, *Pops: A Life of Louis Armstrong*, 206–7, 364. Riccardi, *Heart Full of Rhythm*, 164–65, provides greater detail in his account of the legal problems connected with Glaser's predilection for young girls.

11. Hodgson, "A Hell of a Businessman."

12. Riccardi, Teachout, and Cogswell each offer insightful accounts of Armstrong's earlier managers, Tommy Rockwell and Johnny Collins. Riccardi's account offers the greatest detail among these various sources.

13. George Avakian, correspondence with the author, April 30, 2010.

14. Cogswell, *Louis Armstrong: The Off-Stage Story of Satchmo*, 23. He details Armstrong's troubles with his earlier managers on pp. 160–68. See also Teachout, *Pops: A Life of Louis Armstrong*, 160–96; and Riccardi, *Heart Full of Rhythm*, 16–45 and 140–43. Riccardi notes that unlike today's comprehensive artist manager's role, Johnny Collins handled live performance bookings for Armstrong, while at the same time Tommy Rockwell was in charge of the trumpeter's recording agreements, repertoire, and scheduling. As a result, the trumpeter had two managers with sometime competing interests calling the shots for him.

15. Clark, *Dave Brubeck: A Life in Time*, 61. In 1970, Dave Brubeck ended his business relationship with Associated Booking.

16. Darius Brubeck, interview with the author, December 15, 2018.

17. Chris and Tish Brubeck, interview with the author, December 8, 2018. Philip Clark provides additional evidence of how organized crime was involved in the jazz world, as Birdland, one of New York City's most prominent jazz clubs, had ties to Morris Levy, who required artists to begin and end all live broadcasts from the club by playing the tune "Lullaby of Birdland," for which Levy controlled the copyright. Clark also shared a story told by Dave Brubeck of once turning down a "gift" of $10,000 from an unnamed and unknown "friend" late one night after finishing a gig at a jazz club. The implication was that, if he accepted it, there would come a time when that "friend," someone from the crime world, would demand a favor in return. Brubeck declined the money. Clark, *Dave Brubeck: A Life in Time*, 161–66.

18. George Avakian, correspondence with the author, May 3, 2010.

19. Cogswell, *Louis Armstrong: The Off-Stage Story of Satchmo*, 168.

20. James Bancroft, a Brubeck attorney, shared this anecdote, which typifies Glaser's approach to getting what he wanted. "Michael Maloney, an attorney renegotiating Brubeck's agency contract with Glaser, went to New York in 1961 to finalize the deal in person on Brubeck's behalf. Glaser took Maloney to the Bronx to attend a New York Yankees game. Instead of the baby blue Rolls Royce he normally drove around the city, Glaser drove to the ballpark in a nondescript sedan. He pulled to a fire hydrant adjacent to the stadium and spoke to a policeman who knew him on sight. The officer agreed to keep an eye on his car, as Glaser slipped him five dollars. Glaser related to Maloney that this was his 'regular parking place,' before proceeding to his usual seats directly behind home plate" (Bancroft, interview with the author, June 3, 2009). Maloney was an associate of Bancroft who took over Brubeck's legal work as Bancroft became too busy for the day-to-day work by the early 1960s; however, Bancroft remained a trusted confidante to Brubeck throughout the pianist's life.

21. Hall and Levy, *Men, Women and Girl Singers*, 72. The 2021 value of this sum adjusted for inflation would be $7.89 million. Cohen led Associated Booking after Glaser's death and spent his entire career of seventy-eight years at the agency, from his start in 1942 as an office assistant to his passing in 2020. He worked with the Dave Brubeck Quartet throughout the group's tenure with the booking agency.

22. Avakian, correspondence with the author, May 3, 2010.

23. Although originally released by Roulette in 1961 as a ten-track album titled *Recording Together for the First Time*, an expanded collection was reissued on CD in 2000 and renamed *The Great Summit: Complete Sessions (Deluxe Edition)* [Blue Note 5245462], with a total of twenty-seven tracks, including alternate takes, false starts, and studio banter among the musicians.

24. Eventually, Ellington's "Portrait of Louis Armstrong," without Louis's performance, came out on a 1970 Atlantic release (SD-1580) titled *New Orleans Suite*.

25. Pop star Tommy James, who sold millions of records in the 1960s and '70s, detailed how Levy and Roulette kept the entirety of his royalties due to the label's Mob connection in his autobiography, *Me, the Mob and the Music* (New York: Scribner, 2010). See also Rick Campbell, "For Tommy James, the Past is the Future," *Houston Chronicle*, July 5, 2010, https://blog.chron.com/40yearsafter/2010/07/for-tommy-james-the-past-is-the-future/.

26. The pairing of Armstrong with the Dukes of Dixieland resulted in two albums on the Audio Fidelity label. Details of their collaboration may be found in an informative essay by Ricky Riccardi, "55 Years of Louie and the Dukes of Dixieland," *The Wonderful World of Louis Armstrong* (blog), accessed November 21, 2019, http://dippermouth.blogspot.com/search?q=Dukes+of+Dixieland.

27. Thanks to Armstrong biographer and archivist Ricky Riccardi for sharing the backstory on the Audio Fidelity releases Armstrong recorded via an email. Studio and recording dates for *Satchmo Plays King Oliver* (AFSD 5930) are cited on Discogs, https://www.discogs.com/Louis-Armstrong-His-Orch-Satchmo-Plays-King-Oliver/release/2084061 (accessed July 16, 2020).

28. The agency still operates today in New York City, handling a roster of mostly legacy artists, under the guidance of Lisa Cohen, Oscar Cohen's daughter. See http://www.associatedbooking.com/ab.html.

29. Ricky Riccardi, email to the author, June 12, 2020.

30. Grove Music Online, s.v. "Wein, George," by Barry Long, accessed August 6, 2020, https://o-doi.org.pacificatclassic.pacific.edu/10.1093/gmo/9781561592630.article.A2258690.

31. George Wein with Nate Chinen, *Myself Among Others: A Life in Music* (Boston: Da Capo Press, 2004), 300.

32. Ricky Riccardi, "Louis Armstrong, Joe Glaser and *Satchmo at the Waldorf*," *The Wonderful World of Louis Armstrong* (blog), January 26, 2016, https://dippermouth.blogspot.com/2016/01/louis-armstrong-joe-glaser-and-satchmo.html. Riccardi's arguments attempt to debunk Wein's attributed quote of Armstrong denigrating Glaser after the manager's death, drawing on a wealth of primary materials, and although it is lengthy, it is an excellent example of the scholarly use of evidence. All of the financial data I rely on in this section is drawn from this informative essay.

33. Terry Teachout, *Satchmo at the Waldorf* (New York: Dramatists Play Service Inc., 2015). The play's preview version may be accessed at https://www.dramatists.com/previews/4976.pdf.

34. Dave Brubeck, *A Time to Remember* (unpublished autobiography, coauthored with Iola Brubeck). The couple graciously shared relevant excerpts from this work with the author.

CHAPTER 6. STANDING UP TO SEGREGATION

1. "Satchmo and Trumpet Dull Knoxville Blast," *New York Times*, February 20, 1957.

2. According to the article "Louis Armstrong and Little Rock: 60 Years Later" by Ricky Riccardi, both the Associated Press and United Press International circulated Armstrong's incendiary remarks on the Little Rock struggle, so it was page-one news across the

nation's papers and nightly radio and television broadcasts (http://dippermouth.blogspot
.com/2017/09/louis-armstrong-and-little-rock-60.html, accessed June 3, 2019). Another
insightful look at the impact of Satchmo's calling out of our nation's leaders at that time may
be found in David Margolik's "The Day Louis Armstrong Made Noise," which celebrates the
fifty-year anniversary of Satchmo's diatribe, *New York Times*, September 23, 2017, https://
www.nytimes.com/2007/09/23/opinion/23margolick.html.

3. Bigard and Martyn, *With Louis and the Duke*, 117. All-Star clarinetist Barney Bigard
despised Tallerie and tried to get Armstrong to fire the road manager because he was denigrating members of the band to club owners and promoters every night. Bigard also asserted
that Tallerie must have done some "dirty work," because the FBI maintained a file on him.

4. "Satchmo Tells Off Ike, U.S.," *Pittsburgh Courier*, September 28, 1957, 33.

5. *Louis Armstrong in His Own Words*, ed. Thomas Brothers (New York: Oxford University
Press, 1999), 194.

6. Dave and Iola Brubeck, *A Time to Remember*.

7. Partial lyrics to the song "The Real Ambassador," Brubeck Collection, 1.d.13.

8. Teachout, *Pops: A Life of Louis Armstrong*, 336–39. He recounts the heart attack that
occurred in Spoleto, Italy, as well as some of Armstrong's other health problems, arguing
they were largely the byproduct of playing incessantly for four decades with few breaks.

9. Joe Glaser, letter to Dave Brubeck, November 28, 1958, folder "DB 1963," Brubeck
Collection, 1.c.1.

10. George Avakian, correspondence with the author, May 3, 2010.

11. Speculation continues today as to what percentage of Armstrong's performance and
endorsement income Glaser kept, with some estimates topping 50 percent.

12. Teachout, *Pops: A Life of Louis Armstrong*, 337.

13. Cogswell, *Louis Armstrong: The Off-Stage Story of Satchmo*, 172.

14. Ricky Riccardi, *What a Wonderful World: The Magic of Louis Armstrong's Later Years*
(New York, Pantheon: 2011), 224. The sum of $1 million in 1964 would equal $8.79 million
in 2021.

15. George Avakian, letter to the author, April 30, 2010.

16. Nat Hentoff, "Louis Armstrong and Reconstruction," *Village Voice*, May 26, 1992. The
reference to Glaser's dogs relates to the fact that as a non-music business pursuit, Glaser had
become recognized nationally as a breeder of championship show dogs.

17. Dave Brubeck, letter to Joe Glaser, December 3, 1958, Brubeck Collection, 1.a.2.36.

CHAPTER 7. SECURING SATCHMO

1. The December 27, 1958, engagement at the Empire Room is referenced in Armstrong
scholar Håkan Forsberg's excellent directory, *Louis Armstrong Day by Day*, updated March
6, 2013. A copy was kindly shared with the author by Ricky Riccardi.

2. The New York Philharmonic was renamed the Lewisohn Stadium Symphony Orchestra
for a series of summer concerts held uptown at the twenty-seven-thousand-seat stadium.
CBS Television producer Fred Friendly would film the performance and incorporate it into
his movie *Satchmo the Great*. The program, conducted by Leonard Bernstein on July 14, 1956,

celebrated the life and music of the iconic African American musician and composer W. C. Handy, who was in attendance. It was reportedly the first such concert to feature jazz artists.

3. Teachout, *Pops: A Life of Louis Armstrong*, 15. The author argues that Armstrong met so many people throughout his travels that he settled on the generic sobriquet of "Pops" for everyone he met in passing. Teachout suggests that name stuck to Armstrong in part because, to his multigenerational, global audience he was "the father figure of jazz, and what his children wanted was to be him, or at least come as close as they possibly could."

4. Dave and Iola Brubeck, *A Time to Remember*.

5. Dave Brubeck recounted this anecdote as an introduction to an audio letter (recorded at his home in Oakland on reel-to-reel tape) that accompanied what was then the most recent version of the show's songs, with Brubeck singing the melodies (Louis Armstrong House Archives, tape 1987.3.63, disc 2). Although the song was recorded at the September 1961 sessions, it was not released until the 1994 reissue, nor was it performed at Monterey.

6. Dave and Iola Brubeck, *A Time to Remember*. As a teenager in the 1930s, Brubeck had performed regularly as a member of regional territory bands at weekend dances up and down California's Central Valley, so he was familiar with many of that era's standards that the All-Stars performed.

7. Dave and Iola Brubeck, *A Time to Remember*.

8. *You Asked for It*, January 3, 1959, ABC television, transcript of audio clip found in Louis Armstrong House Museum, audio tape 1987.3.0063.

9. Dave and Iola Brubeck, audio letter to Louis Armstrong, January 3, 1959, Brubeck Collection, Audio Recordings, 4.b.19.1.

10. Grove Music Online, s.v. "McRae, Carmen," by Ed Bemis, revised by Barry Kernfeld, 2003, accessed May 27, 2020, https://doi.org/10.1093/gmo/9781561592630.article.J990125. Carmen McRae Discography, Discogs, accessed May 27, 2020, https://www.discogs.com/artist/34183-Carmen-McRae.

11. Dave Brubeck, letter to to Joe Glaser, January 3, 1959, Brubeck Collection, 1.a.3.21.

12. Dave Brubeck, telegram to Oscar Cohen, January 4, 1959, Brubeck Collection, 1.a.3.21.

13. Joe Glaser, letter to Dave Brubeck, January 5, 1959, Brubeck Collection, Business Correspondence, 1.a.3.21.

14. Glaser goes on to detail Armstrong's commitments between January 5 and 12, leaving little doubt that he was committed to a mix of performances, rehearsals, and a television appearance on *The Timex Hour* variety show in the days leading up to his departure. However, Glaser did not dispute the Brubecks' assertion that January 13 was free.

15. Dave Brubeck, letter to Joe Glaser, January 8, 1959, Brubeck Collection, 1.a.3.21.

16. Dave Brubeck, letter to Joe Glaser, January 8, 1959, Brubeck Collection, 1.a.3.21.

CHAPTER 8. GATHERING MOMENTUM

1. James Bancroft, interview with the author, June 3, 2009.

2. James Bancroft, letter to Dave Brubeck, December 1, 1954, Brubeck Collection, Business Correspondence, 1954.

3. Bancroft's other clients increasingly took more of his time, so that by the early 1960s his associates handled Brubeck's day-to-day legal needs. As of this writing, a former Bancroft associate, Richard S. Jeweler, still represents Brubeck's musical catalog.

4. Iola Brubeck, letter to the author, April 5, 2010.

5. Joshua Logan, letter to Dave and Iola Brubeck, Brubeck Collection, 1.a.3.4.

6. George Avakian, correspondence with the author, April 30, 2010.

7. Iola Brubeck, letter to James Bancroft, March 8, 1959, Brubeck Collection, 1.a.3.21. The Brubecks also considered Glaser as a possible investor. Dave had asked Glaser in his November 20, 1958, letter if he might consider investing in the show. No reply from Glaser exists in the extant archives.

8. Iola Brubeck, letter to James Bancroft, March 8, 1959.

9. Dorothy Kilgallen, "Brubeck Pens 25 Songs for Musical," *New York Journal American*, March 9, 1959. Her syndicated audience was estimated at more than twenty million readers, and she was also a cast regular on the weekly game show "What's My Line?" John Simkin, "Dorothy Kilgallen Bio," Spartacus Educational, accessed January 4, 2021, https://spartacus -educational.com/JFKkilgallen.htm.

10. Larry Bennett, letter to to Iola Brubeck, March 17, 1959, Brubeck Collection, 1.e.7.6. Handwritten by Bennett at the bottom of the letter is the note, "I planted the seed for this story the day I last spoke to you." Bennett had been a bassist in Wingy Manone's band in 1941, according to George Avakian, and joined Glaser's agency after the war. He and his colleague Bert Block, a former bandleader, did the majority of music bookings for ABC, according to Avakian (George Avakian, correspondence with the author, May 3, 2010).

11. Mort Lewis, letter to to Art Thurston, March 28, 1959, Brubeck Collection, 1.a.3.2.

12. Iola Brubeck, letter to Mary Jeanne Sauerwein, March 30, 1959, Brubeck Collection, MSS 325, Letters, Folder 4. Mary Jeanne (Anzalone Marbury) Sauerwein (1923–1999) first met Iola Brubeck in San Francisco in the late 1940s, when they became close friends and frequently babysat for each other. The collection consists of dozens of letters and postcards from Iola Brubeck to Sauerwein between 1947 and 2000. The correspondence gives researchers a better understanding of Iola Brubeck and her role as a mother while Dave Brubeck's career rose through the 1950s and later. Researchers will find a fascinating collection of personal correspondence that not only discusses personal matters as each woman's family evolved, but also refers to seminal ideas that lead to Dave Brubeck's success, like Iola's idea to move from clubs to playing concerts at college campuses.

13. Iola Brubeck, letter to Mary Jeanne Sauerwein, May 26, 1959, Brubeck Collection, MSS 325, Letters, Folder 4.

14. Darius Brubeck recalled the family spending parts of the summers of 1958 and 1959 at the Music Inn (interview with the author, December 15, 2018). The Music Inn was the Lenox, Massachusetts–based summer residency program and school of jazz from 1957 to 1960, featuring teachers including artistic director John Lewis; his Modern Jazz Quartet colleagues, Max Roach, Jim Hall, and Jimmy Giuffre; as well as arranging and composition teachers Herb Pomeroy, Gunther Schuller, and George Russell. Jazz musicology was taught by Marshall Stearns and Willis James. Faculty cited in a letter from Iola Brubeck to Krzysztof and Sofia Komeda, October 7, 1959, Brubeck Collection, 1.c.1, 1958 Personal Correspondence. A documentary film on the School of Jazz at the Music Inn was completed in 2011 (http://

www.musicinnfilm.net/). Lenox is also the summer home of the Boston Symphony Orchestra and the Tanglewood Music Festival.

15. Marshall Jamison, letter to to Dave Brubeck, August 12, 1959, Brubeck Collection, 1.a.3.14.

16. Dave and Iola Brubeck, interview with the author, July 22, 2009.

17. Dave Brubeck, letter to Jerome Robbins, June 20, 1959, Brubeck Collection, 1.a.3.21.

18. Jerome Robbins, letter to Dave Brubeck, July 9, 1959, 1.a.3.4.

CHAPTER 9. A PROMISING PROPOSAL: *THE REAL AMBASSADORS* IN LONDON

1. Dave Brubeck, letter to Harold Davison, May 27, 1959, Brubeck Collection, 1.a.3.21. This letter also referred to plans the Brubecks had to create a musical adaptation of A. A. Milne's children's tale, *Winnie the Pooh*, which never developed beyond the idea stage, due to the publisher's failure to either refuse or grant the Brubecks' adaptation rights request.

2. Iola Brubeck, letter to Harold Davison, July 1, 1959, Brubeck Collection, 1.a.3.21. This letter was written just a week after the aforementioned heart attack Armstrong suffered while on tour in Italy.

3. Chuck Wheat, "Sermon in Jazz May Help Man Love His Brother," *Tulsa Daily World*, November 11, 1959, Brubeck Collection, 1959 Clippings.

4. Dave Brubeck, interview with Ken Burns, *Jazz: A Film by Ken Burns* (2004), coproduced by Florentine Films and WETA.

5. Brubeck, interview with Ken Burns.

6. Harold Davison, letter to Dave Brubeck, June 18, 1959, Brubeck Collection, 1.a.3.14.

7. Harold Davison, letter to Dave Brubeck, November 5, 1959, Brubeck Collection, 1.a.3.14.

8. Joe Glaser, letter to Harold Davison, October 29, 1959, Brubeck Collection, 1.a.3.2.

9. Joe Glaser, cover letter to Dave Brubeck, October 29, 1959, Brubeck Collection, 1.a.3.2.

10. Joe Glaser, letter to Iola Brubeck, December 30, 1959, Brubeck Collection, 1.a.3.2. Glaser evidently maintained a working relationship with many top television executives, including Edward R. Murrow, who had helped produce the very successful *Satchmo the Great* documentary in 1957. Unfortunately, this film has never been reissued since its original run on television and briefly in theaters in the late 1950s.

11. Iola Brubeck, letter to the author, April 5, 2010.

12. Cathy Brubeck Yaghsizian, interview with the author, December 8, 2018.

13. "Why the Richest Bachelor Girl Became a Landlady," *Philadelphia Inquirer*, May 16, 1937, 117. This article documents DeLamar buying up adjacent properties and making them available to artists for modest rents.

14. Cathy Brubeck Yaghsizian, interview with the author, December 8, 2018.

15. Darius Brubeck, interview with the author, December 15, 2018.

16. The pony was a gift from Hugh Hefner and *Playboy* magazine, according to Catherine Yaghsizian. "My dad did an interview with *Playboy* but wouldn't accept any money for it due to his moral streak, which he sometimes had to work around. So he said to them, 'I'll do the interview but I won't accept any money, instead, you can buy a pony for the children.' Of course, we named him 'Playboy.' He turned out to be a little rascal and would dump most of us except for Michael" (Yaghsizian, interview with the author, December 8, 2018).

17. Dave Brubeck, letter to Harold Davison, May 18, 1960, Brubeck Collection, 1.a.4.38.

18. Dave Brubeck, letter to Dick Irving Hyland, August 15, 1960, Brubeck Collection, 1.a.5.31. Glaser himself was likely the source for focusing the Brubecks on doing the show for TV, since he had strong ties to CBS Television and any production would necessarily be done in New York City and approved by Glaser.

19. The Dave Brubeck Quartet's 1961 UK tour program, presented by Harold Davison, Brubeck Collection, 1.f.2.2. In a 2018 interview, Chris recalled being shown around London by a tour guide as well as seeing the immense water tanks used as the set in the seaborne battle scenes for the film *Cleopatra*, which was being made at Pinewood Studios at the same time he and his father were there.

20. Dave Brubeck, letter to Bob Roberts, July 14, 1961, Brubeck Collection, 4.1.a.5.

21. *A Raisin in the Sun* by Lorraine Hansberry premiered in 1959 and ran on Broadway for 531 performances (International Broadway Database page for *A Raisin in the Sun*, accessed January 4, 2021, https://www.ibdb.com/broadway-production/a-raisin-in-the-sun-2083). Jean Genet's avant-garde play *The Blacks* ran for more than 1,400 shows off Broadway and introduced the play-going public to the talents of a host of Black actors, including James Earl Jones, Roscoe Lee Browne, and Cicely Tyson (Robert Simonson, "Classical Theater of Harlem Presents Genet's The Blacks, October 11–28," Playbill.com, accessed January 4, 2021, https://www.playbill.com/article/classical-theatre-of-harlem-presents-genets-the-blacks-oct-11–28-com-99086).

22. Dave Brubeck, letter to Bob Roberts, July 14, 1961, Brubeck Collection, 4.1.a.5.

23. Brubeck, letter to Bob Roberts, July 14, 1961.

24. In theater parlance, the "book" refers to the plot or story line that a musical follows, and is also sometimes referred to as a libretto. Interestingly, the surviving correspondence contains only a single critique of any of the music for *The Real Ambassadors*, a question about the lyrics to "My One Bad Habit" by Columbia president Goddard Lieberson. In contrast, every seasoned producer that the Brubecks met with commented that the aspects of the work that needed substantial revision were the book and the couple's complicated production and staging ideas.

25. Bob Roberts, letter to Dave Brubeck, July 29, 1959, Brubeck Collection 1.a 5.23.

CHAPTER 10. RECORDING *THE REAL AMBASSADORS*

1. Some of these "audio letters" feature Brubeck's rhythm section, while on others he sits at the piano and plays, giving instruction, sometimes with additional commentary and directions from Iola. On one of these preview recordings, Dave can be heard apologizing profusely for his poor vocal abilities before he sings for Armstrong. On another audio letter to Armstrong, Carmen McRae stopped by the Brubeck home to join Dave in singing "You Swing, Baby" for Satchmo. Brubeck's vocal ability was certainly adequate to relate a melody to another musician.

2. Armstrong worked incessantly to document his life using unedited audio recordings he made of everyday life, both at his home and on the road, where he used a carefully constructed steamer trunk with two reel-to-reel recorders in it. For more on Armstrong's obsession with recording his life, see Ben Alexander's fascinating "For Posterity: The Personal

Audio Recordings of Louis Armstrong," *The American Archivist* 71, no. 1 (Spring/Summer 2008): 50–86. Armstrong biographer Ricky Riccardi mined the hundreds of private tapes in the Armstrong Archives in crafting the two critically acclaimed biographies on Satchmo cited earlier.

3. A number of the tapes are extant in both the Brubeck Collection (4.b.19.1 and 2) and the Louis Armstrong Collection (CD 63, 192, and 546) at Queens College in New York. They include an audio introduction to the plot, cast, and characters from Iola Brubeck. The first tape in the Brubeck Collection dates from January 3, 1959, while the second is undated.

4. Dave and Iola Brubeck, *A Time to Remember*. A worn envelope held the cards, addressed in Iola's hand to Louis, care of Joe Glaser's office. Also enclosed was a typewritten page titled "List of Louis Armstrong Songs for 'Blow Satchmo,'" arranged in categories based on which ones were solos, duets with Carmen McRae, or performed with the chorus.

5. Lampley was a talented Julliard graduate who caught the eye of George Avakian while working in the tape editing department at Columbia. He soon rose to be a producer, collaborating on projects with Brubeck, Armstrong, Miles Davis, Duke Ellington, and Leonard Bernstein, among others. Clark details that Lampley served as producer for Brubeck's successful album *Jazz Impression of Eurasia*, written, recorded, and released in fall 1958 after Brubeck's global tour (*Dave Brubeck: A Life in Time*, 229). Lampley biographic information from Jacques Kelly, "Cal Lampley, Producer of Records, Music Educator" (Obituary), *Baltimore Sun*, July 8, 2006, https://www.baltimoresun.com/news/bs-xpm-2006-07-08-0607080026-story.html.

6. There are a number of references to a chorus in correspondence relating to the show as well as on a song sheet. Since Cal Lampley had assumed a number of Avakian's Columbia producer responsibilities after he departed Columbia to help found Warner Brothers Records, it is logical to conclude that Lampley would have been the go-to resource for Brubeck to ask for help in recording a choral demo. In a letter from the Brubecks to Jerome Robbins they also mentioned that an onstage chorus and dancers would be integral to a fully staged version of the musical.

7. Marc Myers, "Dave Lambert: Voice of Reason," *All About Jazz—JazzWax*, July 24, 2014, https://news.allaboutjazz.com/dave-lambert-voice-of-reason.php.

8. Tracklist for *Annie By Candlelight*, PYE NJT-504, Discogs, accessed June 4, 2020, https://www.discogs.com/Annie-Ross-With-The-Tony-Crombie-4-Tet-Annie-By-Candlelight/master/633134.

9. John Bush, "Annie Ross Biography," AllMusic.com, accessed May 27, 2020, https://www.allmusic.com/artist/annie-ross-mn0000590265/biography. Grove Music Online, s.v. "Ross, Annie," by Jeffrey Holmes, 2015, accessed May 27, 2020, https://o-doi.org.pacificatclassic.pacific.edu/10.1093/gmo/9781561592630.article.A2276414. The actress and singer passed away on July 23, 2020, at the age of eighty-nine in her New York City home.

10. Peter Keepnews, "Jon Hendricks, 96, Who Brought a New Dimension to Jazz Singing, Dies," *New York Times*, November 22, 2017, https://www.nytimes.com/2017/11/22/obituaries/jon-hendricks-96-who-brought-a-new-dimension-to-jazz-singing-dies.html.

11. Tracklist for *Sing a Song of Basie*, ABC-Paramount (ABC-223), 1958, Discogs, accessed June 2, 2020, https://www.discogs.com/Lambert-Hendricks-Ross-Sing-A-Song-Of-Basie/master/204145. Critic Will Friedwald cited Creed Taylor, then a staff producer at ABC, who green-lighted the project, and noted that the album was one of Taylor's first significant

credits, an early indication of his future success as a music producer ("Lambert, Hendricks & Ross Sing a Song of Basie," *New Standards* [WNYC], October 2, 2017, https://www.wnyc .org/story/great-jazz-and-pop-vocal-albums-lambert-hendricks-and-ross-sing-song-basie/).

12. Lara Pellegrinelli, "Jon Hendricks, Genre-Pushing Jazz Vocalist, Dead at 96," *The Record: Music News from NPR*, November 22, 2017, https://www.npr.org/sections/the record/2017/11/22/529907015/jon-hendricks-genre-pushing-jazz-vocalist-dead-at-96; Grove Music Online, s.v. "Lambert, Hendricks and Ross," by Philip Greene, 2003, accessed May 27, 2020, https://0-doi.org.pacificatclassic.pacific.edu/10.1093/gmo/9781561592630.article .J498600.

13. Jon Hendricks, interview with the author, July 25, 2009, New York City.

14. Iola Brubeck, interview with Mike Lawless, *The Dave Brubeck Show*, September 8, 1961, 99.9 WJZZ, Brubeck Collection, 4.c.1.a. A recording of one of the rehearsals at Armstrong's home in Corona survives as part of the Louis Armstrong Collection, CD 551-2. The rehearsal fragment is followed by a dub Armstrong likely made from a test pressing of the Columbia LP of *The Real Ambassadors*, provided by the Brubecks in summer 1962 to aid Armstrong in learning his parts for the Monterey Jazz Festival concert performance.

15. Darius Brubeck, interview with the author, December 15, 2018.

16. Iola Brubeck, WJZZ interview with Mike Lawless.

17. Leonard Feather, "There's a Lot in Me the Public Hasn't Heard," *Melody Maker*, April 28, 1962.

18. "Jazz With a Capital W," an anonymous clipping in the Brubeck Collection, recounts the chance meeting between Cooper and Brubeck (Brubeck Collection, 1.d.2.3). Hartford, Connecticut, broadcast historian John Ramsey verified this information via correspondence. Ramsey is webmaster for a website called Hartford Radio History, which at the time of this writing was undergoing an update. According to Ramsey, the station was not able to sup-port itself financially and for a time became listener supported. It switched over to classical music in 1964 before changing its call letters to WEZN (John Ramsey, email correspondence with author, August 6, 2021).

19. This and the following excerpts are transcribed from the previously cited live radio interview with Iola Brubeck by Mike Lawless, WJZZ, September 8, 1961. The hectic schedules of the cast were still giving the Brubecks headaches, as the day prior to her on-air appearance, Iola reported that Lambert, Hendricks & Ross were still not confirmed for the first recording session, which was then less than a week away.

20. David Johnson, "Jump for Joy: Duke Ellington's Celebratory Musical," Indiana Public Media, February 5, 2008, http://indianapublicmedia.org/nightlights/jump-for-joy-duke -ellingtons-celebratory-musical/. This is a one-hour radio documentary on Ellington's World War II–era jazz musical, which Iola refers to in her interview. Johnson argues that the musical, which originally ran for 122 shows in Los Angeles in 1941, represents an important but often overlooked chapter in Ellington's career. Its careful avoidance of stereotypical representa-tions of Blacks led to mostly positive reviews, but also to death threats to cast members for challenging the narrow roles Blacks were limited to in the entertainment industry.

21. Brown's musical had a short run off Broadway in 1965, while *The Connection*, writ-ten by playwright Jack Gelber, ran for 722 shows off Broadway and was recognized as a groundbreaking theater piece for its unstinting portrayal of the daily lives of drug addicts.

22. *Jazz Impressions of the U.S.A.* was released in 1957 by Columbia (CL-984).

23. Earlier in the interview, when describing which songs were "all new" in the musical, Iola stated that "Summer Song" allows Pops to explain to Rhonda, the singer in his band, his philosophy of life.

24. An extensive McRae discography documenting 282 record releases under her name may be found here: https://www.discogs.com/artist/34183-Carmen-McRae (accessed January 5, 2021).

25. A crowd estimated at more than one hundred thousand welcomed Armstrong and his All-Stars to the gigantic soccer grounds in Kinshasa, Republic of Congo, during his 1960 State Department tour of Africa.

26. Further analysis of the show's lyrics, framed in the context of the turbulent civil rights years in which it was conceived and performed, may be found in Von Eschen, *Satchmo Blows Up the World*, 81–91.

27. Hatschek, "The Impact of American Jazz Diplomacy," 279. In one touching example of the People-to-People program's effects, Andrzej Kurylewicz, one of the leading Polish jazz musicians of the day, moved up his forthcoming wedding so the invited Brubeck Quartet could attend and play a number during his marriage ceremony to Polish actress and singer Wanda Warska.

CHAPTER 11. THE MOST EXPENSIVE DEMO EVER MADE

1. Joe Glaser, letter to Dave Brubeck, September 12, 1961, Brubeck Collection, 1.a.5.5. Glaser's reluctance is also cited by Michael Meckna's entry for the musical found in *Satchmo: The Louis Armstrong Encyclopedia*, 47. The run-through by the Brubecks and Armstrong at his Queens home is referenced in a previously cited September 8, 1961, radio interview with Iola Brubeck by Mike Lawless on WJZZ.

2. Joe Glaser, letter to Iola Brubeck, September 17, 1961, Brubeck Collection, 1.a.5.5.

3. Columbia Records Talent Budget Request Forms "Louis Armstrong," "Carmen McRae," and "Lambert, Hendricks & Ross," Macero Collection, *Real Ambassadors* folders, b.6, f.11, New York City Library for the Performing Arts. There are three folders of documents in this archive pertaining to *The Real Ambassadors*: b.6f.9–11. Interestingly, McRae received no advance, only union scale for her performance on the ensemble or duet pieces and future royalty of 1 percent of sales. However, for her solo pieces, "My One Bad Habit," "In the Lurch," "Easy as You Go," et al., her Artist Job Sheet for the December 19, 1961, session lists "5% on her solos split with Dave Brubeck ???????" reflecting the fact that even to Macero and his assistant, Felice Faust, the complicated royalty splits engendered by this project were a bit murky. The fixed advance payments are also reflected on each artist's Artist Job Sheet, a standard form used at each recording session to document artist costs aside from union fees and future royalty obligations. Another tally sheet on yellow legal paper extant in the same folder is in the handwriting of Iola Brubeck and breaks down the detailed musician, union, cartage, and rehearsal studio rental fees incurred for the four sessions that produced the bulk of the album.

4. Columbia Records Talent Budget Request Forms. A document titled "Request to Make Additional Recording with Contract Artists" dated August 31, 1961, shows an approved budget

of $10,000 for the album's recording to be done in four three-hour sessions, commencing with the September 12 and 13 dates at Columbia's 30th Street Studio. To form a benchmark for typical album recording costs at that time, a June 7, 1961, memo from Teo Macero to Goddard Lieberson requested funds to make what amounted to three more albums that year with Miles Davis and three more with Dave Brubeck. He requested a $10,000 aggregate budget for Davis and an equal sum for Brubeck, including the information that one of each artist's next three albums would be done with a large orchestra, virtually doubling the cost for that recording project as compared to the lower costs of working with a quartet or quintet as Davis and Brubeck normally did. ($10,000 in 1961 represents $91,000 in 2021.) Columbia owned its own studios in New York City, and so the studio and personnel costs were reflected in the label's overall cost of doing business, a convention that would end as the time needed by artists in the early 1970s spiraled to greater and greater lengths, with a concurrent rise in the cost of album production.

5. Columbia Records Talent Budget Request Forms, Memorandum draft titled "DB RA Royalty Liability."

6. Columbia Records Talent Budget Request Forms, Walter Dean, memo to Goddard Lieberson, Subject: Dave Brubeck, May 31, 1962.

7. Iola Brubeck, email to the author, June 23, 2010. In May 4, 2010, correspondence, Brubeck attorney Richard Jeweler stated that a separate royalty statement was sent by Columbia for *The Real Ambassadors*, confirming that its costs and recoupment were not tied to any other Brubeck album's earnings.

8. Macero Collection, b.6, f.10. The Artist Job Sheet for the September 20, 1961, session was typed up in advance with the artist designated as "Dave Brubeck + Louis Armstrong." Right after Armstrong's name, Teo Macero added in pen "+ Band." Macero's notes adjacent to each song recorded helpfully confirm that the actual players, for instance, on "Summer Song," which featured both Billy Kyle and Dave Brubeck playing piano together, created a rich harmonic base for Satchmo's timeless reflection on aging and life's broader meaning. These changes escaped the notice of Columbia's legal department, and eight months after the recordings were completed in May 1962, a memorandum was issued from Walter Dean to Clive Davis titled "May 8, 1962 Memo Walter Dean to Clive Davis; Subject: Real Ambassadors" (b.6f.11). Mr. Davis, then a rising star in Columbia's legal department, documented a verbal agreement in the memo, reached with Joe Glaser, that the sums paid to Armstrong's band would be charged against Armstrong's future royalties, even though the original contract from August 1961 did not reflect this stipulation.

9. Frank Laico, interview with the author, November 5, 2008. I am indebted to former Columbia engineer Don Puluse for decoding the session tracking sheet engineer's initials, "FL," and then providing an introduction to Mr. Laico, who graciously agreed to an interview.

10. Jon Hendricks, interview with the author, July 25, 2009.

11. Dave and Iola Brubeck, interview with the author, July 22, 2009.

12. In *A Time to Remember*, the Brubecks recall that McRae and Armstrong were leaving for tours on September 14 and 21, respectively, so the timing and personnel for the sessions was based on each performer's availability. There is a slight discrepancy between Klaus Fischer's published Brubeck discography and Brubeck's autobiography with regard to the dates of the sessions in the week of September 16, 1961. As the dates in the autobiography

more closely match the engineer's notes accompanying tapes from each session held in the Brubeck Collection (4.b.19.7 and 9), I have elected to use the dates in that book. The two songs unrecorded in September, "In the Lurch" and "My One Bad Habit," were recorded in December 1961, the next time McRae and Brubeck would both be in New York City, as documented by Fischer, 242–43.

13. Jon Hendricks, interview with the author, July 25, 2009. In this interview Hendricks related that he had grown up five houses away from Art Tatum and would regularly sing with Tatum's group as a youth in Toledo's black and tan clubs. The emphasis noted was highlighted by Hendricks as representing Armstrong's words.

14. Trummy Young was an experienced vocalist in addition to being a gifted trombonist. Prior to his joining Armstrong's All-Stars in 1952, he had established his vocal style as a member of Jimmie Lunceford's orchestra. Grove Music Online, s.v. "Young, Trummy," by Alyn Shipton, 2003, accessed May 27, 2020, https://0-www.oxfordmusiconline.com .pacificatclassic.pacific.edu/grovemusic/view/10.1093/gmo/9781561592630.001.0001/ omo-9781561592630-e-2000494700?rskey=Mhxiol&result=1.

15. Grove Music Online, s.v. "Kyle, Billy," by Johnny Simmen, Howard Rye, and Barry Kernfeld, accessed April 14, 2010, http://www.oxfordmusiconline.com/subscriber/article/ grove/music/J254100. Dates for his recordings as a leader are found at Scott Yanow, "Billy Kyle: biography," AllMusic.com, accessed January 5, 2021, http://www.allmusic.com/cg/amg .dll?p=amg&sql=11:djfqxqr5ldde~T1.

16. Dave and Iola Brubeck, interview with the author, July 22, 2009.

17. Dave and Iola Brubeck, interview with the author, July 22, 2009.

18. In the fortieth-anniversary excerpts performed at Monterey in 2002, the 2013 Detroit Jazz Festival recreation of the entire concert version of the show, and the Jazz at Lincoln Center 2014 revival, two musicians shared Pops's role: one singing and acting, and a second playing the trumpet leads—confirming the considerable challenges presented for anyone tackling Armstrong's dual role in this show.

19. Dave and Iola Brubeck, *A Time to Remember*.

20. "Notes from Real Ambassadors recording sessions," Jack Bradley Collection, Louis Armstrong Archives.

21. Teo Macero, letter to Joe Glaser, September 15, 1961, Macero Collection, b.6, f.11. "Pennies from Heaven" was the song he performed in the 1936 Bing Crosby film of the same name, which cemented Armstrong's place in the eyes of the mainstream audience. He elected to perform it again at the pivotal 1947 Town Hall concert that introduced the small-group format which came to be known as his All-Stars.

22. Dave and Iola Brubeck, *A Time to Remember*.

23. Riccardi, *What a Wonderful World*, 207. Dan Morgenstern's session recollections are reported here.

24. Dave and Iola Brubeck, interview with the author, July 22, 2009.

25. Riccardi, *What a Wonderful World*, 39.

26. Jon Hendricks, interview with the author, July 25, 2009.

27. Chip Stern, Liner notes to *The Real Ambassadors*, 1994 reissue, Columbia/Legacy.

28. Dave and Iola Brubeck, interview with the author, July 22, 2009.

29. Discography of Historical American Recordings, University of California, Santa Barbara, accessed January 5, 2021, https://adp.library.ucsb.edu/index.php.

30. "Ghana—1956," accessed January 5, 2021, http://www.libertyhall.com/stamp/Ghana .html. Documenting his very first trip to the African continent, this intriguing digest of Louis Armstrong's seminal 1956 experiences in Ghana includes some audio clips of the original performances. Ghana would officially declare its independence from Great Britain on March 6, 1957, and as such may have served as inspiration to Iola Brubeck in her invention of the recently independent fictional nation of Talgalla.

31. Snitzer's account is quoted in Nat Hentoff, "Louis Armstrong and Reconstruction," *Village Voice*, May 26, 1992.

32. Riccardi, *Heart Full of Rhythm*, 211.

33. Dave and Iola Brubeck, oral history interview with Shan Sutton and the author, January 30–31, 2007, Sanibel Island, Florida.

34. Two of the more insightful of these essays include Stanley Crouch, "Laughing Louis," *Village Voice*, August 14, 1975; and Garry Giddins's essay on Armstrong's ability to appropriate and reinterpret minstrelsy repertoire in the chapter "Louis Armstrong/Mills Brothers (Signifying)," found in his book *Visions of Jazz* (New York: Oxford University Press, 1998), 27–34.

35. Jon Hendricks, interview with the author, July 25, 2009.

36. Gilbert Millstein and Iola Brubeck, liner notes to *The Real Ambassadors* (original LP), Columbia OL 5850.

37. Dave and Iola Brubeck, *A Time to Remember*.

38. Riccardi, *What a Wonderful World*, 207.

39. Dave and Iola Brubeck, interview with the author, January 30–31, 2007, Sanibel Island, Florida.

40. Dave and Iola Brubeck, *A Time to Remember*. The week before Louis's March 1, 1949, coronation, he was the first African American featured on the cover of *Time* magazine and the subject in that publication of a feature article titled "Louis the First."

41. Meckna, *Louis Armstrong Encyclopedia*, 47.

42. Gilbert Millstein, liner notes to *The Real Ambassadors*, Columbia OL 5850, released September 1, 1962.

43. According to the Brubecks, Armstrong's recording of "Summer Song" was played by New York City's WQXR-FM radio the day news of his death was announced to the public, as a musical memorial. Dave and Iola Brubeck, interview with the author, July 22, 2009.

44. Will Friedwald, "*The Real Ambassadors*—Notes on Program," Jazz at Lincoln Center *Playbill*, April 2014.

45. Dave and Iola Brubeck, *A Time to Remember*.

CHAPTER 12. MESSENGERS OF CHANGE

1. *Coda* 4, no. 1 (November 1961): 15, Louis Armstrong Collection.

2. Iola Brubeck, letter to the author, January 30, 2009.

3. Macero Collection, b.6, f.10.

4. Gilbert Millstein, "Africa Harks to Satch's Horn," *New York Times Magazine*, November 20, 1960, 24, 64–76. Armstrong's eleven-week African tour not only cemented his connection to his African heritage, it also made news around the world as he performed for diplomats, heads of state, and audiences as great as one hundred thousand.

5. *The Real Ambassadors*, piano-vocal folio, 17.

6. Alison Murray, "He Left the Steers for Stravinsky," *Newington Town Crier*, May 31, 1962, 10, Brubeck Collection, 1962 Clippings.

7. Murray, "He Left the Steers for Stravinsky."

8. Murray, "He Left the Steers for Stravinsky."

9. Murray, "He Left the Steers for Stravinsky."

10. Leonard Feather, "There's a Lot in Me the Public Hasn't Heard," *Melody Maker*, April 28, 1962, Brubeck Collection, 1962 Clippings.

11. Feather, "There's a Lot in Me the Public Hasn't Heard."

12. Feather, "There's a Lot in Me the Public Hasn't Heard."

13. Murray, "He Left the Steers for Stravinsky."

14. Iola Brubeck, WJZZ interview with Mike Lawless, September 8, 1961.

15. Dave Brubeck, letter to Joe Glaser, February 6, 1962, 1962 Business Correspondence. This letter makes clear that Columbia Records had by this date settled the matter of the album's title, which would become the musical's title as well.

16. Jule Foster, letter to Dave Brubeck, March 5, 1962, Brubeck Collection, 1.a.6.12.

17. Foster, letter to Dave Brubeck, March 5, 1962.

CHAPTER 13. THE ROAD TO MONTEREY

1. A short essay describing the polyglot programming presented at the first festival in Monterey may be found at http://performingarts.ufl.edu/wp-content/uploads/2007/08/history-of-monterey-jazz-festival.pdf (accessed January 5, 2021).

2. Scott Yanow, "Ralph J. Gleason Biography," AllMusic.com, accessed January 5, 2021, https://www.allmusic.com/artist/ralph-j-gleason-mn0000403583/biography.

3. Joel Selvin, "Don't Let the Tweed Jackets, Trench Coat and Pipe Fool You—Ralph J. Gleason Was an Apostle of Jazz and Rock with Few Peers," *San Francisco Chronicle*, December 23, 2004, https://www.sfgate.com/entertainment/article/Don-t-let-the-tweed-jackets-trench-coat-and-pipe-2661831.php.

4. "Ralph J. Gleason, Jazz Critic, Dead," *New York Times*, June 4, 1975, https://www.nytimes.com/1975/06/04/archives/ralph-j-gleason-jazz-critic-dead-coast-writer-and-editor-58-was.html.

5. Ralph J. Gleason, "Perspectives," *DownBeat*, April 6, 1955, 18. As referenced elsewhere, Columbia Records had one of the most effective PR organizations in the music industry at that time. Brubeck's media promotion was also boosted when his Columbia producer, George Avakian, pitched Brubeck and his meteoric rise on the charts over a lunchtime martini with a *Time* senior editor. See Stephen A. Crist, *Dave Brubeck's Time Out* (New York: Oxford University Press, 2019), 16.

6. Crist, *Dave Brubeck's Time Out*, 33. Crist provides an insightful and detailed analysis of the Brubecks' often tortured relationship with not just Gleason but other members of the press to give context for the chilly reception the artist's most famous album, *Time Out*, received from the media. Crist reports that Iola's letter to the editor was never published in *DownBeat*. The contentious relationship between Gleason and the Brubeck camp is also reported by Clark, *Dave Brubeck: A Life in Time*, 67–68.

7. Ralph J. Gleason, "Perspectives," *DownBeat*, February 18, 1960, and March 17, 1960.

8. Gleason was the driving force for bringing jazz into American homes through his work as a host on National Education Television (NET), the forerunner to PBS. From 1961 to 1968 he created a series of half-hour segments titled *Jazz Casual*, which provided intimate interviews with leading jazz artists, who were predominantly African Americans. Reportedly, twenty-eight of the thirty-one episodes survived. They were reissued by Efor Films in 2004. An *All About Jazz* review of the reissues by Mark Sabbatini is available at https://www .allaboutjazz.com/the-complete-jazz-casual-series-various-artists-by-mark-sabbatini.php (accessed June 4, 2020).

9. For more on Lyons's early relationship with Brubeck see Hall, *It's About Time*, 38–40, which recounts how Lyons helped Brubeck land a steady engagement at Oakland's Burma Lounge, which helped the then-struggling jazz pianist feed his family. Clark provides additional details in *Dave Brubeck: A Life in Time*, 23, 72–73, 96, 104, and 121. See also the summary pages for the documentary film *Rediscovering Dave Brubeck* by Hedrick Smith (2001) at http://www.pbs.org/brubeck/theMan/cowboyToJazzman.htm (accessed January 5, 2021).

10. The 1960 Census reported 22,618 people living in Monterey. See US Department of Commerce, *The Eighteenth Decennial Census of the United States: Census of Population: 1960*, vol. 1, part 6, "California" (Washington, DC: Bureau of the Census, 1961), https://www.census .gov/history/pdf/1960lacapop.pdf.

11. Dave and Iola Brubeck, interview with the author, July 22, 2009.

12. Iola Brubeck, email to the author, May 3, 2010.

13. Brubeck's groups, in various configurations, would headline the Monterey Jazz Festival fourteen different times.

14. Oscar Cohen, letter to Iola Brubeck, April 11, 1962, Brubeck Collection, Business Correspondence (Associated Booking), 1962. Stephen Crist also reports that Brubeck or his attorney had forwarded a taped copy of the September 1961 cast recordings to ABC in advance of the festival to better acquaint them with the material (Crist, *Dave Brubeck's Time Out*, 237).

15. Dave and Iola Brubeck, *A Time to Remember*. Annie Ross had left the vocal trio and returned to England due to health problems, and twenty-six-year-old Ceylonese-born Yolande Bavan, who it would prove had prior ties to Brubeck and Armstrong, had joined the vocal trio as Ross's replacement.

16. Brubeck's contract is in the Brubeck Collection, 1.b.6.13. The remaining contracts are held in the archives of the Monterey Jazz Festival. Special thanks to Tim Jackson, Tim Orr, Rob Klevan, Shawn Anderson, and the rest of the festival's staff for providing the author access to a wealth of archival materials. McRae ended up performing only in the musical, while the other acts each performed a separate set.

17. Bavan, who later in life became a United Nations goodwill ambassador, visited Sri Lanka in 2010 and was regaled by fans who fondly recalled attending the Dave Brubeck Quartet's 1958 jazz ambassador concerts. Bavan, interview with the author, March 30, 2012.

18. Yolande Bavan, interview with the author, March 30, 2012.

19. Bavan, interview with the author, March 30, 2012.

20. While a biography does not yet exist for Bavan, the broad strokes of her musical career may be gleaned from an informative two-part interview of the actress/singer with Mark Meyers, from November 13, 2007, published on his outstanding *JazzWax* music blog, https://www.jazzwax.com/2007/11/a-chat-with-yol.html. In it, she discusses the role Billie Holiday played in mentoring her.

21. Brubeck biographer Philip Clark states that Teo Macero decided to cut the narrator's part on the album (*Dave Brubeck: A Life in Time*, 291); however, the narrator's track was not conceived or written in September 1961, when the excerpts from the musical were recorded. Creating the narrator's part was necessitated by the Brubecks' desire to give the audience the overarching story of Pops and his traveling jazz ambassadors, to better understand the complexities of relying on the mostly African American jazz ambassadors at the height of the civil rights struggles. The first time the narrator's part was recorded was in summer 2009, when Iola Brubeck recreated her original role on tape for the author, to facilitate the creation of a facsimile recording of the 1962 Monterey performance.

22. Michael J. Maloney, letter to Ralph J. Gleason, June 20, 1962, Brubeck Collection, 1.a.6 1962, Attorneys.

23. Iola Brubeck, letter to Jimmy Lyons, June 30, 1962, Brubeck Collection, 1.d.15.8.

24. Dave and Iola Brubeck, *A Time to Remember*.

25. Cathy Brubeck Yaghsizian, interview with the author, December 8, 2018.

26. Howard Brubeck was then chair of the music department of Palomar College in San Diego, so would have been available due to his school's summer break.

27. Cathy Brubeck Yaghsizian, interview with the author, December 8, 2018.

28. Joe Glaser, letter to Dave Brubeck, August 20, 1962, Brubeck Collection, MS4.1.a.6.4. Glaser repeatedly referred to Lyons as "Jimmy Jones" in this letter.

29. Booking Contract, Louis Armstrong and his All-Stars with Monterey Jazz Festival, Monterey Jazz Festival, 1962 Clippings.

30. Joe Glaser, letter to Dave Brubeck, August 20, 1962, Brubeck Collection, 1.a.6.4.

31. "Schedule Announced for Ohio Valley Jazz Festival" (press release), n.d., Jack Bradley Collection. Both men performed on Friday night, August 24, sharing the billing as follows: Duke Ellington and His Orchestra, the Dave Brubeck Quartet featuring Paul Desmond and Joe Morello, and Louis Armstrong and His All-Stars. Like Monterey, the Cincinnati Music Festival, as it is called today, has continued to thrive since its 1962 inception.

32. Dave and Iola Brubeck, interview with the author, July 22, 2009.

33. An audio recording of a rehearsal of the tune "King for a Day" with Brubeck, Armstrong, Young, and Darensbourg exists in the Armstrong archives. At first, it was believed to have been recorded that night in Cincinnati; however, a woman's voice, likely that of Iola Brubeck, can be heard in the background after Louis asks for an adjustment on a particular chart, saying, "We can take care of that." It's likely this audio recording was made by Armstrong just before the September 1961 studio recording dates when the Brubecks came to his Corona home to rehearse and review his parts for the musical (Louis Armstrong House Collection, audio CD 552, disc 2).

34. Dave and Iola Brubeck, *A Time to Remember*.

35. Ralph J. Gleason, "Here's One Good Reason Why Promoters Get Gray Hairs," *San Francisco Chronicle*, September 2, 1962, Brubeck Collection, 1962 Clippings. Gleason mentions that the soundtrack album is "just out," referencing its release the day before by Columbia.

36. The Detroit Jazz Festival's 2013 production of the show followed Iola's original intent and cast a group of extras wearing authentic African garb to play the part of the dancing townspeople who jubilantly welcomed Pops and his jazz ambassadors to Talgalla. They also created a prop airplane fuselage with windows to precisely represent Iola's original script directions.

37. Howard Brubeck, letter to Dave Brubeck, September 9, 1962, Brubeck Collection, 1.d.15.8. This is a five-page memorandum detailing questions Howard Brubeck had about various parts for the performance binders. It also demonstrates the narrowing window to complete all the musical preparations for the extensive cast, as the only day of rehearsal would be just one week later in San Francisco. In the age before fax machines and email, the brothers often used special-delivery mail to send and receive documents as quickly as possible.

CHAPTER 14. A NIGHT TO REMEMBER

1. Iola Brubeck, letter to Jimmy Lyons, September 14, 1962, Brubeck Collection, 1.d.15.8. Iola also requested reserved tickets for her own parents, who would make the drive down to see their daughter back on the stage for the first time since her performances in college.

2. Ralph J. Gleason, "Louis Represents the Human Race: A 'Domestic Peace Corps' Will Gather at Monterey," *San Francisco Chronicle*, September 16, 1962, Brubeck Collection, 1.e.1.a.12.

3. Yolande Bavan, interview with the author, March 30, 2012.

4. Joe Morello, interview with the author, October 24, 2008.

5. Yolande Bavan, interview with the author, March 30, 2012.

6. Bavan, interview with the author, March 30, 2012.

7. Bavan, interview with the author, March 30, 2012. Bavan explained how it stunned her that although Lambert, Hendricks & Ross were winning awards and being lauded by the media, the reality of touring was that top jazz artists were treated as "second-class citizens" in America. She described her experiences touring the US for three years with the vocal trio, giving examples of ways that jazz musicians were taken for granted and not treated as they were overseas. "Here I would be . . . dressing for our performance, wrapping myself in my sari in a kitchen in a club standing in bacon fat. This was the kind of clubs we were put in, while winning the top awards everywhere."

8. Bavan, interview with the author, March 30, 2012.

9. Paul Vieregge, interview with the author, January 26, 2009. Special thanks to Paul's wife, Penny, and the staff at the Monterey Jazz Festival for helping to arrange this interview shortly before Paul's untimely passing. Paul Vieregge (class of 1950) and Dick West (class of 1951) were also alumni of University of the Pacific, as were Dave and Iola Brubeck (classes of 1942 and 1945, respectively).

10. Vieregge, interview with the author, January 26, 2009.

11. Bavan, interview with the author, March 30, 2012.

12. Dave and Iola Brubeck, *A Time to Remember*.

13. Yolande Bavan, interview with the author, March 30, 2012.

14. Dave and Iola Brubeck, *A Time to Remember*.

15. Dave and Iola Brubeck, *A Time to Remember*.

16. Yolande Bavan, interview with the author, March 30, 2012.

17. Iola Brubeck's elegant stole was a gift her husband had acquired for her on his 1958 tour of India, adding a subtle international flavor to her wardrobe, which suited the musical's themes.

18. *The Real Ambassadors* piano-vocal folio, 2.

19. Dave and Iola Brubeck, *A Time to Remember*.

20. Paul Vieregge, interview with the author, January 26, 2009.

21. Iola Brubeck, email to the author, July 24, 2012.

22. Dave and Iola Brubeck, *A Time to Remember*. To this day, low-flying airplanes are regular "performers" at the Monterey Jazz Festival, as the county fairgrounds where the festival is held are on the approach path to Monterey Airport.

23. Yolande Bavan, interview with John Langdon, September 23, 2012, Monterey Jazz Festival, fiftieth anniversary of *The Real Ambassadors*' premiere, Brubeck Collection, Audio Interviews.

24. Ralph J. Gleason, "A Symbolic Finale at Monterey," *San Francisco Chronicle*, September 24, 1962, Brubeck Collection, 1.e.1.a.12.

25. Jerry Coker, "Satchmo Stars in Premiere," *Monterey Peninsula Herald*, September 24, 1962, Brubeck Collection, 1.e.1.a.12.

26. Jose Stell, "If You Want Your Jazz Festival to Go, Just Book Ol' Satchmo," *San Jose Mercury News*, September 26, 1962. The headline references the musical's very last line, sung a cappella by Armstrong: "Now I leave you / Now I go / Now you know as much as ol' Satchmo." Notes in Iola Brubeck's theatrical notebooks reference this as a "curtain line" likely sung as a coda by Pops out front alone after the curtain had fallen. Stell may have received a copy of the LP and thus made a play on words for his title with Iola's curtain line. Brubeck Collection, 1.e.1.a.12.

27. Johnnie Rodrigues, "Monterey Jazz Festival Goes in Orbit," *Berkeley Daily Gazette*, September 26, 1962, Monterey Jazz Festival archives, 1962 Clippings.

28. Joe Morello, interview with the author, October 24, 2008.

29. Eugene Wright, interview with the author, October 22, 2008.

30. Yolande Bavan, interview with the author, March 30, 2012.

31. Charles M. Weisenberg, "It Happened in Monterey," *Frontier: The Voice of the New West*, no. 14 (November 1962): 20–21.

32. Don DeMicheal, "Falling Angel? Monterey Jazz Festival Report," *DownBeat*, November 8, 1962, 13–15.

33. Don DeMicheal, "Falling Angel."

34. Cathy Brubeck Yaghsizian, interview with the author, December 8, 2018.

35. Undated fragment of clipping found in Brubeck Collection, 1.e.3.b, 1962 Reviews. The clipping includes an annotation in the original newspaper as being "Special to the Times" and includes a photo of Armstrong performing in the show onstage with the caption "Louis Armstrong: A Sermon with Humor."

36. DeMicheal, "Falling Angel," 13–15.

CHAPTER 15. RECEPTION AND REACTIONS

1. The series of 1962 audience member interviews cited in this chapter (Harris, Hoffman, Cooper, Ratner, Algoet, and Taylor) was conducted by University of the Pacific history students John Langdon and Ignacio Sanchez-Alonso on September 23, 2012, at the Monterey Jazz Festival as part of the festival's fiftieth-anniversary celebration of the premiere. John and Ignacio managed and interviewed the respondents and did the majority of the transcriptions. Special thanks again to Tim Jackson, Tim Orr, and the rest of the MJF staff for arranging for the interview space and inviting audience members who had attended the 1962 premiere to participate in the oral history project. Thanks also to University of the Pacific archivist, Michael Wurtz, and his staff, as well as professors Greg Rohlf and Jennifer Helgren in the history department at Pacific for their support in the preparation of the students for this opportunity. Transcriptions and the original recordings may be accessed at https://scholarly commons.pacific.edu/tra/.

2. "In the Lurch" is a mid-tempo number from the show in which the character of Rhonda expresses her dissatisfaction with Pops for always putting the band's business before their relationship.

3. As was referenced earlier, the Brubecks knew that to have any chance to find a musical theater producer, the book would have to be largely rewritten.

4. Pianist John Lewis served as the resident musical director for the Monterey Jazz Festival from 1958 to 1983 but was not able to participate in 1962 due to other commitments with the Modern Jazz Quartet; hence, Benny Carter filled in for him.

5. Yolande Bavan, interview with the author, March 30, 2012.

6. Dave and Iola Brubeck, *A Time to Remember*.

7. Howard Brubeck's note is quoted in *A Time to Remember*.

8. Yolande Bavan retains her engraved plate with the inscription and showed it to the author during a visit to her home in 2014.

9. Dave and Iola Brubeck, telegram to Louis Armstrong, September 24, 1962, St. Francis Hotel, San Francisco, Louis Armstrong House Museum, Jack Bradley Collection.

10. Cathy Brubeck Yaghsizian, interview with the author, December 8, 2018.

11. Iola Brubeck, letter to Mary Jeanne Sauerwein, January 10, 1963, Brubeck Collection, MSS 325, Letters, Folder 5.

12. *Forty Great Years*, 1997 Monterey Jazz Festival commemorative program, F3, Brubeck Collection, 1.e.8.9, Brubeck Mentions.

13. Paul Bannister, letter to Iola Brubeck, October 4, 1962, Brubeck Collection, Box 2, 1962, Business Correspondence.

14. Joe Glaser, letter to Michael Maloney, October 5, 1962, Brubeck Collection, Box 2, 1962, Business Correspondence.

15. Glaser, letter to Michael Maloney, October 5, 1962.

16. Glaser, letter to Michael Maloney, October 5, 1962.

17. Howard Brubeck, letter to Dave and Iola Brubeck, October 9, 1962, Brubeck Collection, Box 2, 1962 Business Correspondence.

18. Howard Brubeck, letter to Charles Hansen, October 9, 1962, Brubeck Collection, Box 2, 1962 Business Correspondence. As the Brubecks were also reviewing these arrangements,

Howard Brubeck noted that a few more changes might still be pending before publication by Hansen could proceed. The piano-vocal folio edition came out in 1963.

19. Michael Maloney, letter to Teo Macero, November 2, 1962 (copies sent to Columbia's Walter Dean and Stan West), Macero Collection, b.6, f.11.

20. Peter Jones, "Brubeck Sensitive to Criticism," *New Record Mirror* (UK), December 1, 1962, Brubeck Collection, Clippings, 1962.

21. Bert Willard, "Real Ambassadors May Go on Tour," *Santa Barbara News-Reporter*, November 3, 1962, Brubeck Collection, 1962 Clippings.

22. Jim Bancroft, interview with the author, June 3, 2009.

23. *The Dave Brubeck Quartet*—1962 self-published concert program booklet, New York City Public Library for the Performing Arts, Brubeck, Dave, biography file, 9. The assertion that *The Real Ambassadors* dealt with too controversial a topic to make it past Broadway producers also appeared in the earlier-referenced "He Left the Steers for Stravinsky" article published May 31, 1962, in the *Newington Town Crier*.

24. Paul Gregory, interview with the author, November 5, 2008.

25. Leonard Feather, review of *The Real Ambassadors*, *DownBeat*, October 25, 1962, 35–36.

26. Dan Morgenstern, review of *The Real Ambassadors*, *Jazz*, November–December 1962, 22–23, Brubeck Collection, Box 3b, 1.e.3.14.

27. Morgenstern, review of *The Real Ambassadors*. The innuendo he refers to centered on frequently voiced criticism that Armstrong's artistry had waned and that he had been reduced to recycling the same ten- to fifteen-song set of standards at each of his concerts, replaying his past glories while tackling no new or challenging repertoire.

28. William C. Glackin, "Jazz to Broadway: The Brubecks Write a Musical," *Sacramento Bee*, December 16, 1962, Brubeck Collection, 1.e.3.14.

29. Peter Gammond, "Peter James Clayton (1927–1991), Radio Broadcaster and Author," in *Oxford Dictionary of National Biography*, Oxford University Press, 2004, accessed June 4, 2020, via Internet Archive, https://web.archive.org/web/20150402123624/http://odnb2 .ifactory.com/view/article/49606.

30. Peter Clayton, review of *The Real Ambassadors*, *Jazz News* (UK), November 28, 1962, Brubeck Collection, Box 3b, 1.e.3.14. *Steptoe & Son* was a popular English TV comedy series that starred a blue-collar father and son who made their living as junk men, playing up the cultural differences between the grimy and grasping father and his son, who aspired to a better life. It was adapted for the US television audience as the highly successful series *Sanford and Son*.

31. "Refashioning a Gospel Story in Black Nativity," *NPR Weekend Edition*, December 1, 2013, https://www.npr.org/templates/story/story.php?storyId=248043431. While this report focuses on the 2013 filmed production, which updates Langston Hughes's original musical play, it cites the show's 1961 debut during the civil rights struggle.

32. Joe Goldberg, "Dave and Iola Brubeck: The Real Ambassadors (Columbia OS 2550/OL5850)," *HiFi/Stereo Review*, December 1962, 111, Jack Bradley Collection. For the full review, as well as a press photo of the Brubecks provided by Columbia, see https://worldradiohistory .com/Archive-All-Audio/Archive-HiFI-Stereo/60s/HiFi-Stereo-Review-1962-12.pdf (accessed January 5, 2021). Goldberg authored *Jazz Masters of the 50s* (1983) for DaCapo Press, a

collection of Goldberg's appreciation of twelve jazz masters, which notably includes Gerry Mulligan and Paul Desmond but not Dave Brubeck or his quartet. The book is still in print today.

33. Iola Brubeck, "Before and After Thoughts," liner notes to *The Real Ambassadors*, OL 5850, 1962.

34. Mrs. G. O. (Bette) Davidson, letter to Iola and Dave Brubeck, August 5, 1963, Brubeck Collection, MS 4.1.c.2, 1963 Personal Correspondence. The check she sent would be worth $893 in 2021. Iola added a note on Mrs. Davidson's letter that the check had been returned to her with a thank-you note.

35. Robbie [no last name], letter to Dave Brubeck, July 16, 1963, Brubeck Collection, 1.c.2, 1963 Personal Correspondence.

36. Walter Dean, memo to Teo Macero, May 31, 1962, Macero Collection, b.6, f.10.

37. Richard S. Jeweler, letter to the author, June 12, 2010. Special thanks to Brubeck attorney Richard S. Jeweler for taking the time to track down the album's sales history and share the results.

38. As mentioned before, *DownBeat*'s Don DeMicheal pointed out that the just-released album unfortunately lacked Iola Brubeck's unifying narration, which had been created specifically for the Monterey concert performance just weeks before the show's premiere and nearly nine months after the soundtrack album was recorded.

39. A few small ads for the release are extant in the 1962 Clippings folders of the Brubeck Collection.

40. Teo Macero Collection, b.6, f.10.

41. Dave Brubeck, undated letter to radio stations, Brubeck Collection, 1.d.13. No records exist of any radio stations actually programming any part of the show.

42. Yolande Bavan, interview with the author, March 30, 2012.

43. Ralph Gleason, "A Swinging Finale at Monterey," *San Francisco Chronicle*, September 25, 1963. Gleason also reported that, furthering the call for change initiated by the cast of *The Real Ambassadors* the previous year, and taken up by candidate Gillespie, Jon Hendricks brought the Monterey audience back to earth during one of his onstage moments by declaring a moment of silence in the middle of an otherwise rousing set, to remember the four young girls killed in the September 15, 1963, Birmingham, Alabama, Sixteenth Street Baptist Church bombing, as well as the fourteen others injured from that racially motivated attack, which occurred less than two weeks earlier.

44. Riccardi, *What a Wonderful World*, 216–24.

45. Hatschek and Wells, *Historical Dictionary of the American Music Industry*, 64, s.v. "British Invasion."

46. George Avakian, letter to the author, May 3, 2010.

47. A search of the Discogs website turned up examples of the 45-rpm single from each of these countries. While "Hello, Dolly!" knocked the Beatles out of the number-one slot on the pop music charts in early May, the sales success of "Nomad" is not mentioned in any of the Brubecks' correspondence from this time period, or in the Macero holdings.

48. Cheryl Corley, "Present at Creation: *A Raisin in the Sun*," NPR, March 11, 2002, originally broadcast as a segment of the *Tavis Smiley Show*, https://www.npr.org/templates/story/story.php?storyId=1139728.

49. Corley, "Present at Creation."

50. Dave and Iola Brubeck, interview with the author, July 22, 2009.

51. Iola Brubeck, letter to Michael Maloney, December 3, 1965, Brubeck Collection, 1965 Business Correspondence.

52. Colleen Melott Dimmitt, interview with the author, August 19, 2018. This jazz trio consisted of Paul Melott, bass, and Sten Crissey, drums—the two of whom were college roommates at the University of Oregon—and fourteen-year-old Larry Dunlap (piano), who was still in high school in Forest Grove, Oregon. The trio accompanied the dress rehearsals and actual performances of the show. The author appreciates Paul Melott and Larry Dunlap's willingness to answer questions about their experience performing the work. Dunlap has enjoyed a lengthy career as a respected San Francisco–area jazz pianist, composer, arranger, and educator. "Larry Dunlap Biography," AllMusic.com, accessed June 5, 2020, https://www .allmusic.com/artist/larry-dunlap-mn0000107207.

53. *The Real Ambassadors* concert program, Lebanon Valley Union High School, April 28, 1964. Thanks to Larry Dunlap, who generously donated his original copy of the program to the author.

54. According to the program, the dance numbers were performed as a sequence, immediately after the song "Remember Who You Are" concluded. In order of performance the dance pieces were the changing of the guard (England); the Highland fling (Scotland); the maika (geisha dance, Japan); and the tango (South America).

55. Due to the steady advocacy of the NAACP, Hollywood and Broadway had largely eliminated blackface performances by 1960. However, producers continued to routinely cast white actors in the role of Asian characters, notably in *The King and I* (1951 on Broadway, 1956 Academy award–winning film) and *Breakfast at Tiffany's* (1961). Yul Brynner, of Swiss-German and Russian descent, performed in the role of King Mongkut more than four thousand times before his death in 1985. As Audrey Hepburn's neighbor, Mr. Yunioshi, Mickey Rooney's performance played to the typical stereotypes regarding Asian Americans at the time, enhanced by the character's makeup, thick glasses, and prosthetic buckteeth.

56. Colleen Melott Dimmitt, interview with the author, August 19, 2018.

57. Dave and Iola Brubeck received a copy of the program sent by Dimmitt, which Iola carefully filed away and retained in her records with the rest of the materials pertaining to *The Real Ambassadors*.

58. Dave and Iola Brubeck, interview with the author, July 22, 2009.

59. Hall, *It's About Time*, 71.

60. Clark, *Dave Brubeck: A Life in Time*, 383–84. A twenty-fifth-anniversary reunion was agreed to by all four members of the classic Dave Brubeck Quartet in 1976. The fifteen-city, twenty-five-day tour was a sellout, and plans were underway for a European leg when Joe Morello had to pull out of the last three US dates due to problems with his vision. The band never re-formed, as later in 1976, Desmond was diagnosed with cancer. He passed away from that illness on May 30, 1977, at the age of fifty-three. Morello remained active musically up until his death in 2011, primarily as a drum teacher in the New York area, also leading his own groups on occasion. Grove Music Online, s.v. "Morello, Joe," by Barney Kernfeld (2011), accessed May 27, 2020, https://o-www.oxfordmusiconline.com.pacificatclassic.pacific.edu/ grovemusic/view/10.1093/gmo/9781561592630.001.0001/omo-9781561592630-e-2000311500.

61. The new Dave Brubeck Quartet recorded two albums for Columbia in this configuration in 1968, *Compadres* and *Blues Roots* (CBS 63395, 63517).

62. Hall, *It's About Time*, 81–82, 118.

63. Hall, *It's About Time*, 114–20.

64. As early as 1961, the British Musicians Union had called for a cultural boycott in which all British musicians would decline offers to appear in South Africa.

65. Darius and Cathy Brubeck, email to the author, February 27, 2019.

66. Hall, *It's About Time*, 73.

67. Aggrey Klaaste, "Angry Brubeck Slams Apartheid," *Weekend World*, October 17, 1976, Brubeck Collection, Clippings, 1976.

68. Klaaste, "Angry Brubeck Slams Apartheid."

69. Shan Sutton, interview with Dave and Iola Brubeck, 2007, Brubeck Collection Oral History Project, accessed January 6, 2021, https://scholarlycommons.pacific.edu/bohp/27/.

70. Victor Ntoni cofounded the band Afro Cool Concept with Darius Brubeck in 1989. The group toured Asia, Africa, and Europe during their time together.

71. "Goodbye—Until Segregation Goes Says Brubeck," *Sunday Times*, October 17, 1976, Brubeck Collection, Clippings, 1976.

72. "Goodbye," *Sunday Times*.

73. According to Darius and Cathy Brubeck, while schools at various levels offered individual courses in jazz, no university then offered a degree in jazz studies.

74. Hall, *It's About Time*, 99. Darius and Cathy Brubeck, email to the author, February 27, 2019. See also Joann Stevens, "Dave Brubeck's Son, Darius, Reflects on His Father's Legacy," *Smithsonian*, April 2, 2013.

CHAPTER 16. REDISCOVERING *THE REAL AMBASSADORS*

1. To assess the size of the vast Louis Armstrong discography, one may search the web directory Discogs using his name and see that it lists 2,483 records featuring Satchmo.

2. Ricky Riccardi, "Lonesome Revisited," *The Wonderful World of Louis Armstrong* (blog), April 11, 2009, http://dippermouth.blogspot.com/2009/04/lonesome.html.

3. Crist, "Jazz as Democracy," 155.

4. Scott Yanow, review of *The Real Ambassadors*, AllMusic.com, accessed June 5, 2020, https://www.allmusic.com/album/real-ambassadors-mw0000114315.

5. Richard S. Jeweler, letter to the author, June 12, 2010.

6. In 2019, the University of the Pacific announced that, after twenty years, the Brubeck Institute at Pacific would be shuttered. The Brubeck family established a new Brubeck Living Legacy, which will relocate the Brubeck Collection of papers and documents to the Wilton, Connecticut, Public Library, where a special area is being developed to support researchers and the substantial holdings that have been so essential to this research. For more information, visit http://www.davebrubeckjazz.com/Bio-/Brubeck-Living-Legacy (accessed December 31, 2020).

7. *A Historical Tribute to The Real Ambassadors*, September 22, 2002, performed at the forty-fifth annual Monterey Jazz Festival, Stanford University archives, Items 1564 and 1565 (video), Monterey Jazz Festival collection.

8. *A Historical Tribute to The Real Ambassadors.*

9. *A Historical Tribute to The Real Ambassadors.*

10. Scott Yanow, "The 2002 Monterey Jazz Festival or How to See 60 Groups in 30 Hours," *Jazz Journalists Association Library*, accessed November 24, 2018, www.jazzhouse.org/nlib/index.php3?read=yanow7.

11. Chris and Tish Brubeck, interview with the author, December 3, 2018.

12. *A Historical Tribute to The Real Ambassadors.*

13. Yanow, "The 2002 Monterey Jazz Festival."

14. *A Historical Tribute to The Real Ambassadors.*

15. Program book from 2008 Brubeck Festival, 3.

16. The extensive photo exhibition has been archived on a companion website: http://www.meridian.org/jazzambassadors/ (accessed January 6, 2021).

17. "Inaugural Recipients of the Benjamin Franklin Awards for Public Diplomacy," US State Department archives for 2001–9, accessed January 6, 2021, https://2001-2009.state.gov/r/pa/prs/ps/2008/apr/103121.htm.

18. Arshad Mohammad, "Dave Brubeck Wins Medal for Spreading Jazz Abroad," *Reuters*, April 8, 2008, https://www.reuters.com/article/people-brubeck-dc-idUSN0832843920080409.

19. An intriguing mystery regarding whether or not an audio recording of the Monterey premiere was made surreptitiously surfaced in Stephen Crist's book on the making of Brubeck's most noted album, 1959's *Time Out*. He reported that Jack Eglash, then head of the American Federation of Musicians' Las Vegas local, taped the concert, as clearly referenced by correspondence between Joe Glaser and Brubeck's attorney, Michael Maloney. Crist tracked down Eglash's son, Ryan (Jack Eglash died in 2006), who stated that the tape may still exist in the union's archive (Crist, *Dave Brubeck's Time Out*, 239). The author attempted to contact Ryan Eglash as well as the current Las Vegas Musicians Union staff, neither of whom replied.

20. Dave and Iola Brubeck, interview with the author, July 22, 2009.

21. Special thanks to University of the Pacific faculty member and recording engineer Jeff Crawford and casting director Professor James Haffner for their advice and assistance in completing this project. Thanks also to Brubeck attorney Richard Jeweler for providing copies of the Hansen score and advice on the collaboration with the Brubecks. At the time of this writing, the facsimile copy is not available online due to the aforementioned migration of the Brubeck Collection to its new home in Wilton, Connecticut.

22. Special thanks to archivists Michael Wurtz, Trish Richards, and Shan Sutton for their dedication and efforts to realize this exhibit. Similarly, thanks go to Tim Jackson, Timothy Orr, and the entire staff of the Monterey Jazz Festival, generous partners in the planning and executing the anniversary events.

23. Chris and Tish Brubeck, interview with the author, December 3, 2018. Chris stated that Russell Gloyd served in the same capacity for the Jazz at Lincoln Center performances, where he was credited as creative advisor.

24. Program guide from the 2013 Detroit Jazz Festival, and program sheet for *The Real Ambassadors* performance (author's personal collection). Meyer authored the program sheet copy.

25. Cassandra Spratling, "Claudia House Morcom, Legal Pioneer and Champion for Human Rights, Dies at 82," *Detroit Free Press*, August 20, 2014.

26. Steve Carmody and Emma Winowiecki, "Before 'I Have a Dream,' There Was the 'Great Walk to Freedom' in Detroit," Michigan Public Radio, January 16, 2017, https://www.michiganradio.org/post/i-have-dream-there-was-great-walk-freedom-detroit. More than 125,000 marchers joined Dr. King on June 23, 1963, in what was apparently a test run for the forthcoming March on Washington that would occur in August 1963 and immortalize King's "I Have a Dream" speech.

27. *The Real Ambassadors* day of concert program sheet, September 1, 2013.

28. *The Real Ambassadors* concert recording, September 1, 2013, personal audio recording made by author at performance. The author was a member of the audience for the Detroit Jazz Festival production of *The Real Ambassadors* and is reporting what he observed that day.

29. In doing so, Meyer paid indirect tribute to the tens of thousands of fans around the world who similarly came out day or night, in good or bad weather, to welcome and salute America's jazz ambassadors throughout the twenty-two-year period when the USA sent America's most noted jazz artists abroad.

30. Mark Stryker, "Detroit Jazz Festival: Swinging Styles, Creative High Notes," *Detroit Free Press*, September 3, 2013.

31. Charles J. Gans, "Wynton and Dave Brubeck Playing at Newport Jazz Festival," AP, accessed January 6, 2021, https://wyntonmarsalis.org/news/entry/wynton-and-dave-brubeck-playing-at-newport.

32. Charles J. Gans, "Brubeck Gets Nod from Another Jazz Great," *San Diego Union*, August 9, 2010, https://www.sandiegouniontribune.com/sdut-brubeck-gets-nod-from-another-jazz-great-2010aug09-story.html.

33. Darius Brubeck, interview with the author, December 15, 2018.

34. Simon Rowe, interview with the author, November 10, 2018. Rowe served as executive director of the Brubeck Institute from 2011 to 2016.

35. Chris and Tish Brubeck, interview with the author, December 3, 2018.

36. Chris and Tish Brubeck, interview with the author, December 3, 2018.

37. Jazz at Lincoln Center *Playbill*, April 2014.

38. Simon Rowe, interview with the author, November 10, 2018.

39. Yolande Bavan, interview with the author, November 13, 2018.

40. Will Friedwald, "*The Real Ambassadors*—Notes on the Program," Jazz at Lincoln Center *Playbill*, April 2014.

41. Yolande Bavan, interview with the author, November 13, 2018.

42. Darius Brubeck, interview with the author, December 15, 2018.

43. The string of revivals continued with Rhodes College in Memphis, Tennessee, partnering with Opera Memphis and the Brubeck Institute to stage two acclaimed performances of *The Real Ambassadors* featuring Todd Payne in the role of Pops and Johanna Hunter as Rhonda on April 8–10, 2016. The performance weekend echoed the 2013 Detroit Jazz Festival tribute to the Brubecks in that Memphis also staged Dave Brubeck's Mass, *To Hope! A Celebration*, and three of his sons, Darius, Chris, and Dan, joined with the Memphis Symphony Orchestra to perform the large-scale piece featuring jazz combo, chorus, and vocal soloists. According to Chris Brubeck, *The Real Ambassadors* worked very well in a smaller, more intimate cabaret-style environment and played to sold-out crowds (Chris and Tish Brubeck, interview with the author, December 3, 2018).

44. Although the classic Dave Brubeck Quartet had disbanded in 1967, Wright remained in contact with the Brubecks and joined the group for the reunions in 1985 at the Kool Jazz Festival and the group's historic performance in Moscow in 1988 as part of the Reagan-Gorbachev Summit. He resided in Los Angeles until his passing on December 30, 2020, at the age of ninety-seven. In his post–Brubeck Quartet career, he was active in jazz education, playing on film and television soundtracks and maintaining an active private studio teaching bass. Nate Chinen wrote an informative obituary at the time of his passing, "Eugene Wright, Steadfast Bassist and Longtime Anchor for Dave Brubeck Quartet, Dies at 97," December 31, 2020, WBGO Radio, https://www.wbgo.org/post/eugene-wright-steadfast-bassist-and-longtime-anchor-dave-brubeck-quartet-dies-97#stream/0. For additional background on Wright's career, see Grove Music Online, s.v. "Wright, Eugene," by Brenda Pennell, 2003, updated by Barry Kernfeld, 2003, accessed May 27, 2020, https://0-www.oxfordmusiconline .com.pacificatclassic.pacific.edu/grovemusic/view/10.1093/gmo/9781561592630.001.0001/omo-9781561592630-e-2000492100.

45. *The Real Ambassdors in Concert*, February 9, 2021, https://www.facebook.com/louis armstronghousemuseum/videos/886590842162328. Additional support for this production was provided by the US Embassy in Moscow.

EPILOGUE

1. In an effort to educate Americans on the history and consequences of slavery, in August 2019, the *New York Times* launched the *1619 Project* to help reframe both the struggles and contributions of African Americans from the earliest days of slavery in North America to today. See https://www.nytimes.com/interactive/2019/08/14/magazine/1619-america-slavery .html (accessed August 7, 2020).

2. PBS broadcast a one-hour Peabody award–winning film titled *The Jazz Ambassadors*, directed by Hugo Berkeley in May 2018, further revealing just how impactful the Cold War cultural diplomacy was in its day. See https://www.pbs.org/video/the-jazz-ambassadors -efcogw/ (accessed August 7, 2020). The concept of soft power was identified by the political scientist Joseph Nye in the 1980s. He argued that it could be best defined as the ability to influence others' behavior by co-opting or influencing them rather than using threats, intimidation, or military power.

3. Riverside OJCCD-0667-2.

4. Sonny Rollins, liner notes to *Freedom Suite*, Riverside OJCCD-0667-2.

5. Steve Huey, review of *Mingus Ah Um*, by Charles Mingus, AllMusic.com, accessed July 15, 2020, https://www.allmusic.com/album/mingus-ah-um-mw0000188531.

6. An informative retrospective on Cadence's history, which featured more than one hundred best-selling singles, titled "Archie and the Metronome" by Mike Callahan and David Edwards, may be found here: http://www.bsnpubs.com/cadence/cadencestory.html (accessed June 30. 2020). Callahan and Edwards also provide a discography of Candid releases here: http://www.bsnpubs.com/cadence/candid.html (accessed June 30, 2020).

7. Ingrid Monson, *Freedom Sounds: Civil Rights Call out to Jazz and Africa* (New York: Oxford University Press, 2010), 182. I am indebted to the comprehensive research and

reporting provided in Monson's book, which is to date the most detailed analysis of how musicians and celebrities worked in partnership with civil rights leaders to fight for equality during this turbulent period.

8. Monson, *Freedom Sounds*, 172.

9. Monson, *Freedom Sounds*, 175.

10. For a brief summary of this civil rights initiative, see Marian Smith Holmes, "Freedom Riders—Then and Now," *Smithsonian Magazine*, February 2009, https://www.smithsonian mag.com/history/the-freedom-riders-then-and-now-45351758/.

11. Art Blakey & the Jazz Messengers, *The Freedom Rider*, Blue Note BST 84156.

12. Mike Micucci, "November 18, 1963: John Coltrane Records 'Alabama,'" *JazzIz*, November 18, 2016, https://www.jazziz.com/nov-18-1963-john-coltrane-records-alabama/.

13. Grove Music Online, s.v. "Simone, Nina," by Mark Anthony Neal, accessed August 9, 2021, https://o-doi.org.pacificatclassic.pacific.edu/10.1093/gmo/9781561592630.article. A2258277. Simone features prominently in the excellent 2021 documentary film *Summer of Soul*, directed by Amir "Questlove" Thompson (Searchlight Pictures). Performing at the 1969 Harlem Cultural Festival, artist/activist Simone in her remarks between songs challenges the predominantly Black audience with the notion that it may require violent overthrow to actually bring about the end of segregation.

14. Beyond the jazz genre, Bob Dylan's 1962 composition "Blowin' in the Wind" became an anthem of the civil rights movement. That song inspired soul singer Sam Cooke to add his voice to those of other artists with his moving gospel-tinged 1964 hit single, "A Change is Gonna Come," which he composed and recorded two months after Coltrane's "Alabama," demonstrating that musicians from all genres were challenging segregation.

15. Unlike the advice offered by the diplomats in his song "Remember Who You Are," which directed artists to "Never face a problem, always circumvent," Brubeck spoke candidly about the ills of racism when touring as a jazz ambassador. See Hatschek, "The Impact of American Jazz Diplomacy," 278.

16. Von Eschen, *Satchmo Blows Up the World*, 249.

17. Von Eschen, *Satchmo Blows Up the World*, 316.

18. Corinna da Fonseca-Wollheim, "America's Musical Ambassadors," *Wall Street Journal*, June 16, 2010.

19. See Crist, "Jazz as Democracy," for multiple references to the various US Embassy reports on the positive outcomes that were generated by the jazz ambassadors during their foreign tours.

20. For more on the Rhythm Road program, see da Fonseca-Wollheim, "America's Musical Ambassadors"; Misani, "Jazz at Lincoln Center, U.S. State Department Create Cultural Exchange Legacy," *New York Amsterdam News*, November 17, 2011; Moises Velasquez-Manoff, "U.S. Send a Jazzy Message Overseas," *Christian Science Monitor*, 99, no. 197 (September 2007): 13–16; US State Department, "U.S. Department of State, Jazz at Lincoln Center Announce 2011–2012 Lineup of The Rhythm Road: American Music Abroad," *Media Note*, February 15, 2011.

21. Velasquez-Manoff, "U.S. Sends a Jazzy Message Overseas."

22. da Fonseca-Wollheim, "America's Musical Ambassadors."

23. Tracy Smith, "U.S. Diplomacy: Hitting the Right Notes." *CBS Sunday Morning*, July 4, 2010. Companion article at https://www.cbsnews.com/news/us-diplomacy-hitting-the-right-notes/ (accessed July 2, 2020).

24. da Fonseca-Wollheim, "America's Musical Ambassadors."

25. Smith, "U.S. Diplomacy: Hitting the Right Notes."

26. Monson, *Freedom Sounds*, 201–6. The June 1963 SCLC benefit featured forty-two jazz artists performing at baseball great Jackie Robinson's Stamford, Connecticut, home. The SNCC benefit was held at Carnegie Hall on November 23, 1963, the day after President John F. Kennedy was assassinated in Dallas. Monson (chapter 6) provides a detailed review of how active jazz artists were during this time, not only raising much-needed funds for these grassroots organizations, but also becoming outspoken advocates for change, thereby further raising awareness among jazz fans worldwide.

27. Monson, *Freedom Sounds*, 157.

28. *Dave Brubeck—In His Own Sweet Way* is a documentary film from 2007 directed by Bruce Ricker that offers a retrospective of Brubeck's life, while interweaving the creative story of how the *Cannery Row Suite* was written, rehearsed, and brought to the 2006 Monterey Jazz Festival stage.

29. Matt Collar, review of *From the Plantation to the Penitentiary*, by Wynton Marsalis, AllMusic.com, accessed November 17, 2020, https://www.allmusic.com/album/from-the-plantation-to-the-penitentiary-mw0000577573.

30. Li Onesto, review of *From the Plantation to the Penitentiary*, by Wynton Marsalis, *Revolution*, March 18, 2007.

31. Onesto, review of *From the Plantation to the Penitentiary*.

32. Wynton Marsalis, liner notes to *From the Plantation to the Penitentiary*, Blue Note 0946 3-73675-2-0.

33. In the summer of 2020, Marsalis once again created a powerful new recording addressing exactly how he saw the dire state of America with regard to institutional racism, greed, social decay, and the dehumanizing efforts used against immigrants—a powerful song cycle titled *The Ever Fonky Lowdown* (Blue Engine Records BE-0025). The nearly two-hour work uses a construct similar to *The Real Ambassadors* by adding the role of a narrator, dubbed "Mr. Game," who employs various tones, from that of a snake oil salesman to Shakespeare-like soliloquies, to make false promises of wealth as well as instill fear of "the other," all in order to manipulate the "glorious people" into taking actions that are clearly against their own self-interest. The musicianship is stellar throughout, but the sometimes strident messages found in the work leave no doubt that Marsalis wanted to send a strong wake-up call to his audience, stating clearly just how troubling the nation's situation had become. See https://wyntonmarsalis.org/discography/title/the-ever-fonky-lowdown (accessed December 21, 2020).

34. Dave Brubeck, *Young Lions & Old Tigers*, Telarc CD-83349. Jon Hendricks also appears on this album, on a duet with Brubeck that does not feature McBride.

35. Matt Collar, review of *The Movement Revisited*, by Christian McBride, AllMusic.com, accessed July 15, 2020, https://www.allmusic.com/album/the-movement-revisited-a-musical-portrait-of-four-icons-mw0003338868.

36. Christian McBride, liner notes to *The Movement Revisited: A Musical Portrait of Four Icons*, Mack Avenue Records, MAC-1082.

37. Brandon Harden, "Jazz Great Christian McBride Has New Music to Go with Famous Civil Rights Speeches," *Philadelphia Inquirer*, February 20, 2020, https://www.inquirer .com/entertainment/music/christian-mcbride-album-musical-portraits-icons-mlk-rosa -parks-20200220.html.

38. Jazz musicians are among the hundreds of African American culture workers who have formed Black Artists for Freedom, an outgrowth of the Black Lives Matter movement. The organization was founded as a collective of Black workers in the culture industries dedicated to using their agency to declare a five-point manifesto urging action, not words, as the only sure way to change racial prejudice in America. See www.blackartistsforfreedom .com (accessed August 7, 2020).

39. Jim Harrington, "John Legend Torn on Artists Speaking Out About Politics," *San Jose Mercury News*, July 16, 2020.

40. A 2016 production of *The Real Ambassadors*, cited in an earlier note, was staged by Opera Memphis.

INDEX

269

ABOUT THE AUTHOR

Keith Hatschek is author of three other books on the music industry and directed the music management program at University of the Pacific for twenty years. Prior to becoming an educator, he spent twenty-five years in the music business as a musician, producer, studio owner, and marketing executive.

CPSIA information can be obtained
at www.ICGtesting.com
Printed in the USA
BVHW030621090122
625101BV00001B/7